BONEYARD

SoCal's Aircraft Graveyards at Night

TROY PAIVA

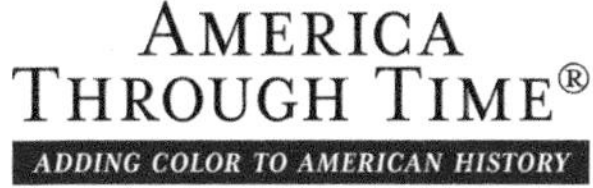

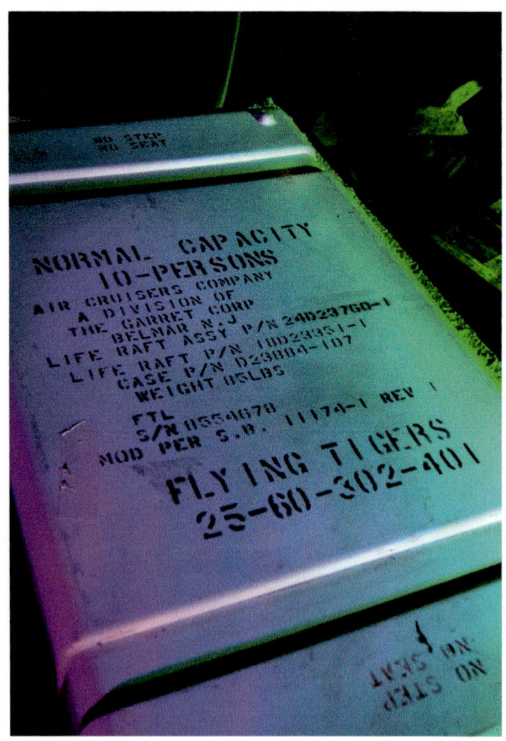

America Through Time is an imprint of Fonthill Media LLC
www.through-time.com
office@through-time.com

Published by Arcadia Publishing by arrangement with Fonthill Media LLC
For all general information, please contact Arcadia Publishing:
Telephone: 843-853-2070
Fax: 843-853-0044
E-mail: sales@arcadiapublishing.com
For customer service and orders:
Toll-Free 1-888-313-2665

www.arcadiapublishing.com

First published 2019

ISBN 978-1-63499-136-0

Typeset in Trade Gothic
Printed and bound in England

CONTENTS

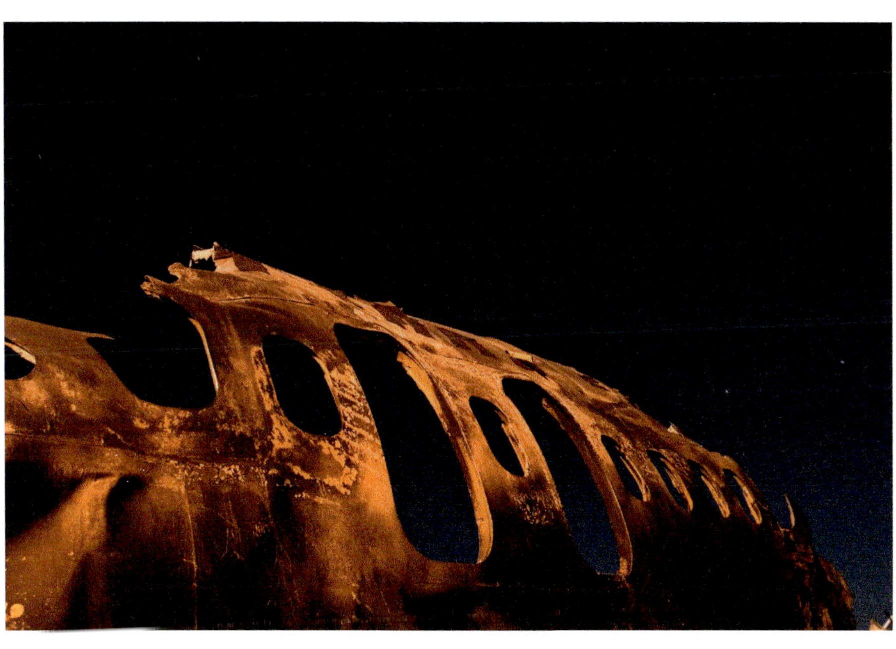

ACKNOWLEDGMENTS

This book is dedicated to my father, Joe Paiva.

Special thanks to:

Mark Thomson and the Thomson family, at Aviation Warehouse.

The owner and caretaker of The Secret Boneyard.

My traveling companions: Julie Paiva, Jeff Hayden, Joe Reifer, Ron Pinkerton and Hunter Luisi. Fun times!

Ryan Baxter, Ron Pinkerton and Jeff Breitenstein for their inestimable editorial help.

Steve Harper, for inspiring a whole generation of photographers, and my brother Tom, for the influence and encouragement to pursue night photography.

And always, my love and gratitude to my mom, Mother Stella, who allowed me to grow and bloom as an artist, encouraging me every step of the way. She lives on in my heart.

I love Julie.

For more fun, visit www.lostamerica.com.

1

THE SECRET BONEYARD

Joe, Hunter and I were making the long drive into the desert to shoot the Secret Boneyard. It was a waxing full moon, and the entire West Coast was in the grip of a late winter storm. In the Mojave, temperatures were in the thirties, with wind, rain and possible snow in the forecast. But that hadn't kept the weekend warriors from rolling out of LA in their RVs to party in the desert. The highways were crazy. We blasted down hundreds of miles of dippy two-lane roads, managing to survive each of Hunter's hair-raising 100-mph passes.

Once we were close to the yard, we pulled off at a giant AM/PM store, the last-chance stop at the turnoff for a popular off-road vehicle playground. The oversize lot was clogged with RVs towing dune buggies and sand-rails. A dozen vehicles with trailers jockeyed for a spot at the pumps. Hoonigans on ATVs buzzed in figure-eights around them.

Inside, a million gallons of beer were stacked in ceiling-high pyramids, while a hundred sunburned tweakers itched to put all of it inside them, ASAP. The place was pandemonium, and it made me squirm. I longed for the quiet and solitude that another trip to the Secret Boneyard—my altar at the church of dead technology—would bring me. I had to hold out for one more hour on the road, but at least I could stock up on Good & Plentys.

Boneyard ... It's a loaded word for me.

I grew up in a household obsessed with aviation. My dad was a flight engineer—the guy in the seat behind the pilot and copilot in old movie cockpit scenes. He started his career in the 1950s on Lockheed Constellations for Eastern, then switched to DC-8s at Seaboard World Airlines and Flying Tigers in the sixties and seventies, and finished in the eighties, flying cargo 747s for FedEx.

In his spare time, he flew volunteer search and rescue missions for the Civil Air Patrol in a T-6 Texan. It was all flying, all the time. At home, the TV room's bookshelves were packed with obscure and technical airplane books, and I had devoured all of them by the time I was twelve. Even before my voice broke, I could point out the differences between a P-39 and a P-63, and could recount the sad fate of the spectacularly cool XB-70.

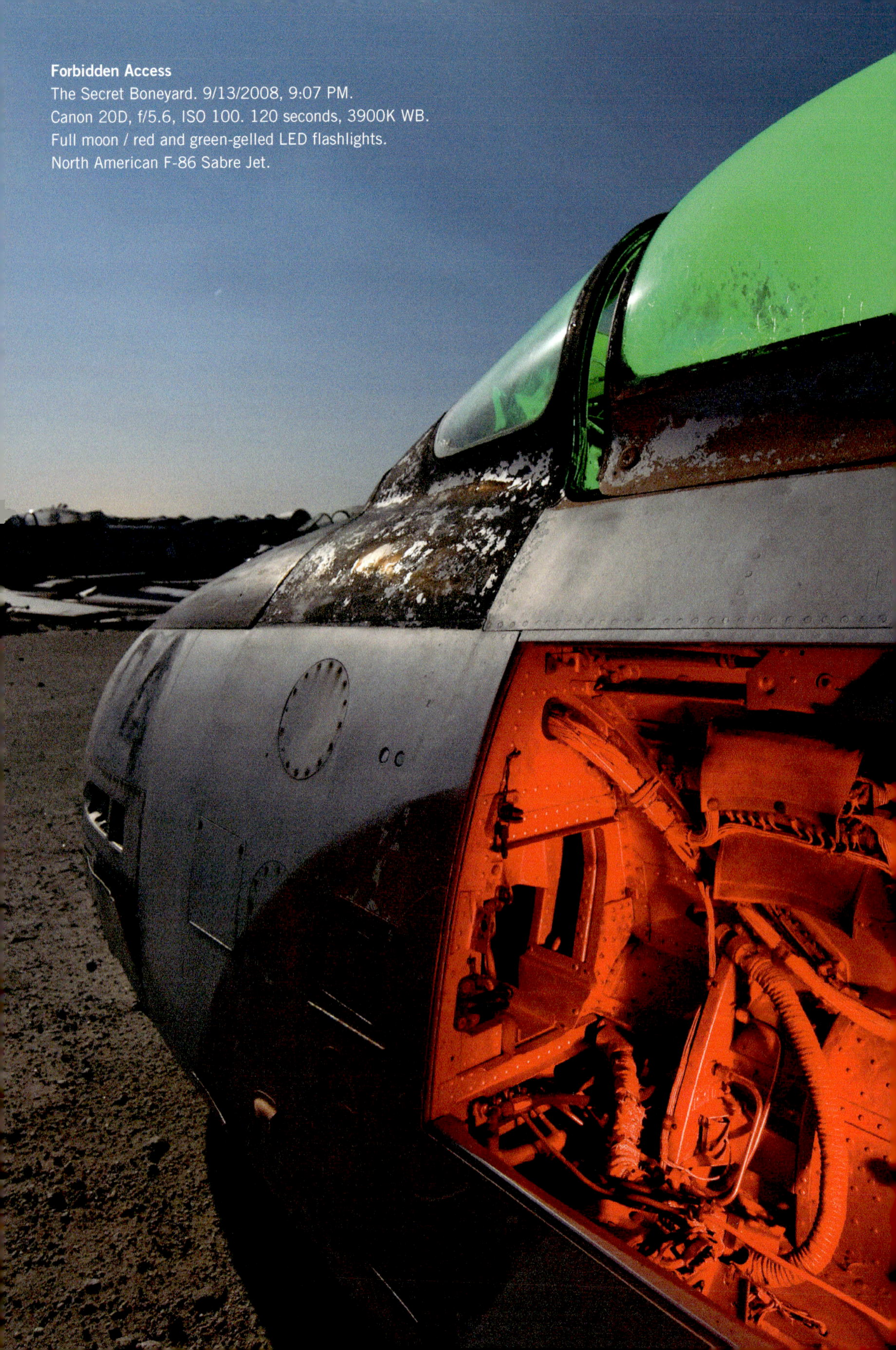

Forbidden Access
The Secret Boneyard. 9/13/2008, 9:07 PM.
Canon 20D, f/5.6, ISO 100. 120 seconds, 3900K WB.
Full moon / red and green-gelled LED flashlights.
North American F-86 Sabre Jet.

Dad was based out of San Francisco International Airport, so we lived close by. In my early teens, Mom would drop my friend, Jeff, and I off at the SFO terminals. It was the early seventies—long before 9/11—and the only security was an occasional metal detector, so we had free run of the sprawling terminal complex, even the international gates. We'd hang out all day, people watching in the departure lounges, soaking up the atmosphere spiced by travelers from far-away places, traversing the globe. The streamlined shapes and gleaming metal, the fantasy of flight and the romance of travel at the peak of the jet-set machine age ... it was intoxicating.

Even as a kid, I recognized that flight was one of mankind's greatest achievements. While most people take it for granted, for me the experience of flight will always be a thrill. Yes, I've had my share of horribly cramped eighteen-hour flights, loaded with screaming children and overflowing toilets—but I get swept up in the space age, sci-fi fantasy every time I step into the cabin. A few hours later, and I'm on a different continent, another world. It's something that a hundred years ago would have only been the stuff of dreams.

Even so, most people see aircraft as unchanging fixtures in their everyday lives. They have always been there, and they will always be there. This work reveals the flip side, the finite nature of even *this* amazing technology.

After a lifetime obsession with light painted night photography in all kinds of modern ruins, I've come to embrace the painful beauty in the impermanence of *everything* humans create.

Aircraft are no different. For me, their boneyards are the most evocative of modern ruins—not just because of my own personal history, but because flight epitomizes a true high point in human accomplishment.

And now look at them. Forgotten. Irrelevant. Junk.

:::::

In early 2008, my friend, Joe, told me about a little-known airplane graveyard located in the Southern California desert. "It's in the middle of nowhere, miles down an unmarked dirt road, so no one will ever find it. They have F-86s and B-29s, dozens of planes!" I wrangled the approximate coordinates out of him and filed them away in the back of my mind.

In September of that same year, I was vacationing in the desert with my wife, Julie, and I convinced her that we should try to find this legendary place. It was a full moon and I was dying to take some pictures. Using Google Earth, I was able to locate the site and find the dirt roads to follow. We must have passed seven or eight "No Trespassing" signs on the way in.

"Didn't you see that sign?" Julie asked.

"What sign? I'm too busy driving to see any signs. Besides, we'll just see if there's anyone around … and then try to ask for permission."

We arrived at the lot just at sundown. The gate was open, so I parked in the large turnaround area. I hopped out of the car with my camera, and we started exploring. It was a comfortably dry 100 degrees and totally still. The sky was darkening from pink to purple. On one side of the yard stood a house surrounded by blue-gray willows. No cars. The silence was broken only when the swamp cooler on the roof occasionally buzzed back to life. No one was around, so we began to relax.

The hard-packed dirt yard was jammed with disassembled airframes and decaying wooden crates—filled with ancient, but factory-new parts. Airliners and civil aircraft are one thing, but it's the military angle that made this yard special. That, and the age of that military equipment: many of the planes dated back to World War II. There were B-17 parts, two ready-to-assemble B-29s and complete B-25 nose sections tied to pallets and ready to ship.

Rows of Korean War-era F-86s lay on their bellies in the sand, with their wings and tails clipped off and crated for long-term storage. These airframes have been stored here for decades, so everything had a perfectly baked desert patina—an untouched quality. I was overcome with emotion, the feeling of history lost and the palpable passage of time.

With about thirty minutes of daylight remaining, we had explored every corner of the yard, including an unexpected collection of Chevy Corvairs tucked off to one side. When it became dark enough to shoot, I unlimbered the tripod and got down to the real work. I shot like a maniac for about two hours, methodically pounding out images as fast as I could, just in case …

And sure enough, just as I was getting started on the B-29s, a pair of headlights appeared in a cloud of dust at the gate, a hundred yards away, right next to my car. My wife, who was stretched out, moon tanning on a dismembered bomber wing, sprang to her feet. "He's here," she whispered.

I quickly broke my tripod down, and we started making our way towards the car, hoping we could just slip away—but as we got halfway back, we were intercepted by the silhouette of a man with a flashlight. Wow, was *he* pissed … and rightly so. "Did you *not* see all the 'No Trespassing' signs? Do they have *no* meaning for you?" Steam was practically coming out of his ears. He looked ready to brain me with his D-Cell Maglite. I think if Julie hadn't been there with her calming influence, he just might have.

I tried to calm him down by sticking to my usual script. "I'm a photographer, not a vandal, not a thief." I added that I trespassed because coming to this place was like a religious pilgrimage for me. I handed him a copy of my book, *Night Vision*,

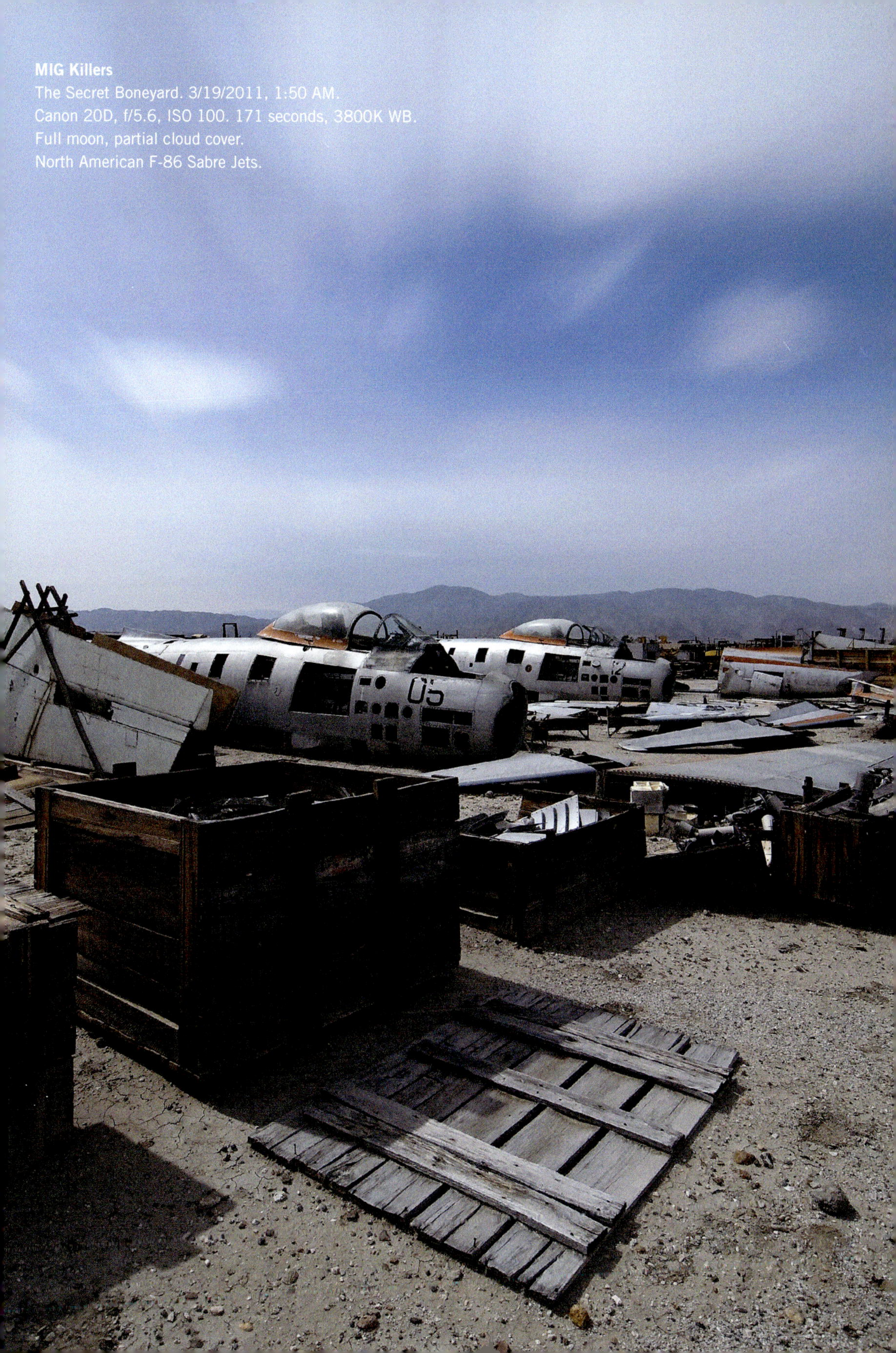

MIG Killers
The Secret Boneyard. 3/19/2011, 1:50 AM.
Canon 20D, f/5.6, ISO 100. 171 seconds, 3800K WB.
Full moon, partial cloud cover.
North American F-86 Sabre Jets.

turned to the Aviation Warehouse work, dropped the owner's name, and saw a flash of recognition in his eyes. He calmed down a little, but hissed, "If the owner of this yard ever sees your pictures of this place in a book or on the Internet, you'll be sued. Now get the hell out of here!"

Feeling lucky that he didn't call the sheriff or make me delete the images, we made the two-hour drive back to our motel on pure adrenaline. When I got home, I did some research and uncovered the owner's name. I sent him an envelope full of 8x12s and a letter that struck a balance between conciliatory and impassioned, but never heard back.

In early 2011, while talking to another aircraft owner about accessing a different boneyard, I related the story. He laughed and said, "You sent your pictures to the wrong guy." He shared the real owner's name with me, and I contacted him with some fresh prints. Fascinated by the illicit work, he granted me access to the yard for the March full moon. He said I could do whatever I wanted with any of the images, with the stipulation that I not disclose his name or the yard's location. He's rightly concerned about vandals and salvagers and doesn't want to be bothered with tourists snooping around, so "The Secret Boneyard" is all you'll get out of me.

:::::

Joe, Hunter and I saw the caretaker only once that March when he pulled into the yard late the first night and dashed into the house. I can't say I blamed him, given our past history and all. Besides, those two nights were bitterly cold and windy. I spent half my time hunkered down on the lee side of a fuselage thinking no sane person would be out in this.

At the beginning of the second night, while gearing up beside the car, a combination of gusting wind and an accidental bump knocked my tripod over. The fall smashed the body and tore the camera off the tripod. The camera's screw mount was completely ripped out. It still took pictures, but I couldn't attach it to the tripod.

Rather than sit in the car and wring my hands, I taped the camera to the tripod. Using about ten feet of heavy-duty gaffer's tape, I wrapped it around and around until everything was stable. I had to cut a window in the tape to access the LCD screen and buttons. It was a laughable kludge-job, but it worked. I shot sixteen set-ups that night and only lost one to camera movement when the tape finally began to sag. It was a classic "shooting junk with junk equipment" moment, an ethos I've always gravitated to.

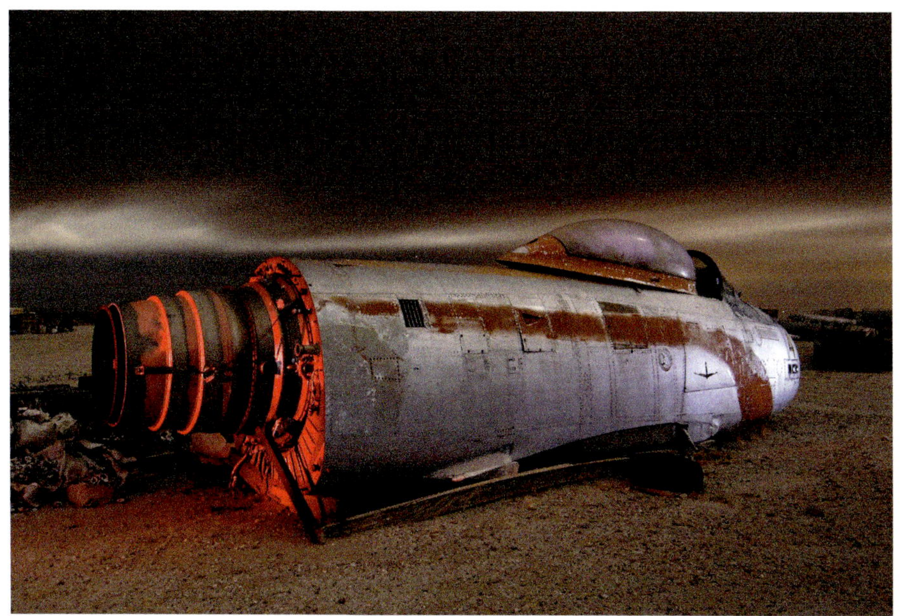

Rocket Sled

The Secret Boneyard. 3/20/2011, 12:26 AM.
Canon 20D, f/5.6, ISO 100. 193 seconds, 4400K WB.
Full moon, partial cloud cover / natural white, red and purple LED flashlight.
North American F-86 Sabre Jet.

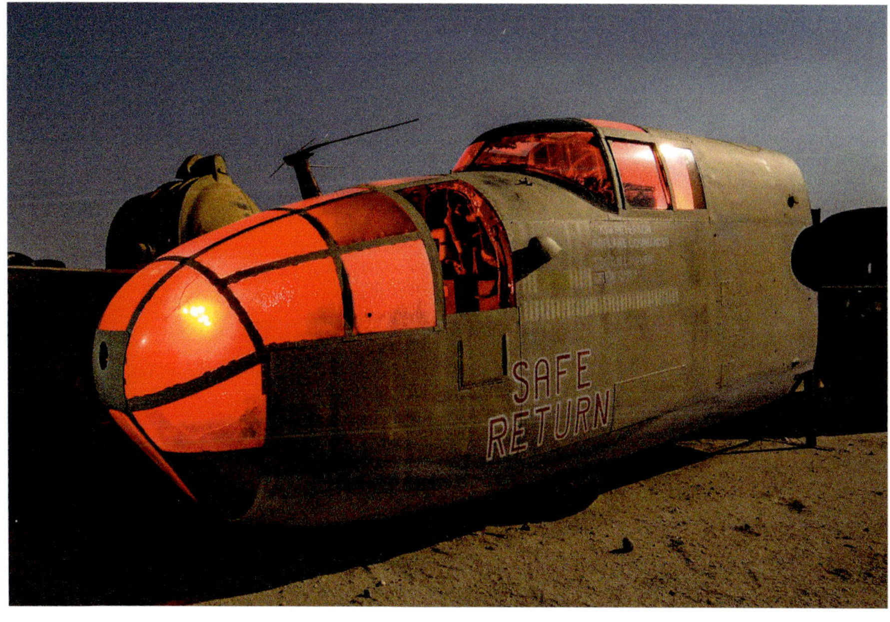

Safe Return

The Secret Boneyard. 9/13/2008, 9:24 PM.
Canon 20D, f/5.6, ISO 100. 120 seconds, 4800K WB.
Full moon / red LED flashlight.
North American B-25 Mitchell.

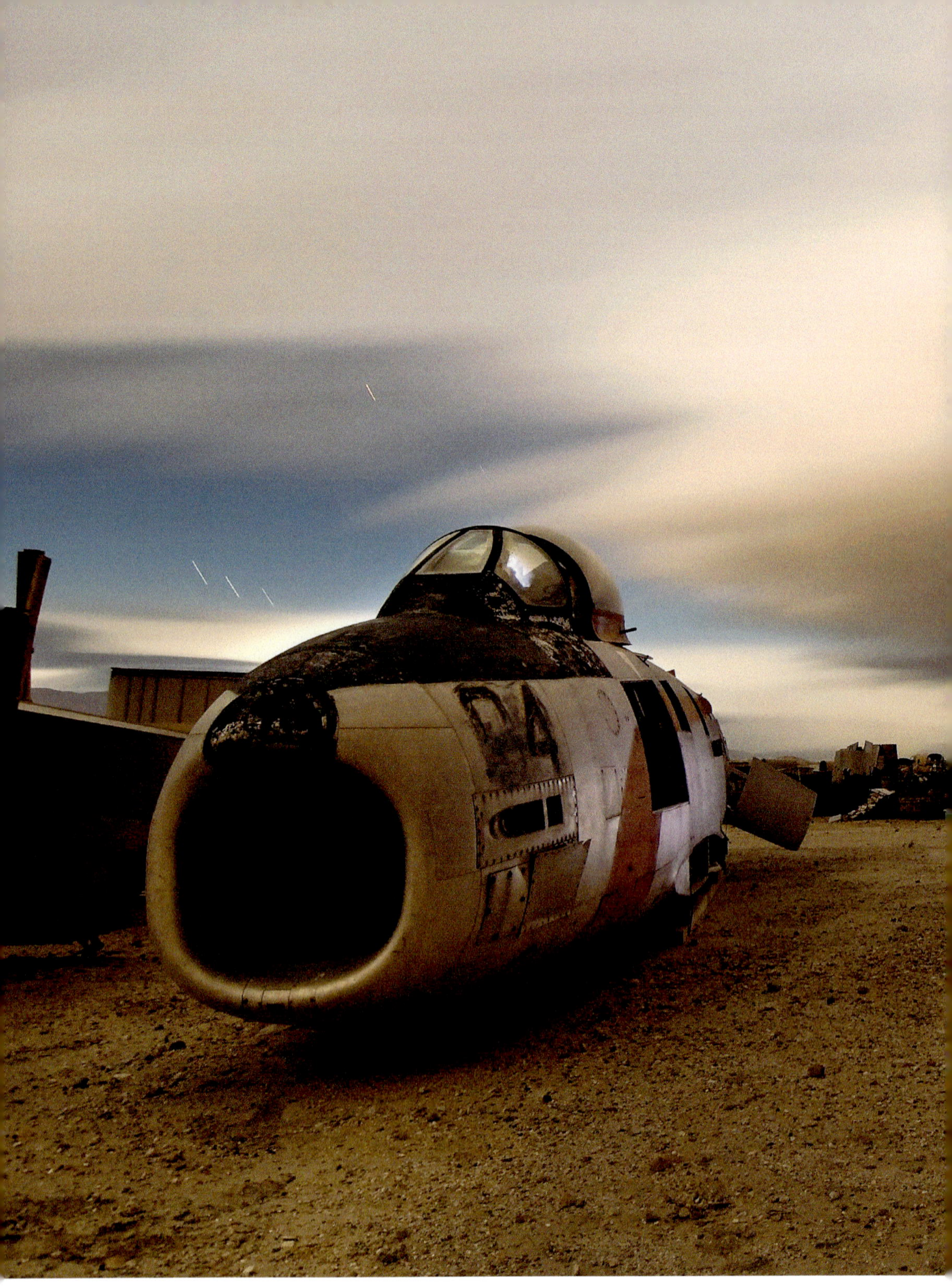

My Evil Twin
The Secret Boneyard. 3/20/2011, 12:14 AM.
Canon 20D, f/5.6, ISO 100. 257 seconds, 5000K WB.

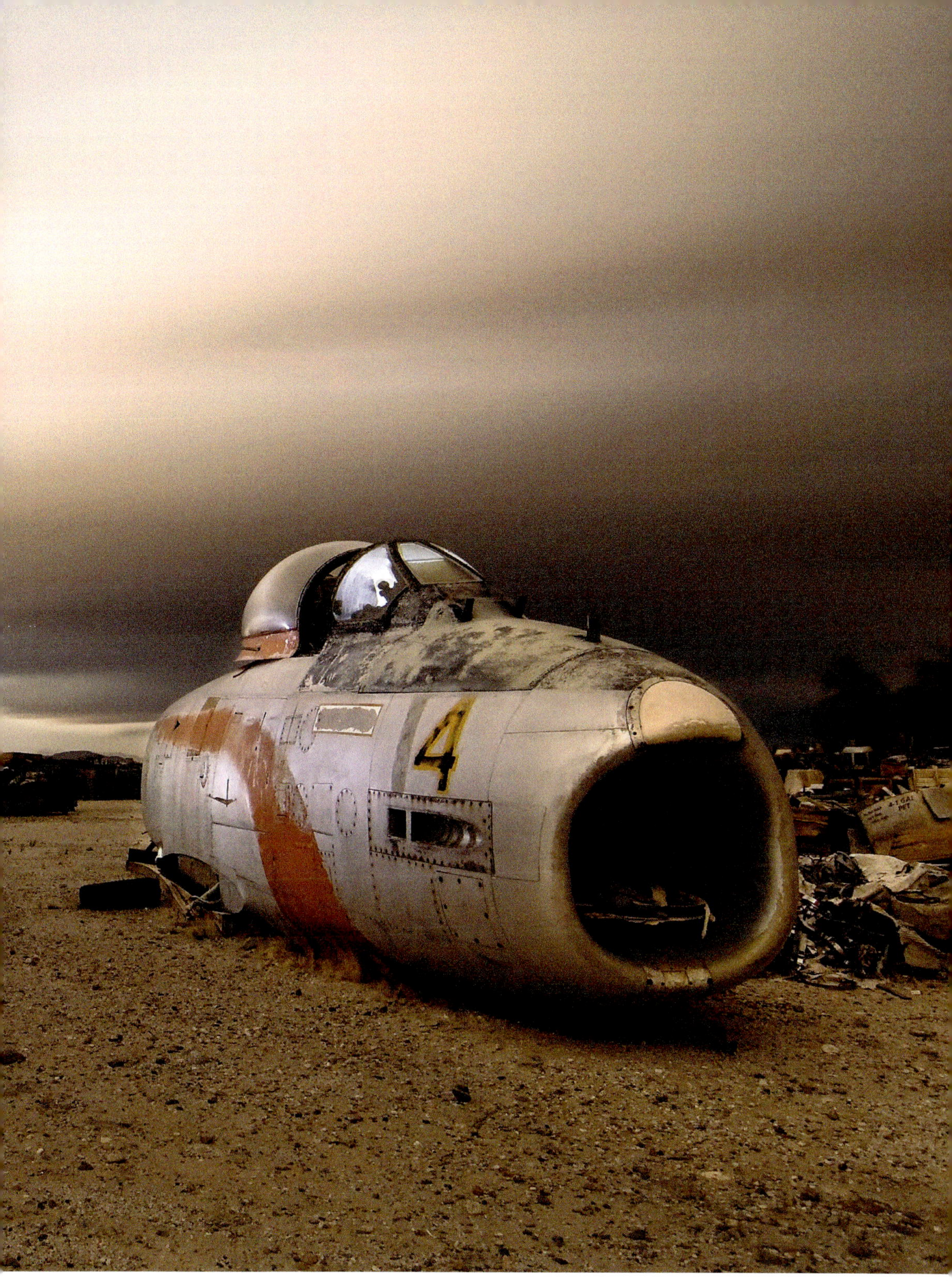

Full moon, partial cloud cover / natural white LED flashlight.
North American F-86 Sabre Jets.

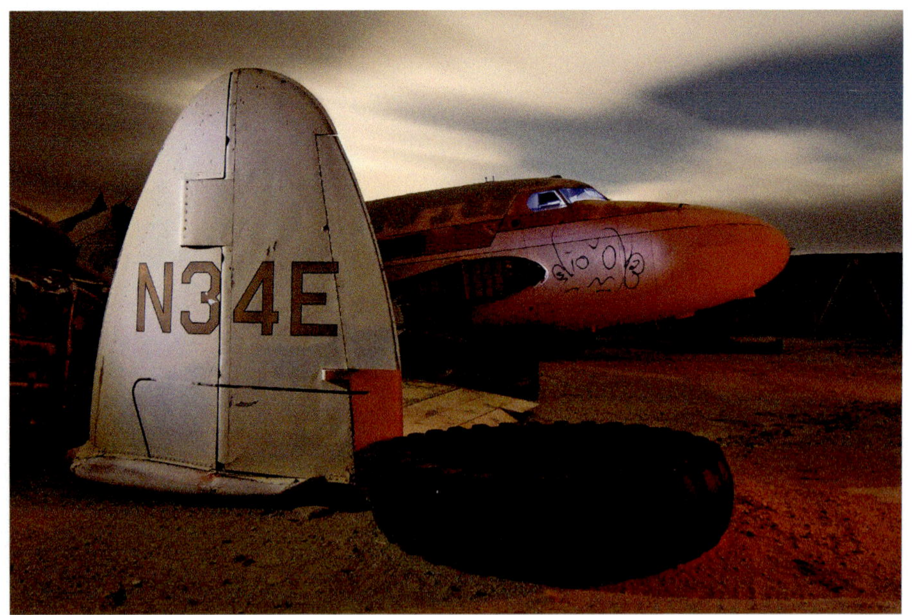

Shedding Her Tail
The Secret Boneyard. 3/20/2011, 12:00 AM.
Canon 20D, f/5.6, ISO 100. 198 seconds, 5000K WB.
Full moon, partial cloud cover / natural white, blue and red-gelled LED flashlights.
Lockheed Lodestar (Howard 350 conversion).

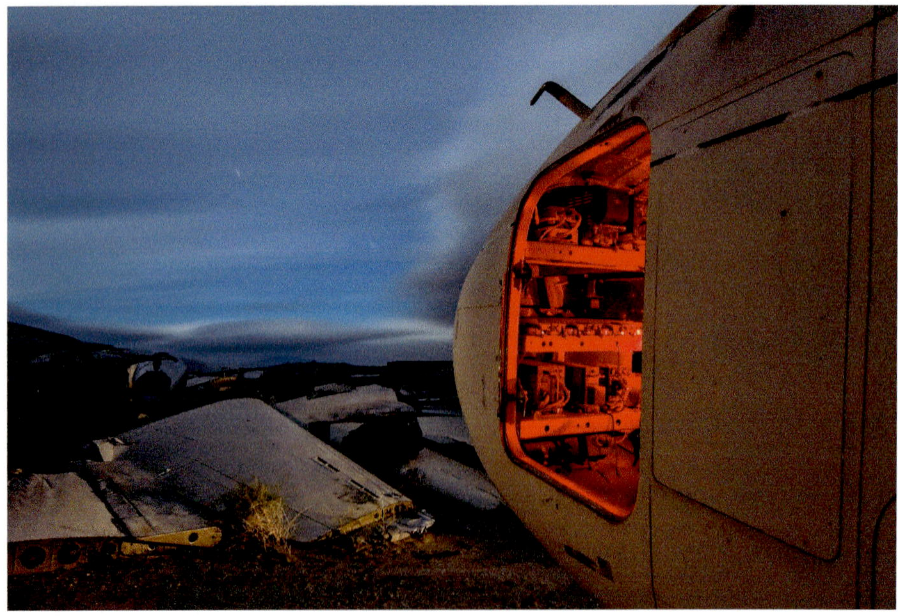

Inside Her Nose
The Secret Boneyard. 3/19/2011, 11:08 PM.
Canon 20D, f/5.6, ISO 100. 141 seconds, 3700K WB.
Full moon, partial cloud cover / natural xenon and red LED flashlights.
Lockheed Lodestar (Howard 350 conversion).

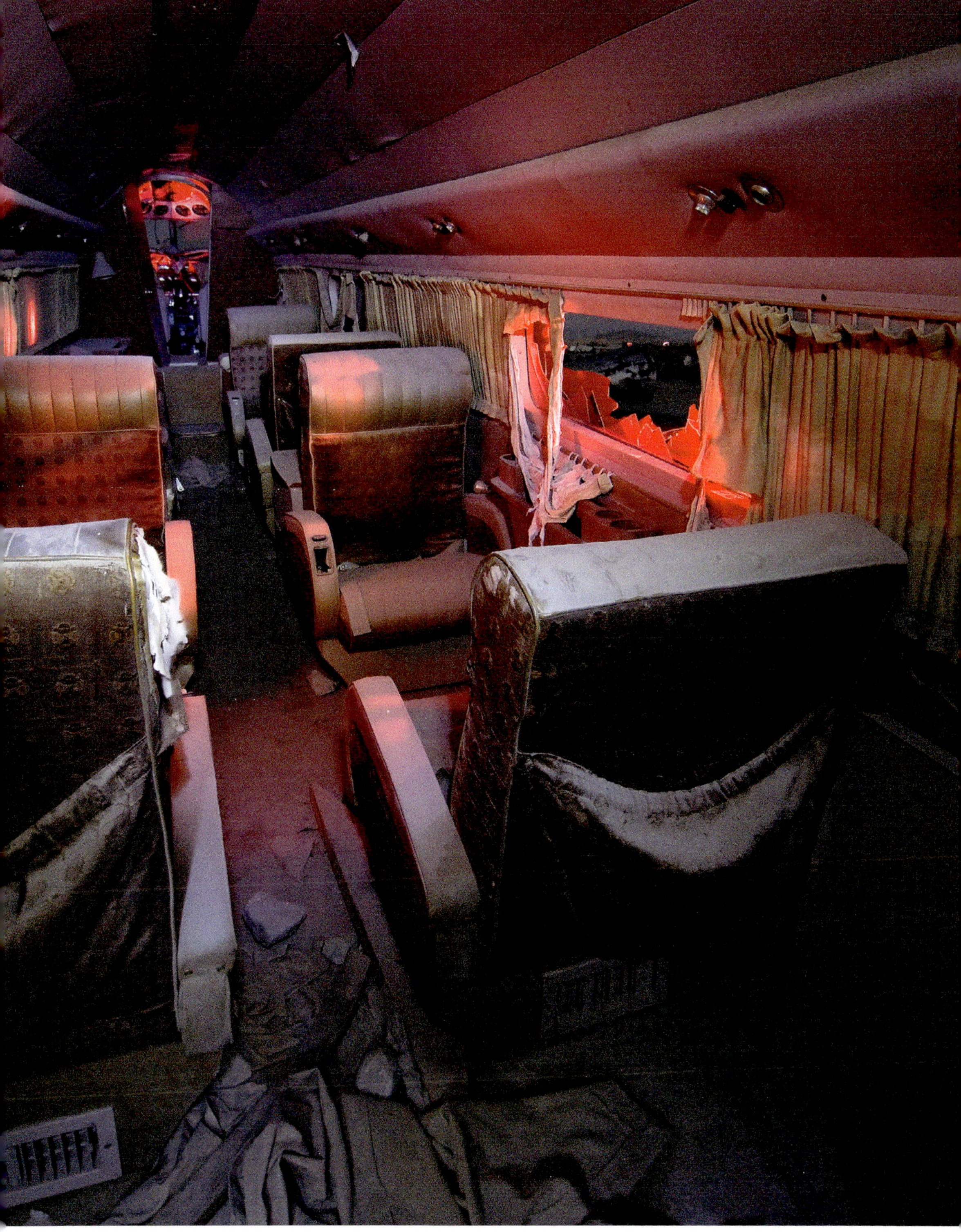

The Bends
The Secret Boneyard. 3/18/2011, 9:17 PM.
Canon 20D, f/5.6, ISO 100. 120 seconds, 3700K WB.
Full moon, partial cloud cover / red and natural white LED flashlight.
Lockheed Lodestar (Howard 350 conversion).

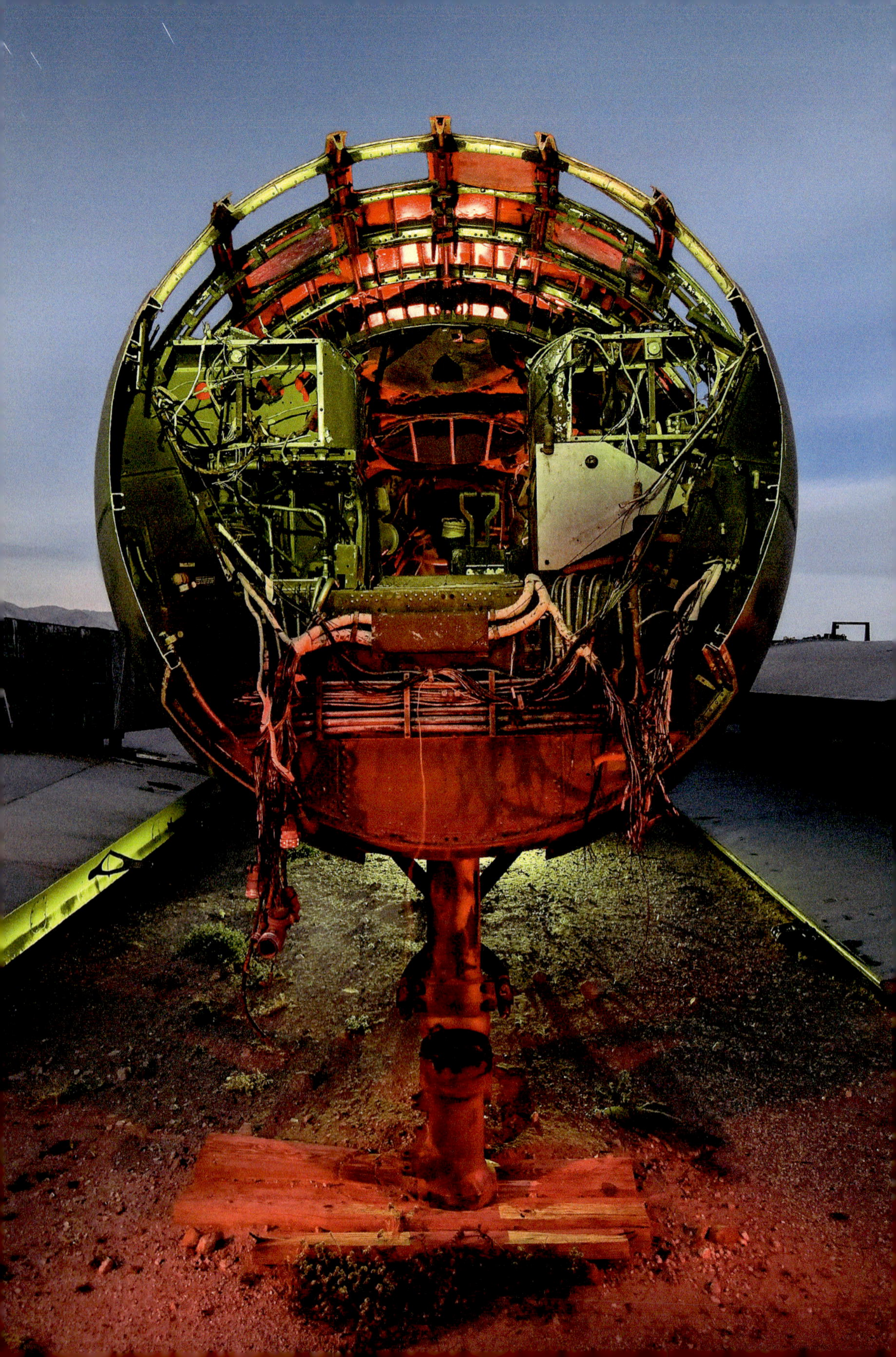

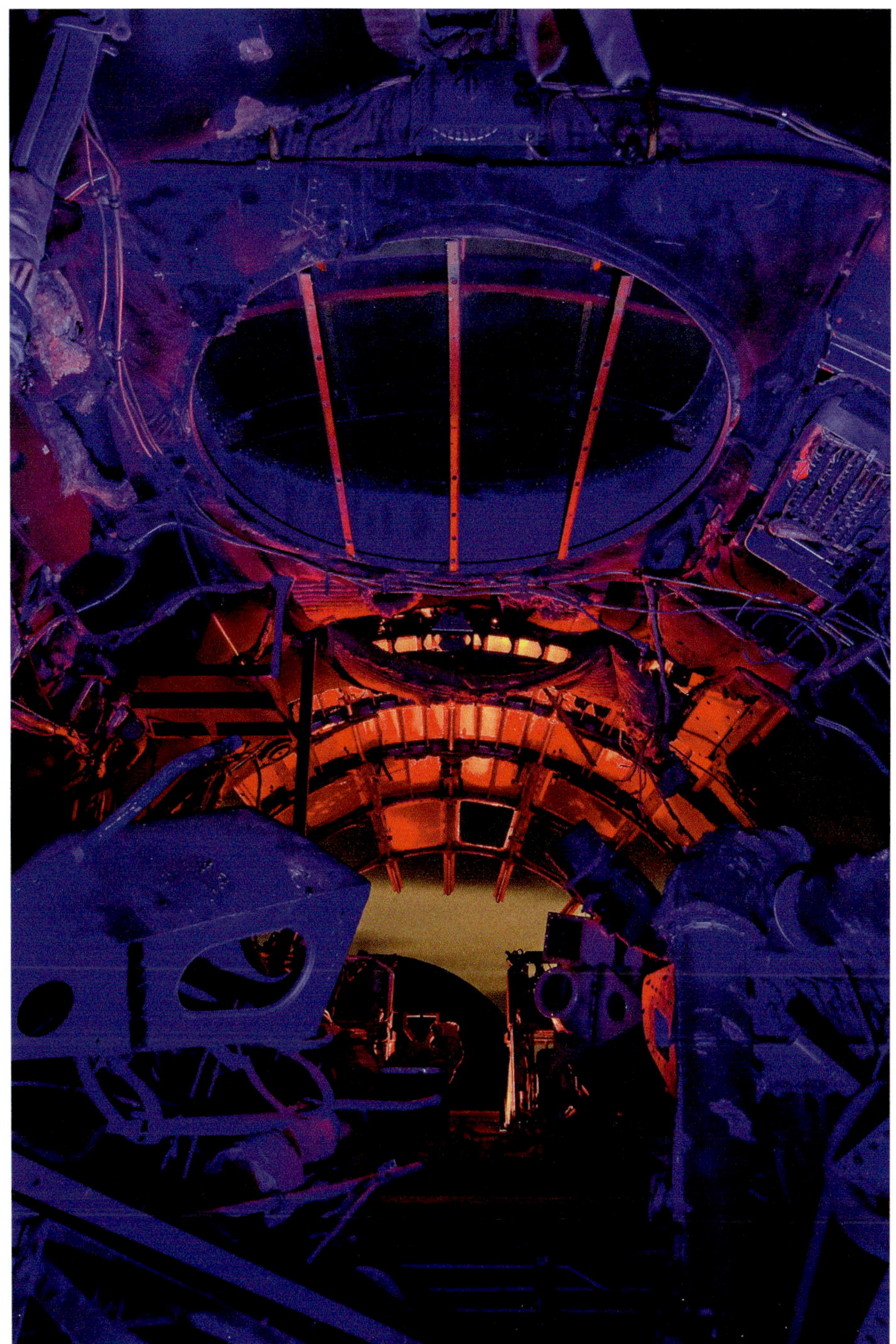

◄ **Flight Deck Amputee**
The Secret Boneyard. 3/18/2011, 10:17 PM.
Canon 20D, f/5.6, ISO 100. 241 seconds, 3800K WB.
Full moon, partial cloud cover / red and lime-gelled LED flashlight.
Boeing B-29 Superfortress.

From the Bomb Bay
The Secret Boneyard. 3/19/2011, 10:21 PM.
Canon 20D, f/5.6, ISO 100. 137 seconds, 6900K WB.
Full moon, partial cloud cover / red and purple-gelled LED flashlight.
Boeing B-29 Superfortress.

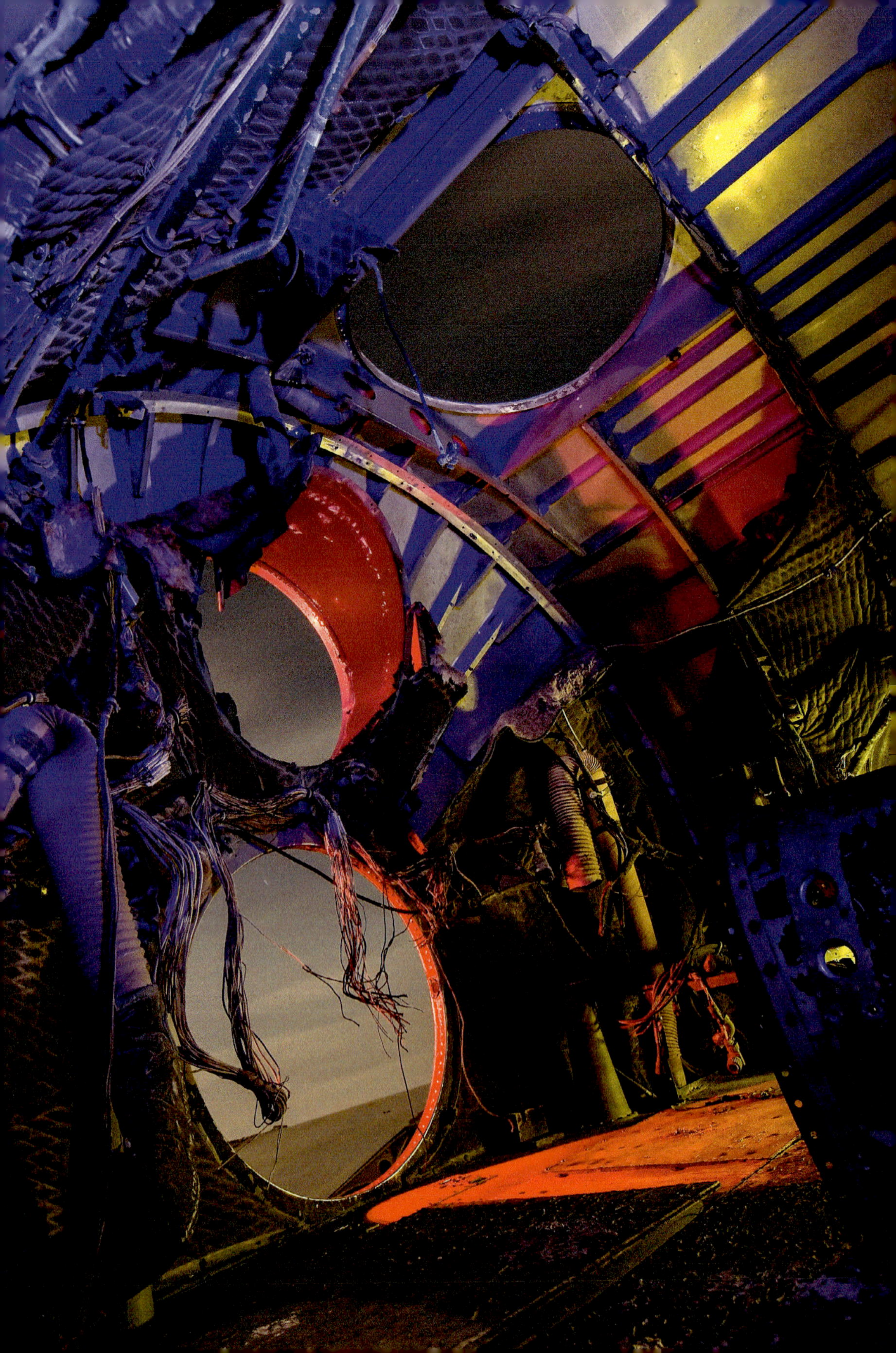

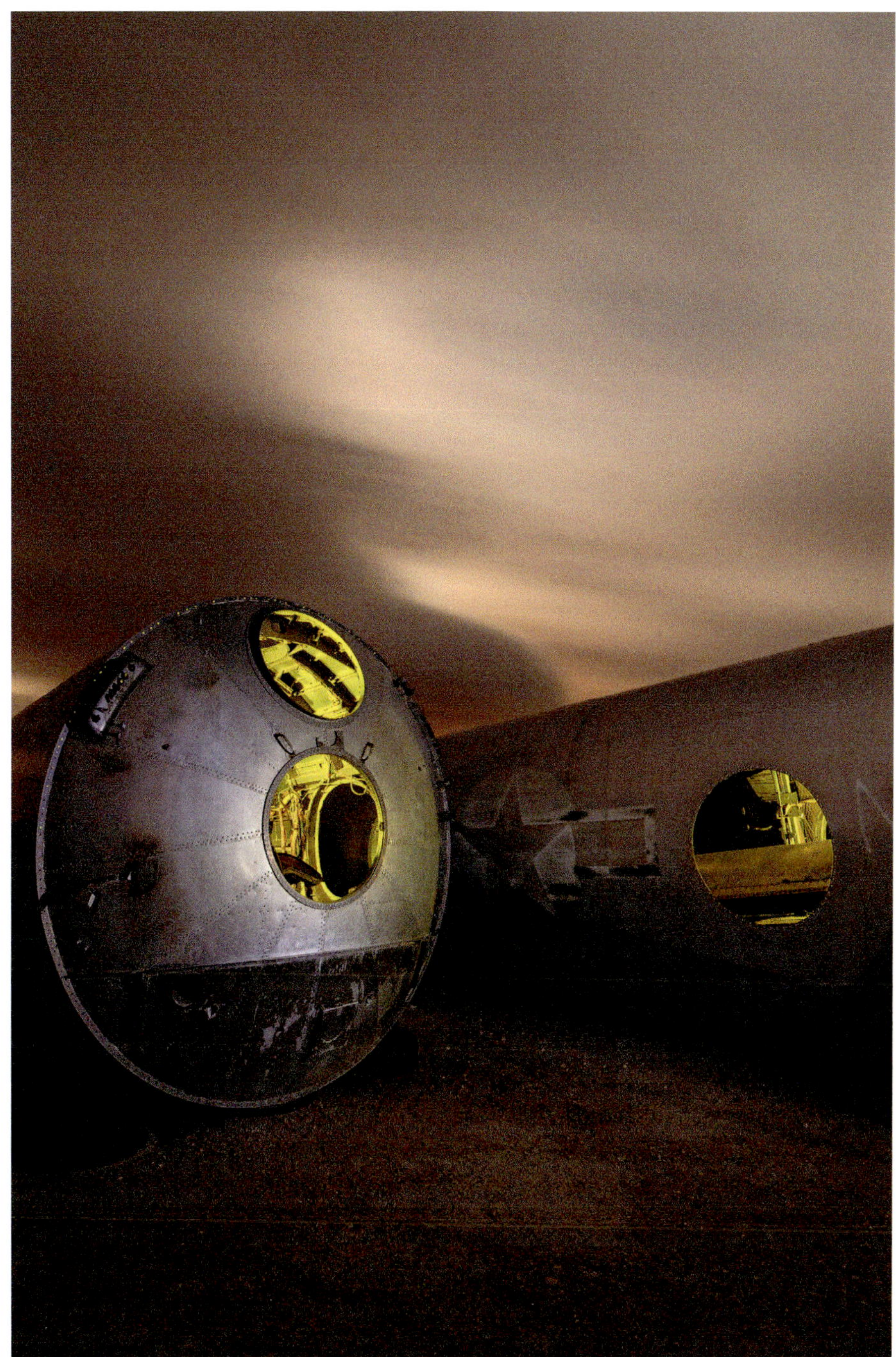

◀ **The Three Portals**
The Secret Boneyard. 3/18/2011, 10:58 PM.
Canon 20D, f/5.6, ISO 100. 120 seconds, 6000K WB.
Full moon, partial cloud cover / red, lime and purple-gelled LED flashlight
Boeing B-29 Superfortress.

Contents Under Pressure
The Secret Boneyard. 3/19/2011, 10:49 PM.
Canon 20D, f/5.6, ISO 100. 196 seconds, 5300K WB.
Full moon, partial cloud cover / lime-gelled and natural white LED flashlight.
Boeing B-29 Superfortress.

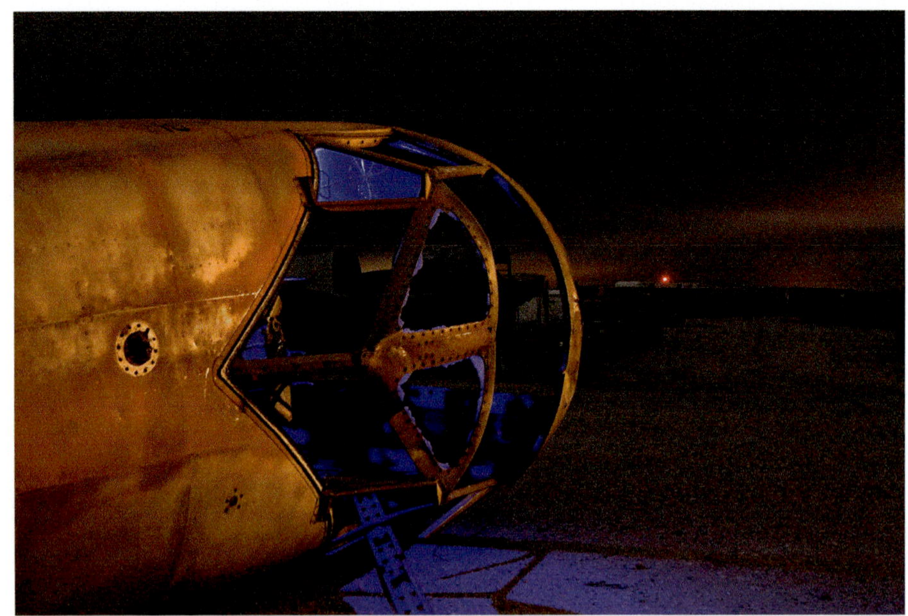

12 O'Clock Sideways
The Secret Boneyard. 3/19/2011, 11:48 PM.
Canon 20D, f/5.6, ISO 100. 198 seconds, 5000K WB.
Full moon, partial cloud cover / natural white xenon and blue-gelled LED flashlights.
Boeing B-17 Flying Fortress.

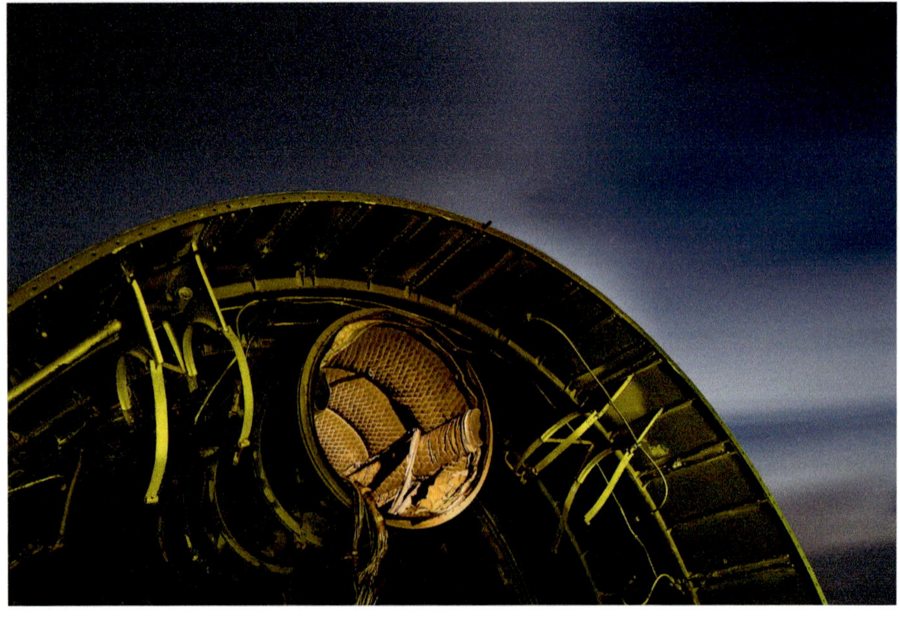

Severed Spine
The Secret Boneyard. 3/19/2011, 10:33 PM.
Canon 20D, f/5.6, ISO 100. 257 seconds, 3750K WB.
Full moon, partial cloud cover / natural xenon and lime-gelled LED flashlights.
Boeing B-29 Superfortress.

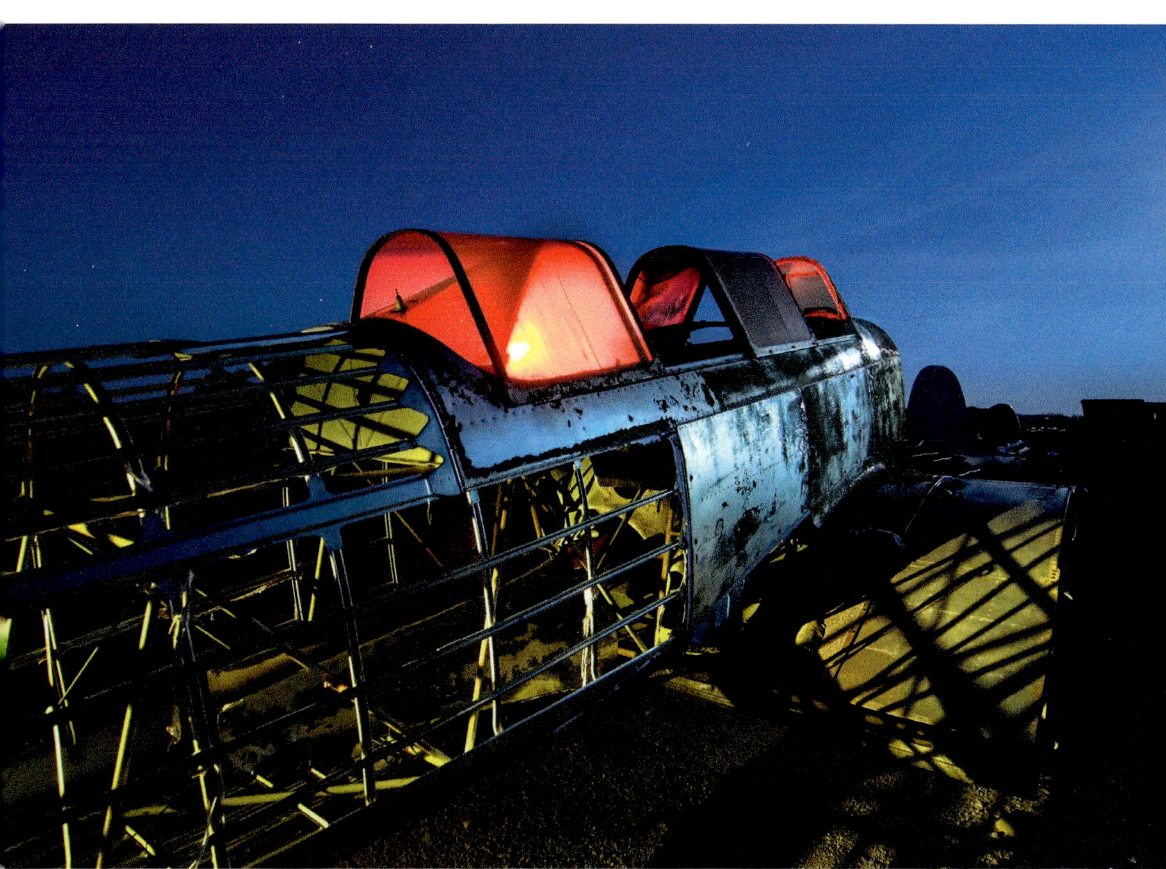

In The Cage
The Secret Boneyard. 9/13/2008, 7:58 PM.
Canon 20D, f/5.6, ISO 100. 60 seconds, 2850K WB.
Full moon / natural white, red and lime-gelled LED flashlight.
North American T-6 Texan.

On the following page:

The 29
The Secret Boneyard. 3/18/2011, 11:08 PM.
Canon 20D, f/5.6, ISO 100. 120 seconds, 3800K WB.
Full moon, partial cloud cover / natural white LED flashlight.
Boeing B-29 Superfortress.

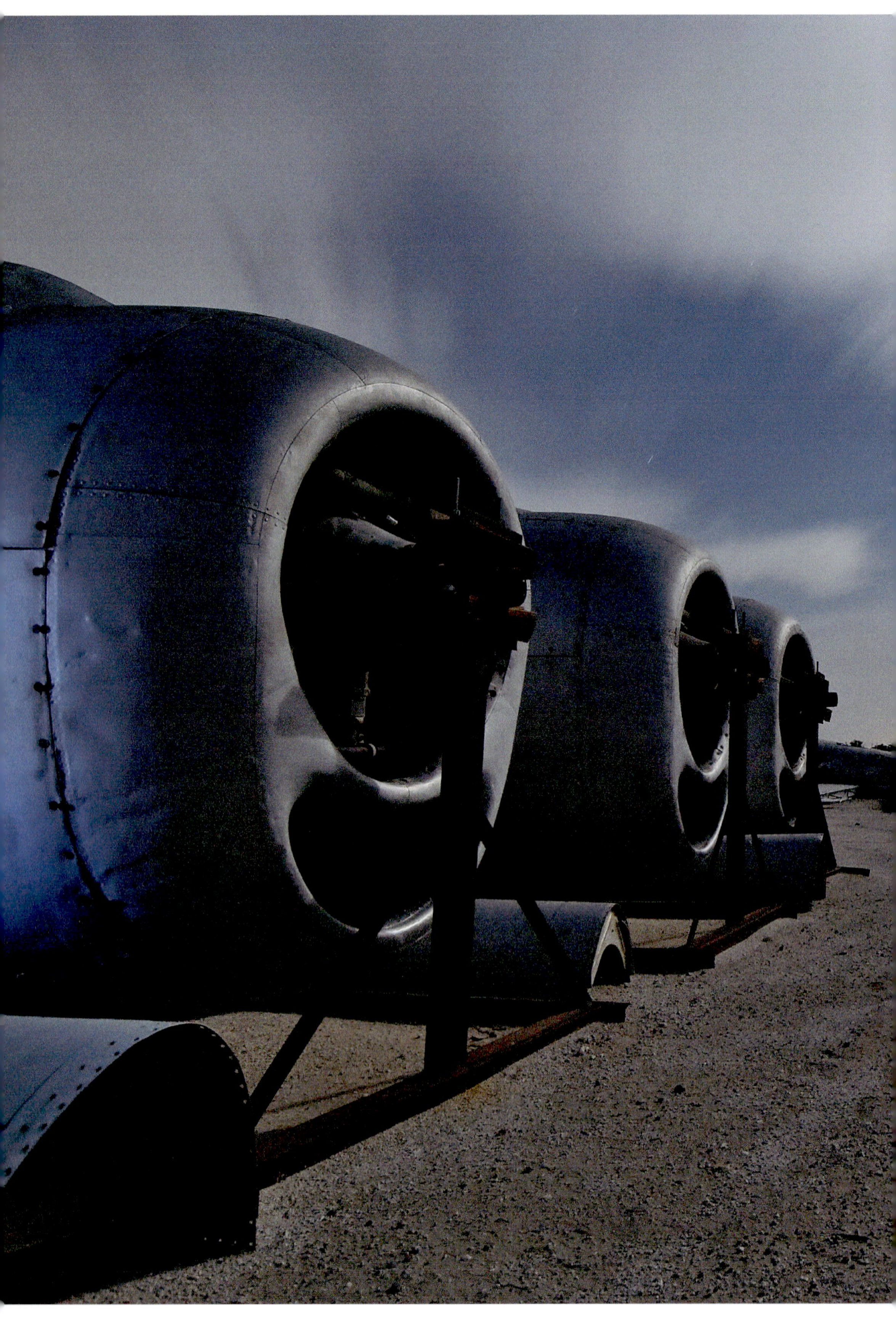

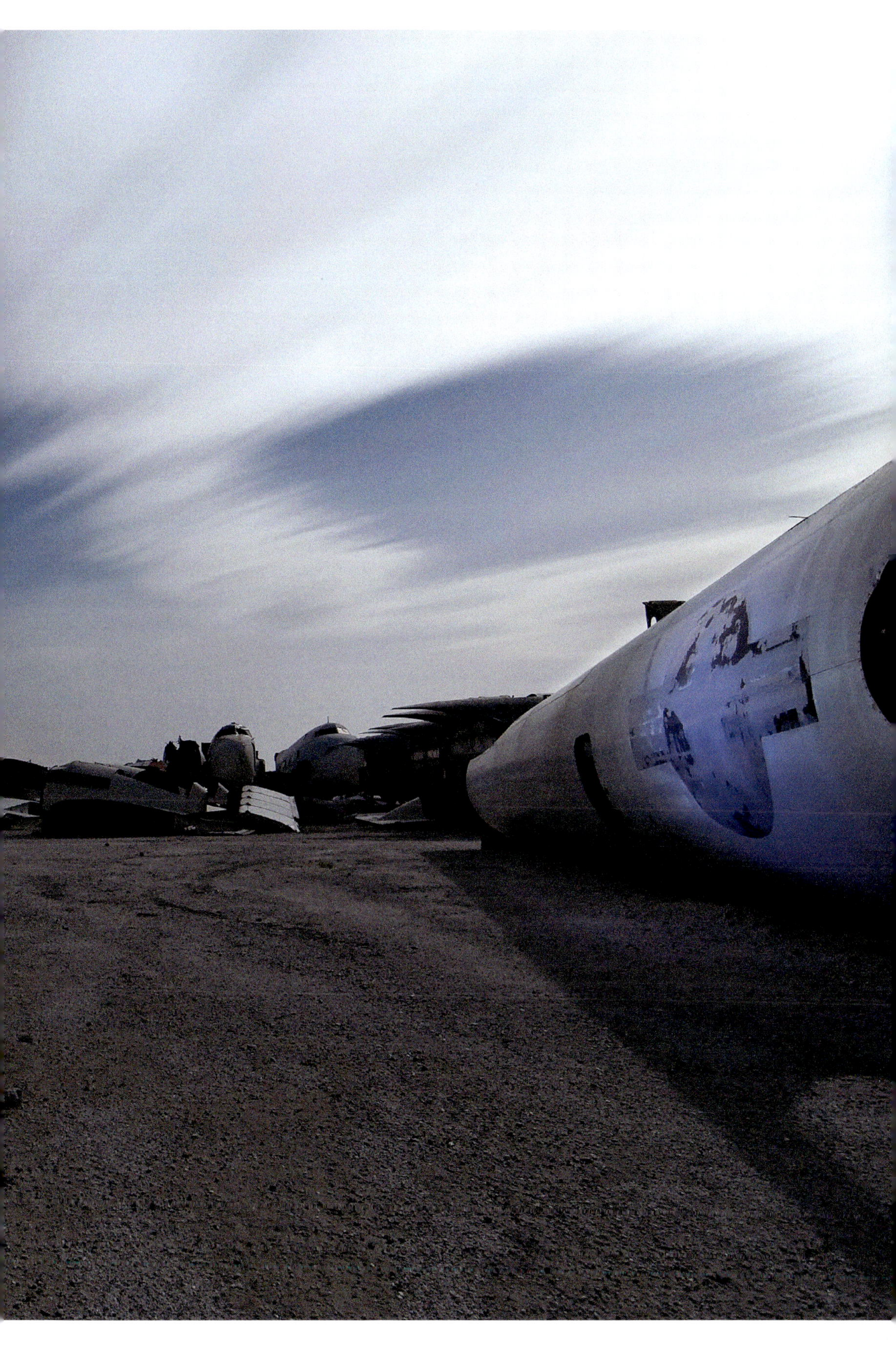

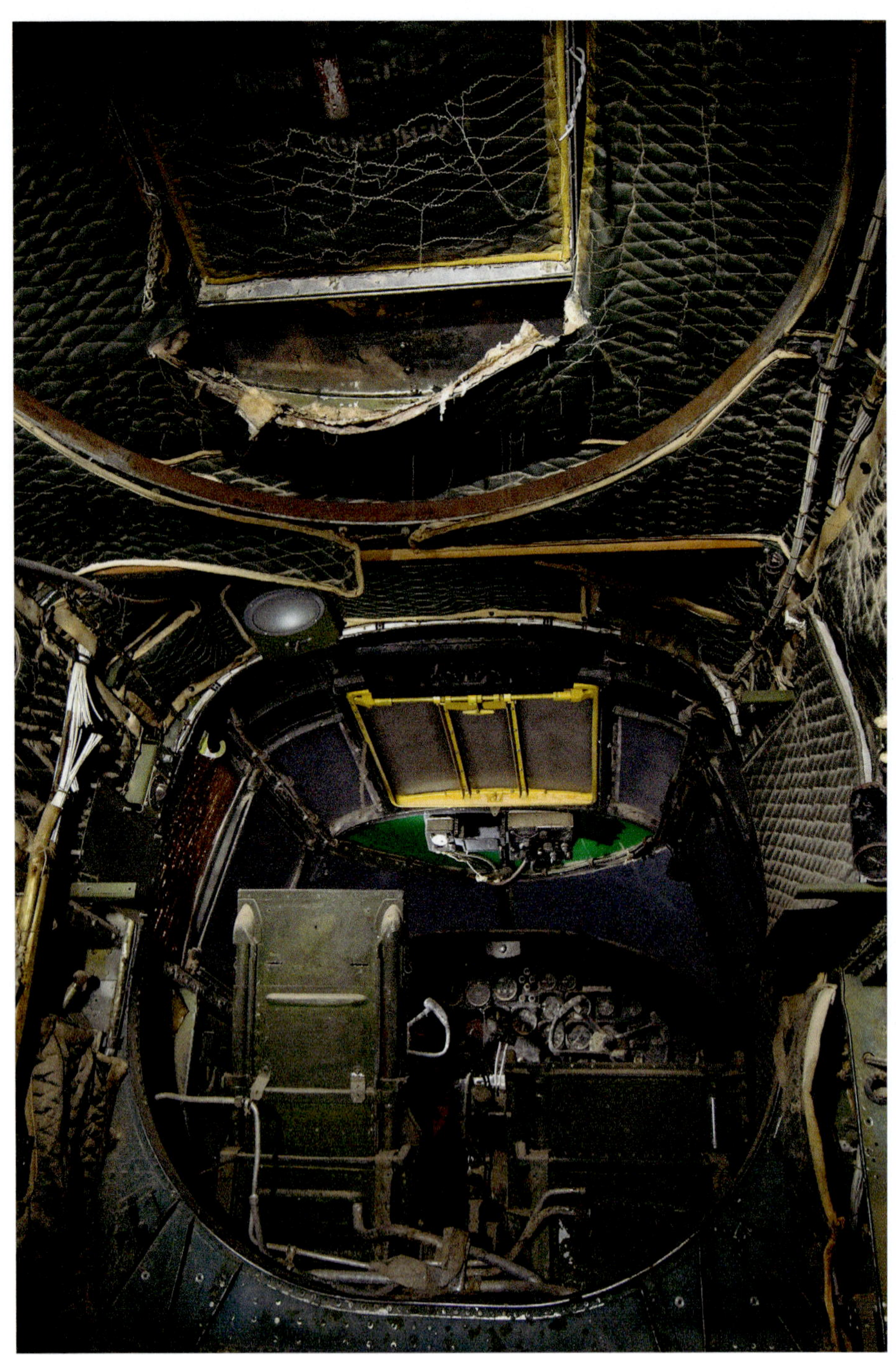

Bombardier to Pilot
The Secret Boneyard. 9/13/2008, 9:36 PM.
Canon 20D, f/5.6, ISO 100. 120 seconds, 4800K WB.
Full moon / natural white LED flashlight.
North American B-25 Mitchell.

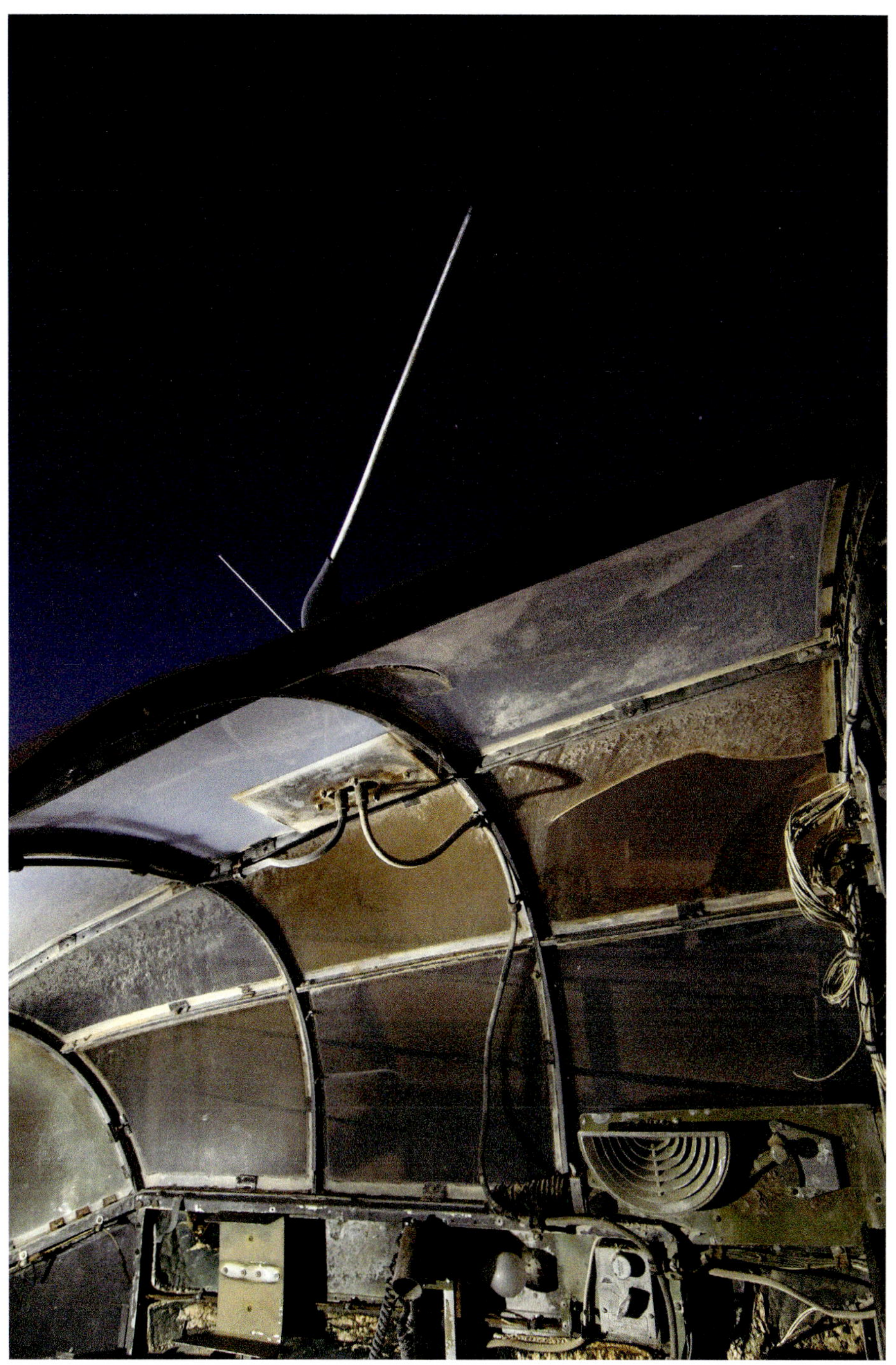

Primitive Radio
The Secret Boneyard. 9/13/2008, 9:40 PM.
Canon 20D, f/5.6, ISO 100, 120 seconds, 4200K WB
Full moon / natural white LED flashlight.
North American B-25 Mitchell.

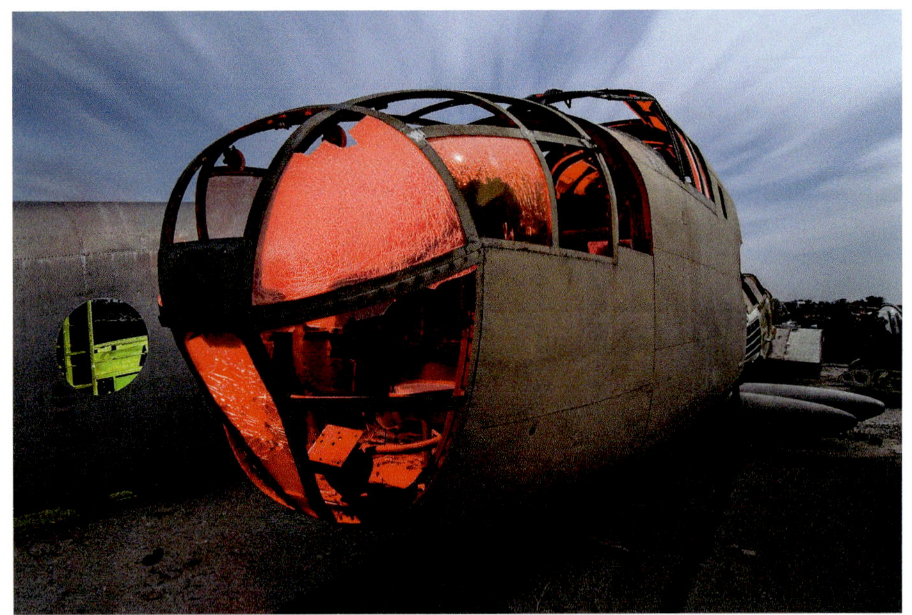

Observer
The Secret Boneyard. 3/18/2011, 11:52 PM.
Canon 20D, f/5.6, ISO 100. 131 seconds, 3700K WB.
Full moon, partial cloud cover / red and lime-gelled LED flashlights.
North American B-25 Mitchell.

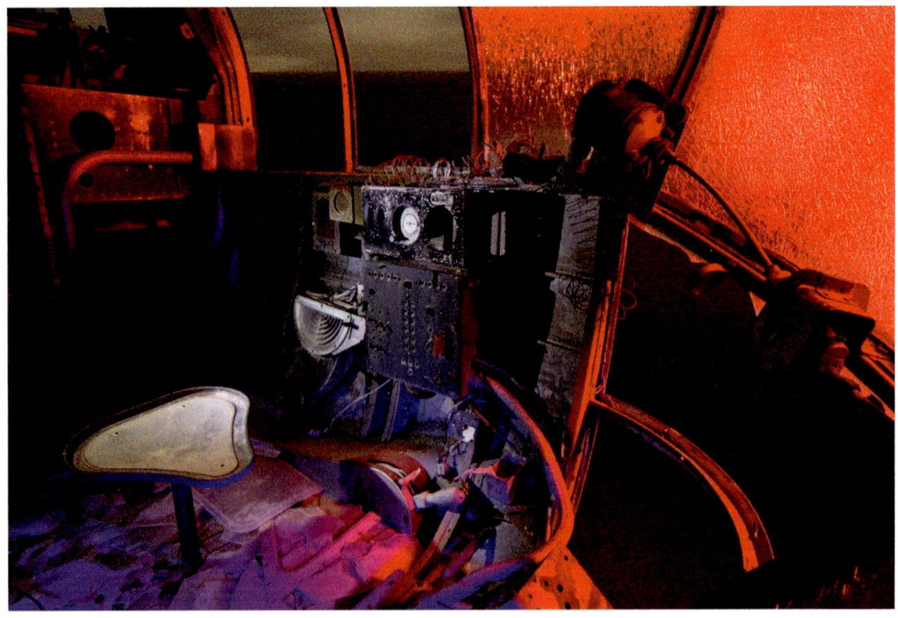

Dropping the Bomb
The Secret Boneyard. 3/19/2011, 12:06 AM.
Canon 20D, f/5.6, ISO 100. 120 seconds, 5300K WB.
Full moon, partial cloud cover / natural white, red and purple-gelled LED flashlight.
North American B-25 Mitchell.

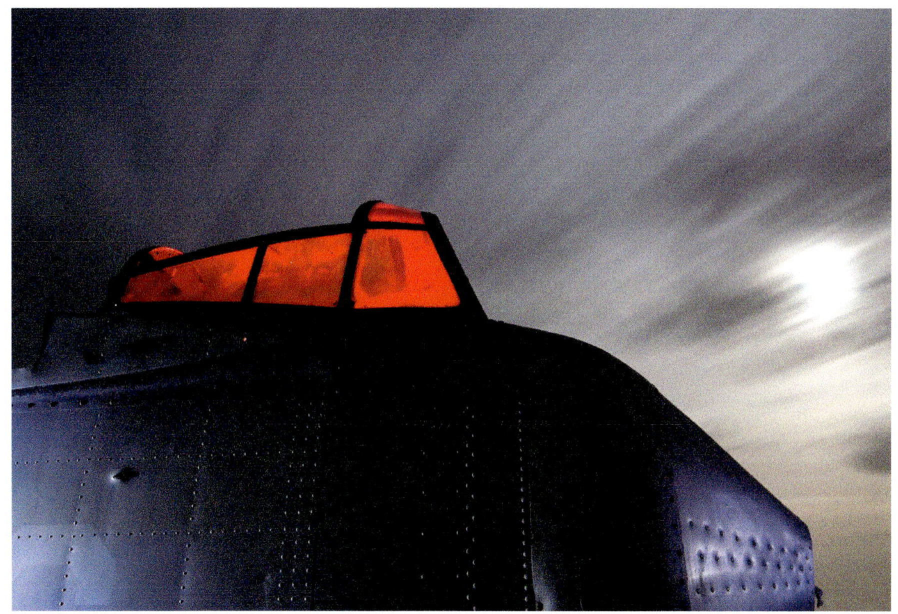

From the Back Seat
The Secret Boneyard. 3/18/2011, 9:46 PM.
Canon 20D, f/5.6, ISO 100. 67 seconds, 3900K WB.
Full moon, partial cloud cover / natural white and red LED flashlight.
North American B-25 Mitchell.

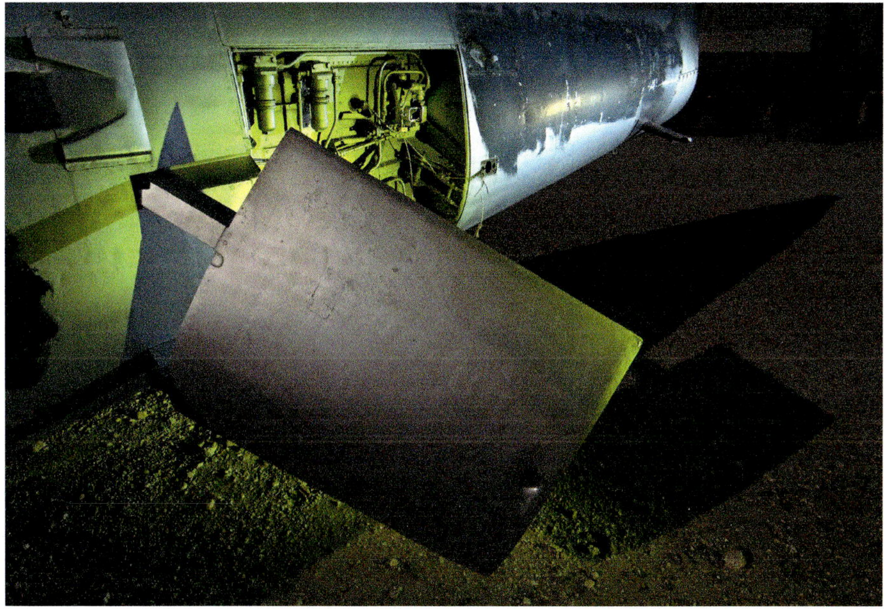

Air Brake
The Secret Boneyard. 9/13/2008, 8:58 PM.
Canon 20D, f/5.6, ISO 100. 61 seconds, 2850K WB.
Full moon / natural white and lime-gelled LED flashlight.
North American F-86 Sabre Jet.

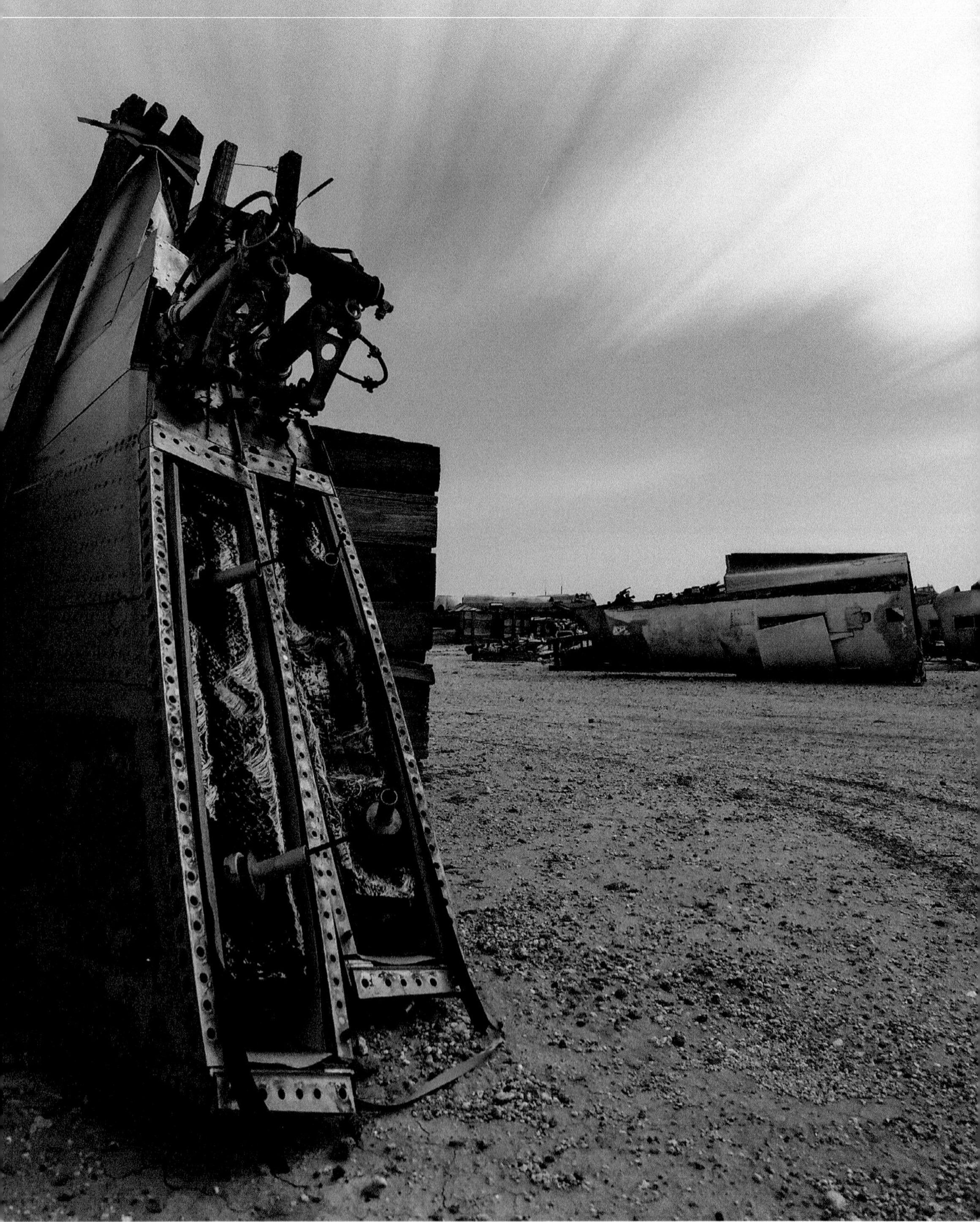

Ready For Reassembly

The Secret Boneyard. 3/18/2011, 11:33 PM.

Canon 20D, f/5.6, ISO 100. 310 seconds, 3700K WB.

Full moon, partial cloud cover.

North American F-86 Sabre Jet.

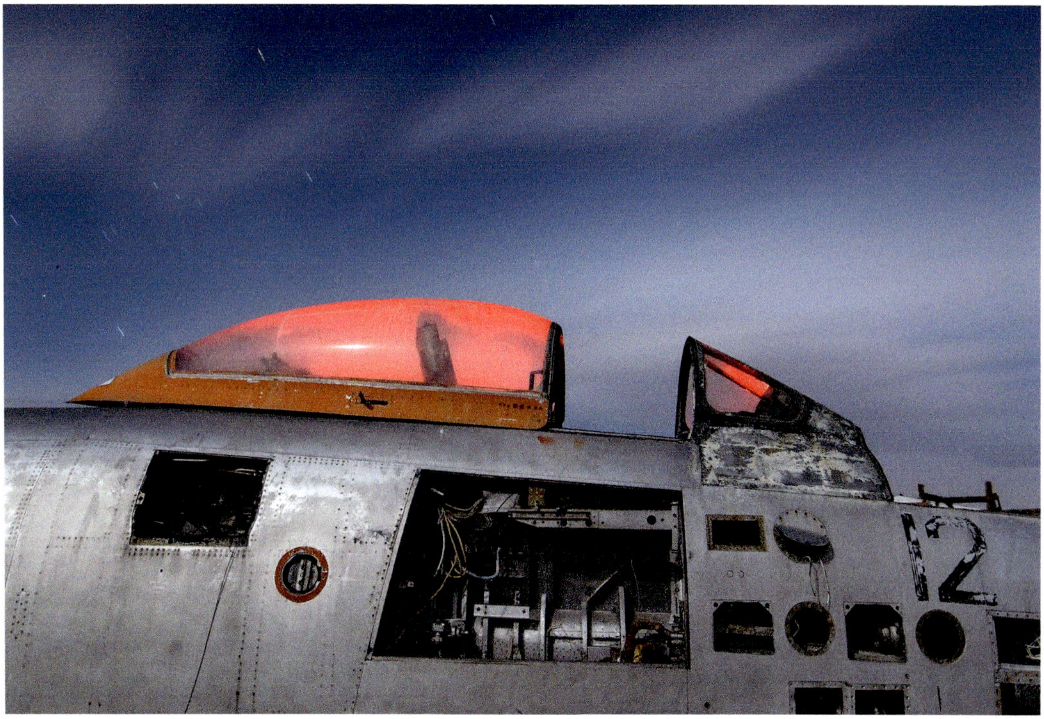

Canopy Number 12
The Secret Boneyard. 3/18/2011,
11:14 PM.
Canon 20D, f/5.6, ISO 100.
170 seconds, 3900K WB.
Full moon, partial cloud cover /
red LED flashlight.
North American F-86 Sabre Jet.

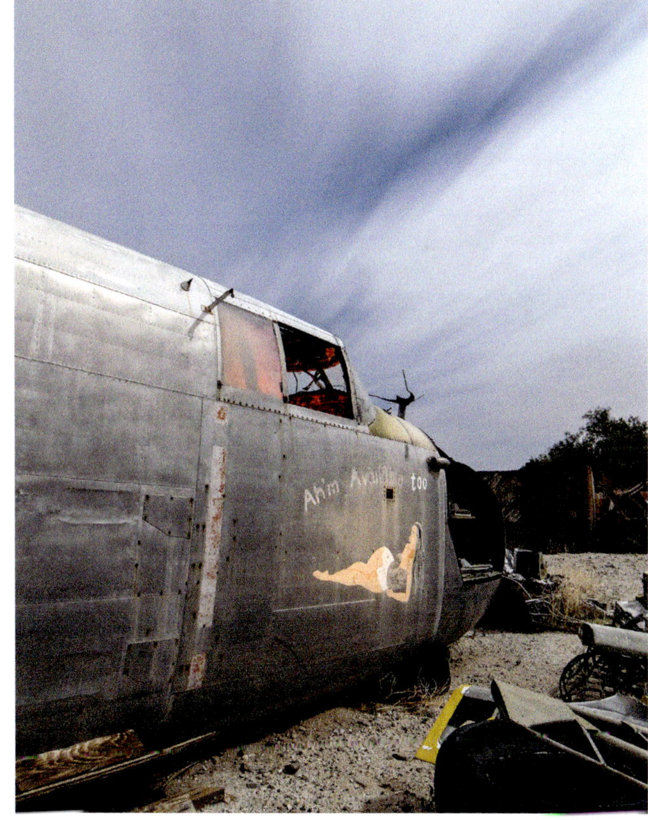

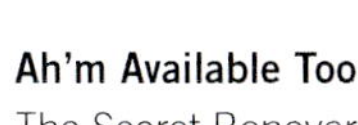

Ah'm Available Too
The Secret Boneyard. 3/19/2011,
12:23 PM.
Canon 20D, f/5.6, ISO 100.
175 seconds, 3900K WB.
Full moon, partial cloud cover /
natural white xenon flashlight.
North American B-25 Mitchell.

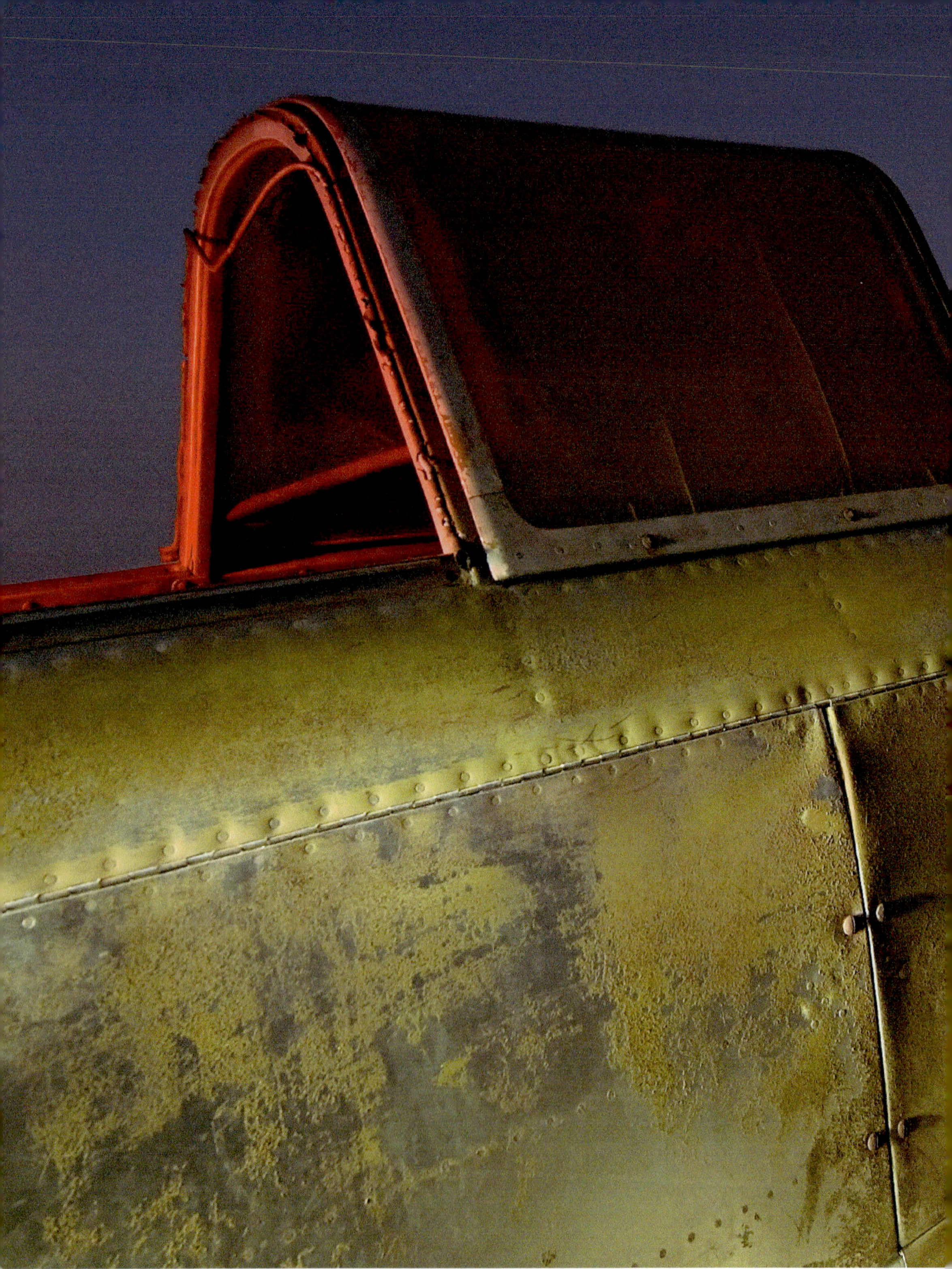

Trainee
The Secret Boneyard. 9/13/2008, 7:44 PM.
Canon 20D, f/5.6, ISO 100. 30 seconds, 5050K WB.

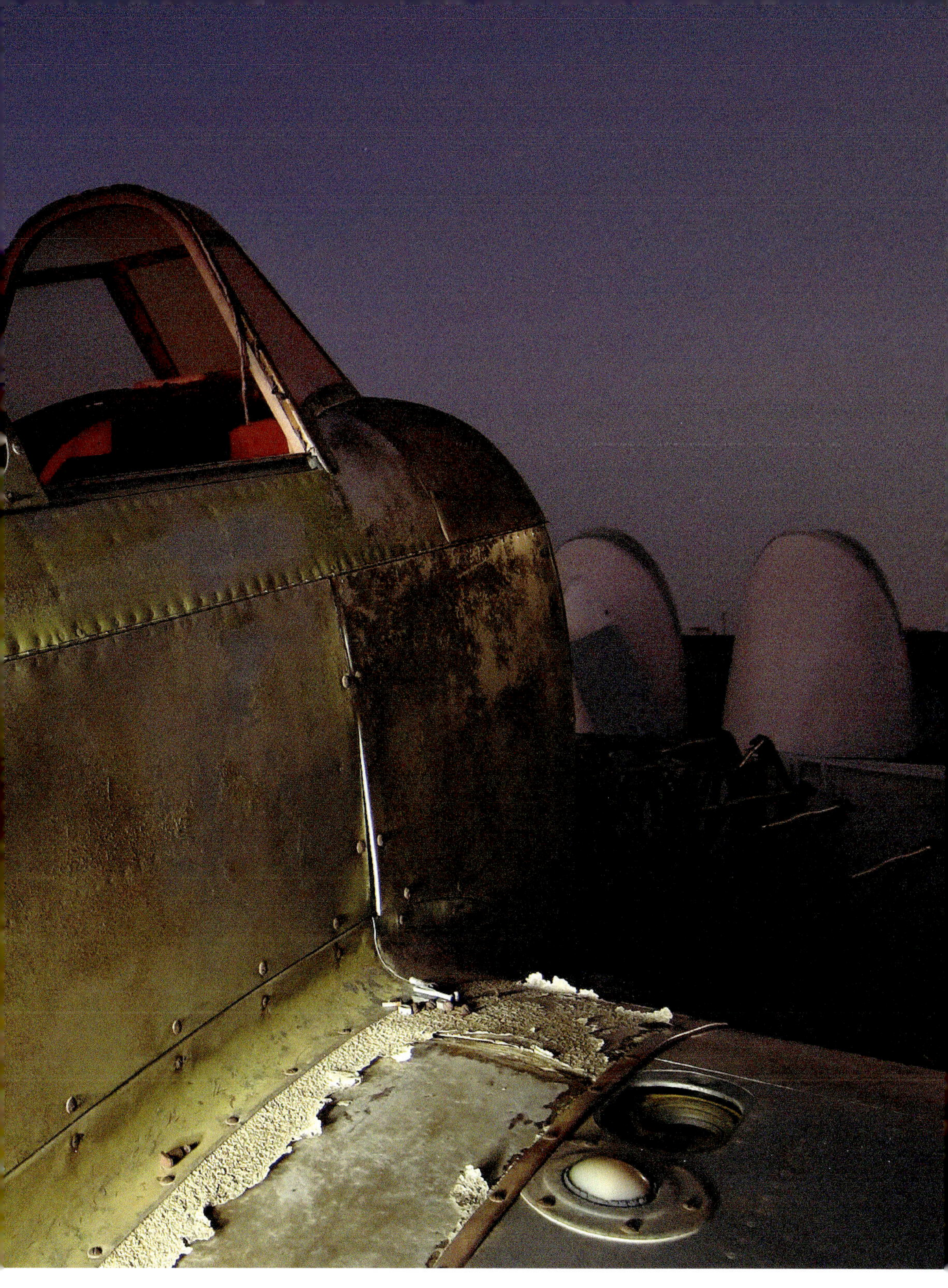

Full moon / natural white and red LED flashlight.
North American T-6 Texan.

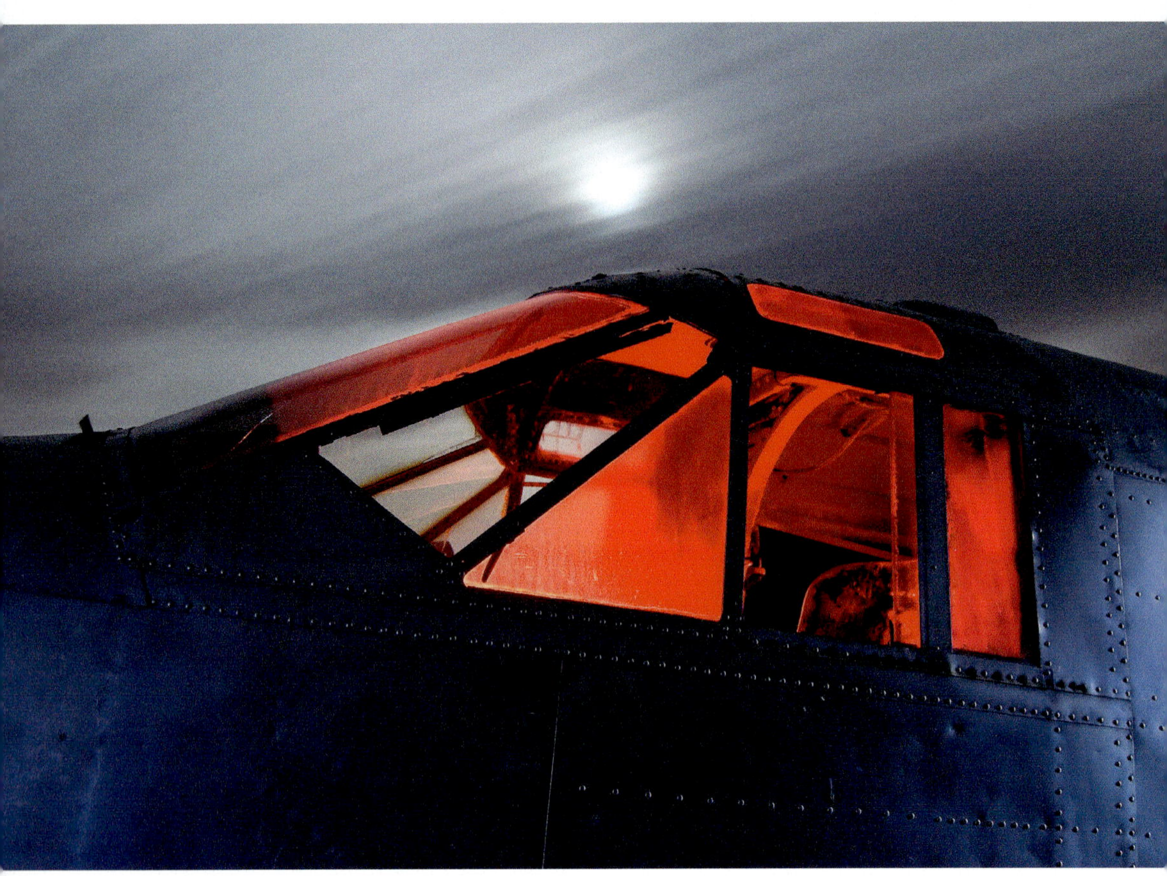

Veee-Efff-Arrrgh
The Secret Boneyard. 3/18/2011, 9:52 PM.
Canon 20D, f/5.6, ISO 100. 107 seconds, 3500K WB.
Full moon, partial cloud cover / natural white and red LED flashlights.
Beechcraft Model 18.

The Tailgunner's Pod ▶
The Secret Boneyard. 3/19/2011, 12:23 AM.
Canon 20D, f/5.6, ISO 100. 104 seconds, 3800K WB.
Full moon, partial cloud cover / natural white LED flashlight.

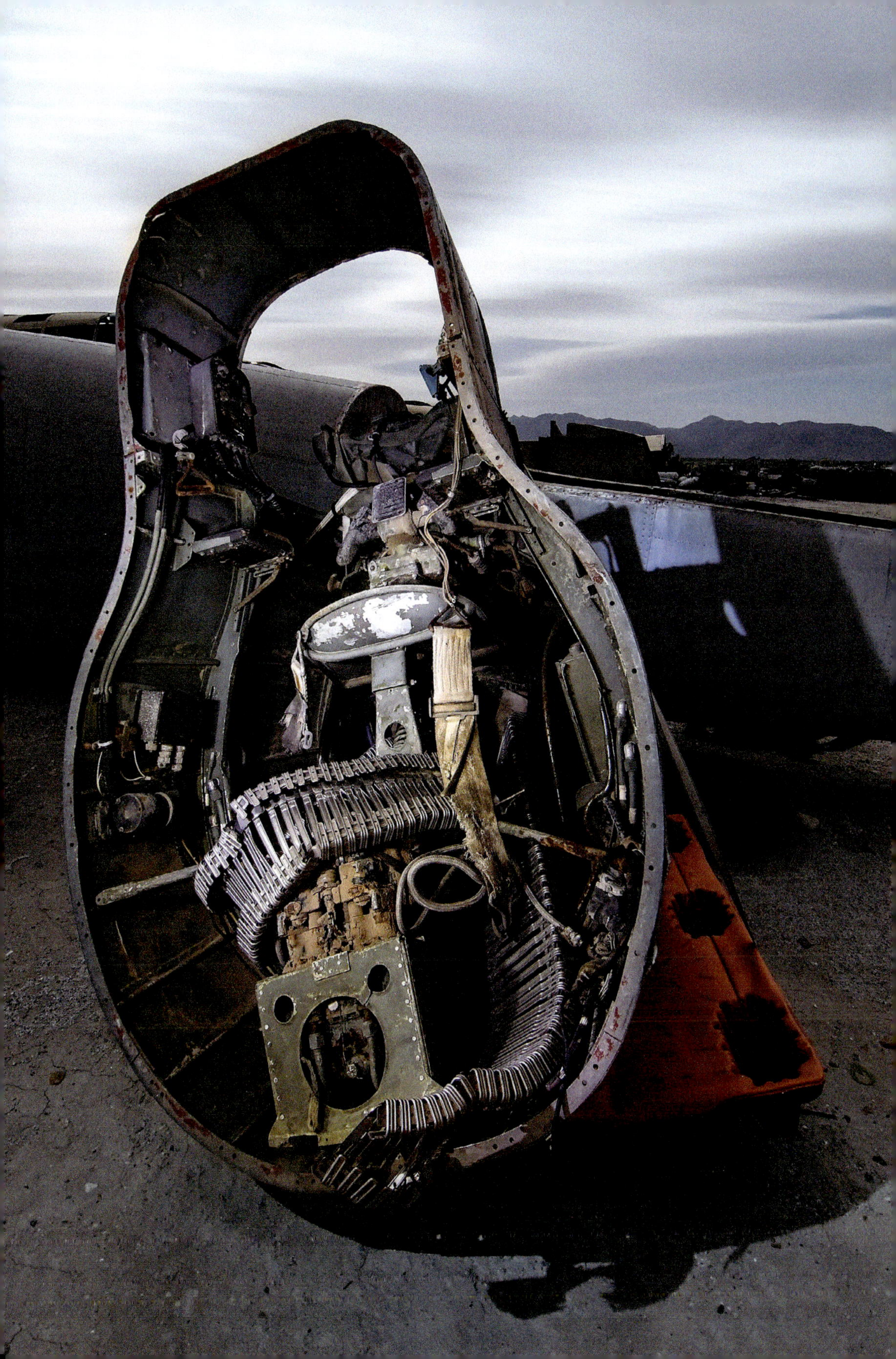

2

THE LAND OF JETS AND JOSHUAS

Idling down the dirt road, headlights off ... the tail is the first thing you see. It slowly grows, black against the deep blue of the night sky. The wedge looms overhead as Ron's Jeep's tires crunch to a stop in the gravel, under the sleek jet's curled wingtip. Like something out of my surreal sci-fi subconscious, I am on another planet, exploring some kind of Robinson Crusoe space wreck. Is that the stringless ghost of Fireball XL5's Steve Zodiac, climbing out of the cockpit? Decrepit, yet majestic, statuesque in its stark setting, silhouetted against the always-strange Joshua trees, this aircraft is one of the most singular sights I've ever seen.

I'm finally visiting Snoopy, the derelict Convair B-58 Hustler (55-0665), lost in the wide open spaces of the Mojave, way out past the end of the seven-mile, dry lake runway, at Edwards Air Force Base. There are many people who think the Hustler is one of the sexiest, most ballistic-looking airplanes ever made. Its elegantly balanced triangular wings, Coke-bottle fuselage and long, thin engine pods were frequently mimicked in automotive design, architecture and science fiction. In early 1960s terms, it's what transportation in *The Future* looked like.

Initially the darling of Strategic Air Command, it was the first bomber capable of supersonic flight: a Mach 2 nuclear sword that could outrun and out climb any other aircraft of the day, even fighters. The 1963 "Greased Lightning" speed record, from Tokyo to London (8 hours, 35 minutes), still stands.

It was also temperamental and dangerous: twenty-six of the 116 built were lost in testing and crashes. Expensive to build and fly, hampered by its short range and the development of faster enemy missiles, the Hustler remained operational for only ten years—retiring in 1970. The eighty-six surviving aircraft were shuttled to the Military Aircraft Storage and Disposition Center (MASDC), the government's own boneyard, in Tucson, Arizona. All but eight ended up in the smelter in 1977.

Seven of the remaining Hustlers have been lovingly restored and are on display in major American aviation museums, leaving airframe 55-0665 as the mystery plane, relegated to a slow death, forgotten in the high desert. This aircraft, the sixth built, only

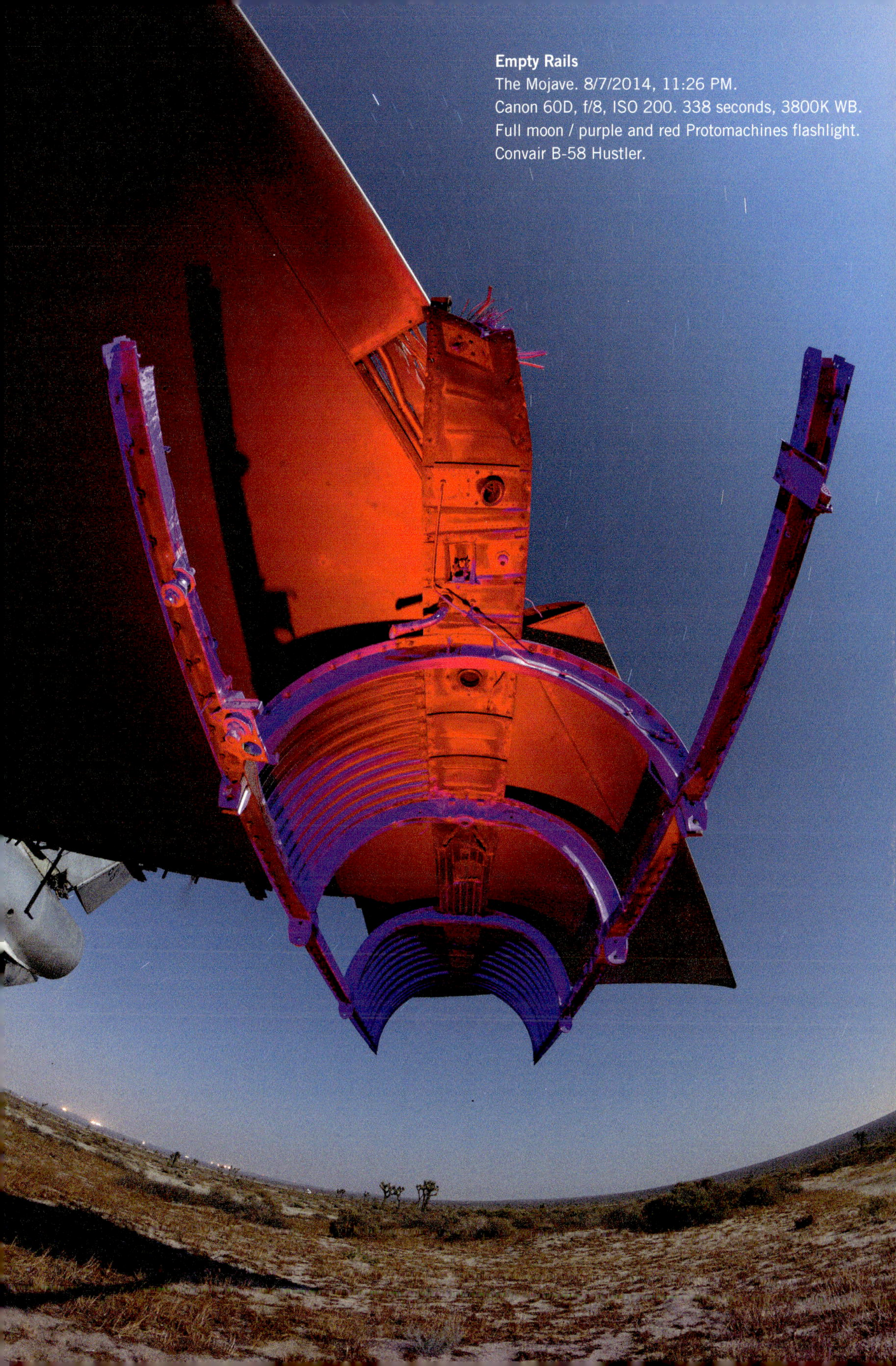

Empty Rails
The Mojave. 8/7/2014, 11:26 PM.
Canon 60D, f/8, ISO 200. 338 seconds, 3800K WB.
Full moon / purple and red Protomachines flashlight.
Convair B-58 Hustler.

saw duty as a test bed, its nose extended and expanded to house experimental radar guidance systems for the next generation of missiles, hence the Snoopy nickname. By the mid-sixties, the test program had concluded and it was towed out to this remote spot and left as a photo recon target and electronic target for virtual bomb runs.

Sitting out in the open for fifty years has taken its toll. As remote as it is, the aircraft has been picked clean. Only hints of its original paint remain. Baked and sandblasted for half a century, the once mirror-like aluminum skin has gone matte, diffusing softly in the moonlight. Dusty underwing panels, streaked with the water stains of summer monsoons, arch just overhead, the delicate wings perched on tall, skeletal landing gear. The modified fiberglass radar cone has delaminated, leaving Snoopy with a fuzzy nose.

Part of me sees this old dog's fate as a tragedy, but at the same time, it's the only B-58 that I'll ever be able to get this intimate with, the only one so exquisitely decayed and in such a picturesque location. I didn't have any trouble spending six meditative hours contemplating its slippery lines while my long exposures burned in. Curse you Red Baron, I love Snoopy.

Bang a right and wind through the patches of sagebrush. Eventually, you crest a rise to the left and drop into a clearing on the fringe of a dry lake. The nose suddenly looms out of the dark and towers over you. I'm out of the Jeep practically before it stops, ready to give the monster a walk-around. Staggeringly big, the first of two abandoned Boeing B-52 Stratofortresses dominates the site. My first reaction: It's amazing something so thick and blunt can fly.

A contemporary to, but complete opposite of the sleek and pointy Hustler, the affectionately nicknamed BUFF (Big Ugly Fat Fucker) was the more conventional and functional design, allowing for varied types of missions and relative ease of upgrade. It's been a constant presence in the American arsenal since 1955, seeing action in Vietnam, Serbia, the Gulf War, and the wars in Iraq and Afghanistan. It's cemented in pop culture lore by the band of the same name and the plane's pivotal role in Stanley Kubrick's *Dr. Strangelove.* Even though the last one was built in 1962, the BUFF is still in service, more than sixty years after its introduction.

This massive plane is structurally intact, still sitting on its flat tires on the desert hardpan. It's gutted though, engines gone, everything removed. The lower fuselage is pocked with holes from vandals. Under the faded U.S. AIR FORCE legend on the fuselage is BARRIER TEST AIRCRAFT in smaller letters. This plane (53-0379) was repeatedly rolled into, and caught by, experimental netting systems, later installed at the ends of Edwards' long runways to catch runaway jets. Written off in 1970, this tweaked and abused airframe was towed out here and forgotten.

Walking under the wing root looming as tall as a cathedral, it seems more building than airplane. It's streaked with dirt and sagging, the outer engine pylons hanging

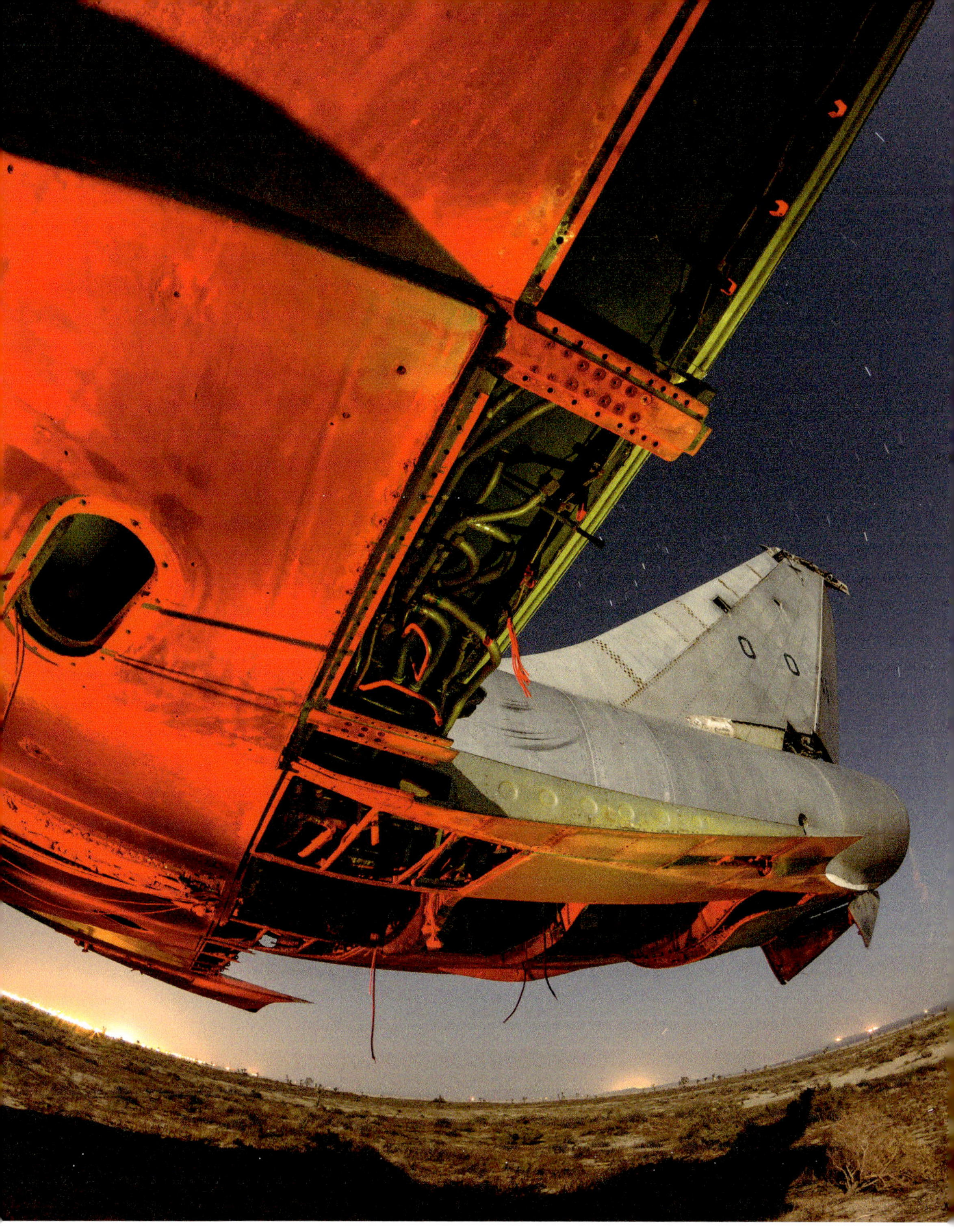

Elevonless
The Mojave. 8/7/2014, 11:51 PM.
Canon 60D, f/8, ISO 200. 237 seconds, 5000K WB.
Full moon / lime and red Protomachines flashlight.
Convair B-58 Hustler.

low enough to touch the Joshua trees dotting the horizon. One eye closes and I bob my head, compulsively composing, even without my camera.

I give in to the temptation to climb into the black hole in the beast's belly; up through the landing gear, shimmying my way through the narrow, totally dark passage and onto the cramped flight deck. Utterly destroyed by time and roosting birds, it is a place immeasurably unique. I tear holes in my clothes on jagged metal and accidentally smash my phone in the tight quarters. On the way out, I naturally find a much easier passage by dropping out through a hatch in the nose. Happy to be out in the open again, I make my way aft, under the endlessly long, slightly wrinkly fuselage.

Under the fluke-like tail, I discover the second B-52, tucked in close behind. Unlike the other aircraft, this one looks like a crash: wings broken off, fuselage shattered into three big chunks and flopped on its belly in the dried and cracked lakebed. Its jumbled appearance, coalescing out of the darkness, is breathtaking. It's so cinematic, it almost seems staged.

This second B-52 (57-0119) was also a sixties testbed aircraft. The GE TF-39 engine, for the upcoming Lockheed C-5A program, was mounted to its right inboard engine pylon and the plane put in hundreds of hours, developing and fine-tuning the all new, high-bypass turbofan. It eventually joined the other B-52, dragged out here to be forgotten among the sage and Joshuas.

Forgotten, that is, until 1991, when the Strategic Arms Reduction Treaty (START) with the Soviet Union called for cutting half the B-52 force. In order to comply, over 350 B-52s in storage at the now renamed Aerospace Maintenance and Regeneration Center (AMARC) in Tucson were broken up and left for ninety days, to allow confirmation by Soviet satellite.

Soon after, the Russians spotted these two "combat ready" strategic bombers in the remote desert. Unaware of their actual condition, they insisted one be destroyed to comply with the treaty. The unlucky plane was quickly rendered and left for satellite confirmation. Unlike the planes in Tucson, which were quickly recycled, this one was left as a stark, unintentional reminder of the costs and madness of war.

The battered nose section lays cockeyed in the sand, trailing off into the exploded and burned center section. At the rear, the tail was neatly sheared off and dragged aside, like a cleaned fish. Meanwhile, the cut fuselage end, relieved of its weight, juts into the sky. The wings were dragged to the side and left in a crumpled heap. It would have been easy to walk around all night in a slack-jawed search for meaning and forget to take the pictures. This raw merging of technology and nature, the blending of past and future and back to past again, this infinite cycle, is readily apparent in these monumental ghosts, these Angels of the Mojave.

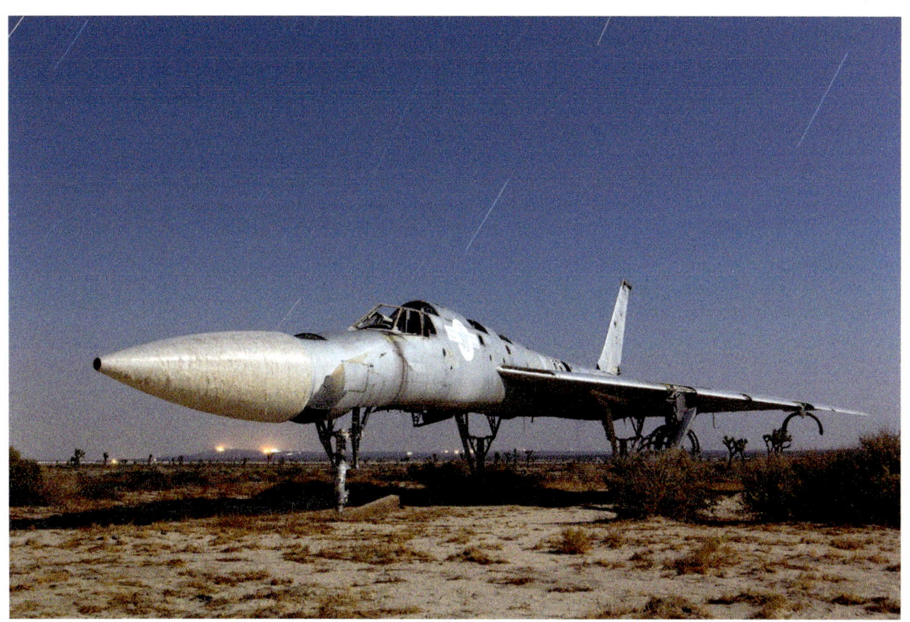

Snoopy's Fuzzy Nose
The Mojave. 8/7/2014, 8:42 PM.
Canon 60D, f/8, ISO 200. 25 minutes, 3800K WB.
Full moon.
Convair B-58 Hustler.

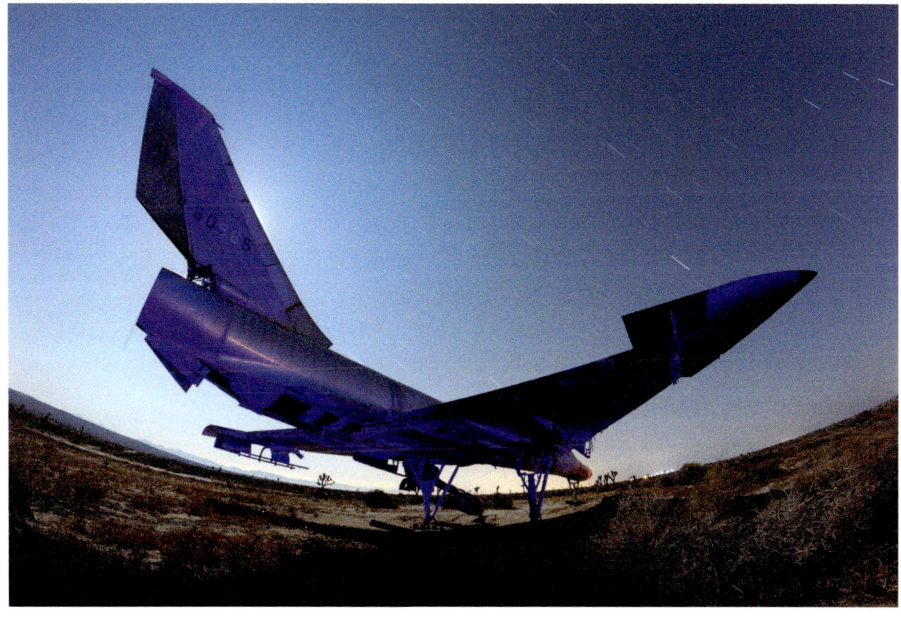

Fail Safe
The Mojave. 8/7/2014, 9:48 PM.
Canon 60D, f/8, ISO 200. 15 minutes, 3800K WB.
Full moon / purple Protomachines flashlight.
Convair B-58 Hustler.

Chicken Legs Dropped His Engine
The Mojave. 8/7/2014, 10:21 PM.
Canon 60D, f/8, ISO 200. 162 seconds, 5000K WB.
Full moon / purple, red and green Protomachines flashlight.
Convair B-58 Hustler.

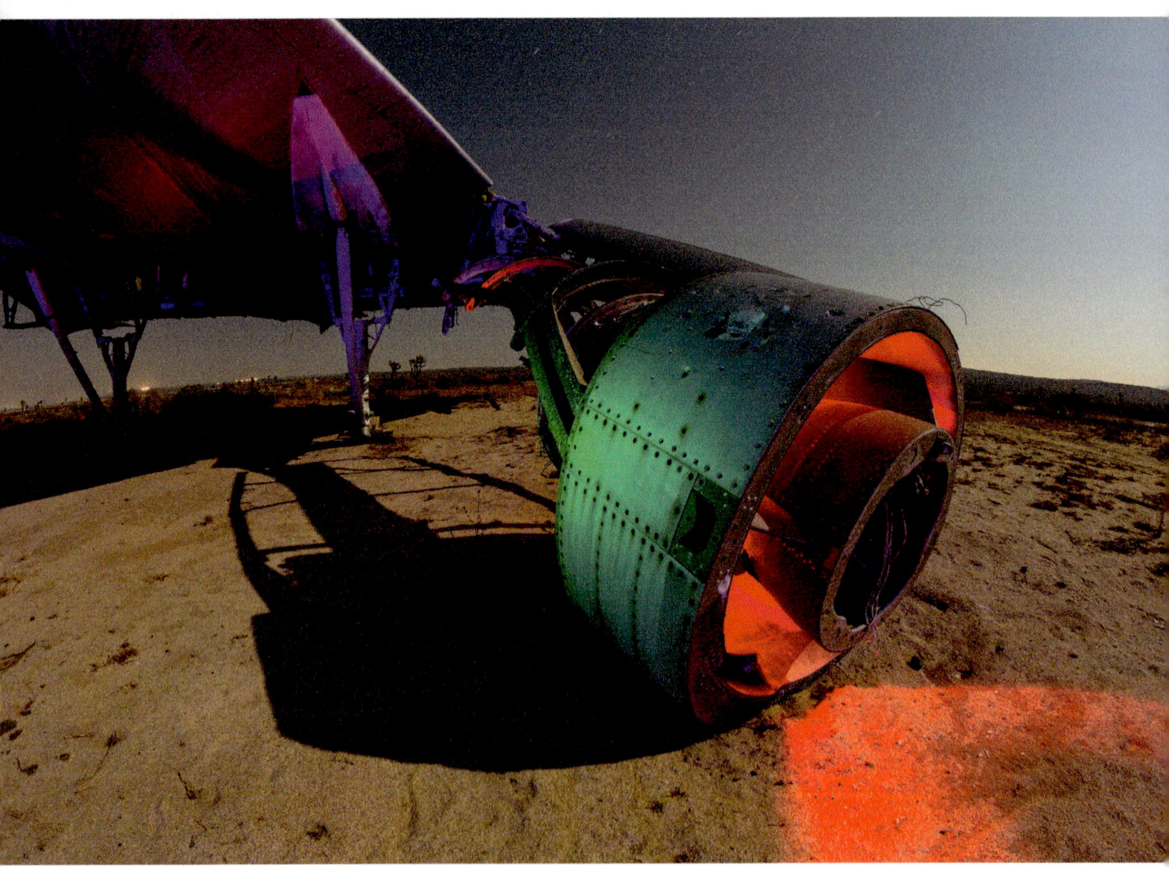

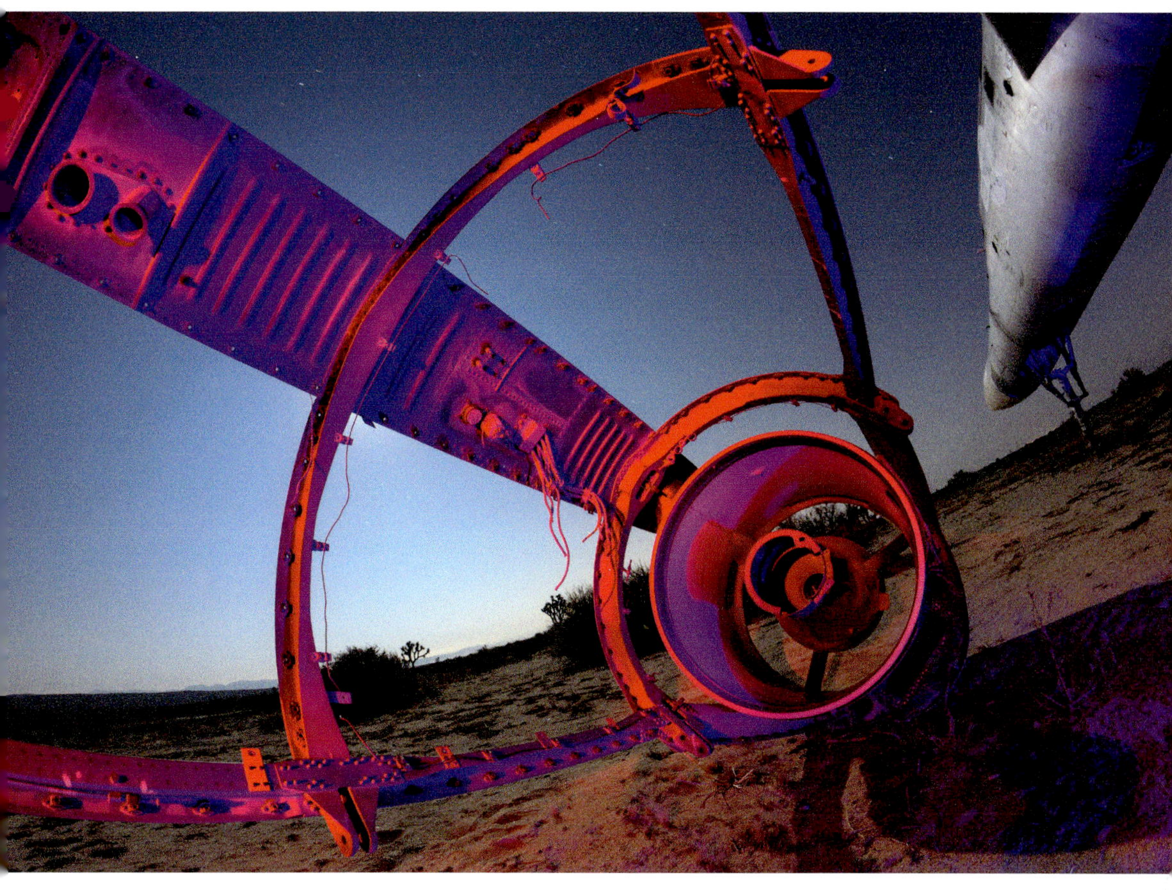

Ghost of the J79
The Mojave. 8/7/2014, 11:05 PM.
Canon 60D, f/8, ISO 200. 95 seconds, 3900K WB.
Full moon / purple and red Protomachines flashlight.
Convair B-58 Hustler.

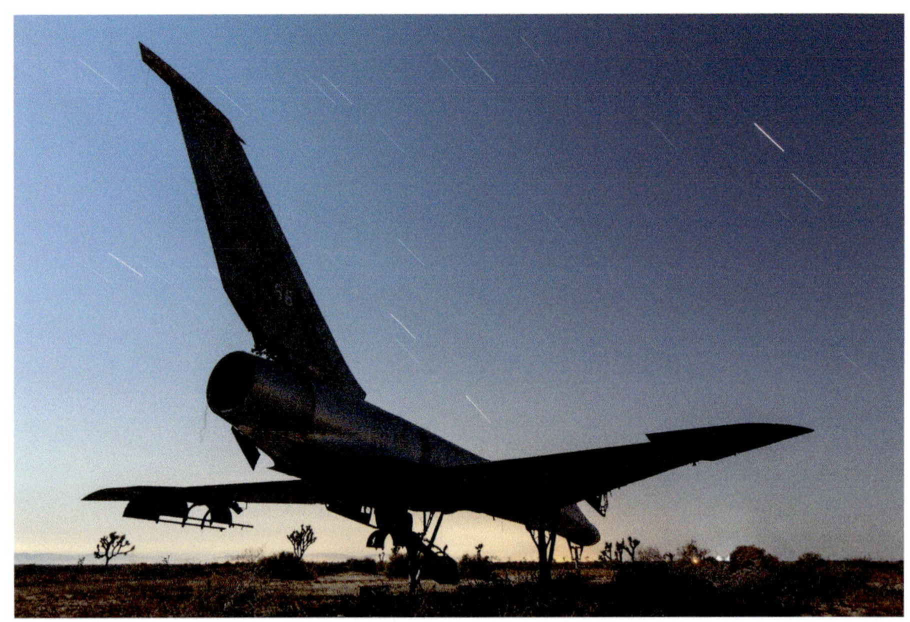

Fireball XL5
The Mojave. 8/7/2014, 9:21 PM.
Canon 60D, f/8, ISO 200. 15 minutes, 3800K WB.
Full moon.
Convair B-58 Hustler.

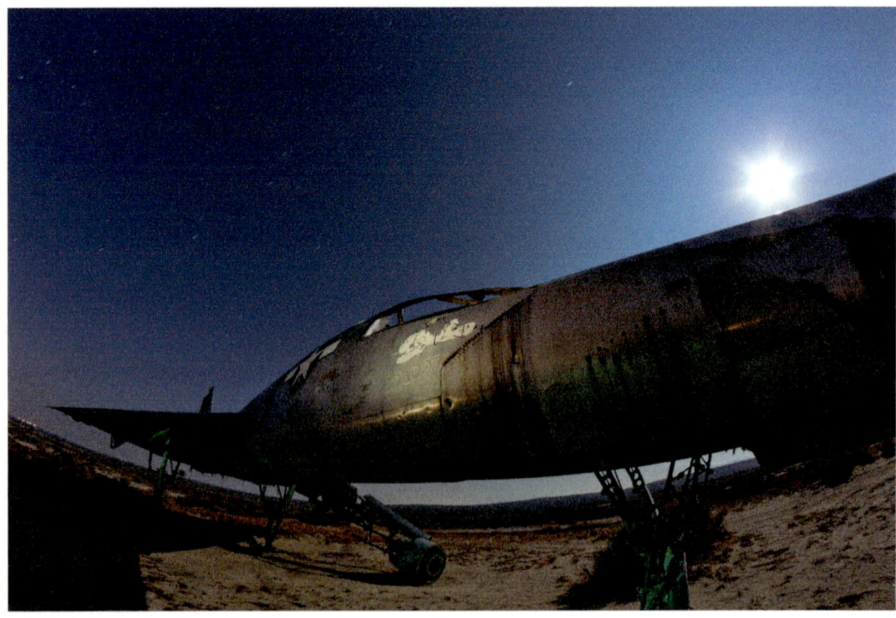

The Snoopy One
The Mojave. 8/7/2014, 10:36 PM.
Canon 60D, f/8, ISO 200. 206 seconds, 3800K WB.
Full moon / green and white Protomachines flashlight.
Convair B-58 Hustler.

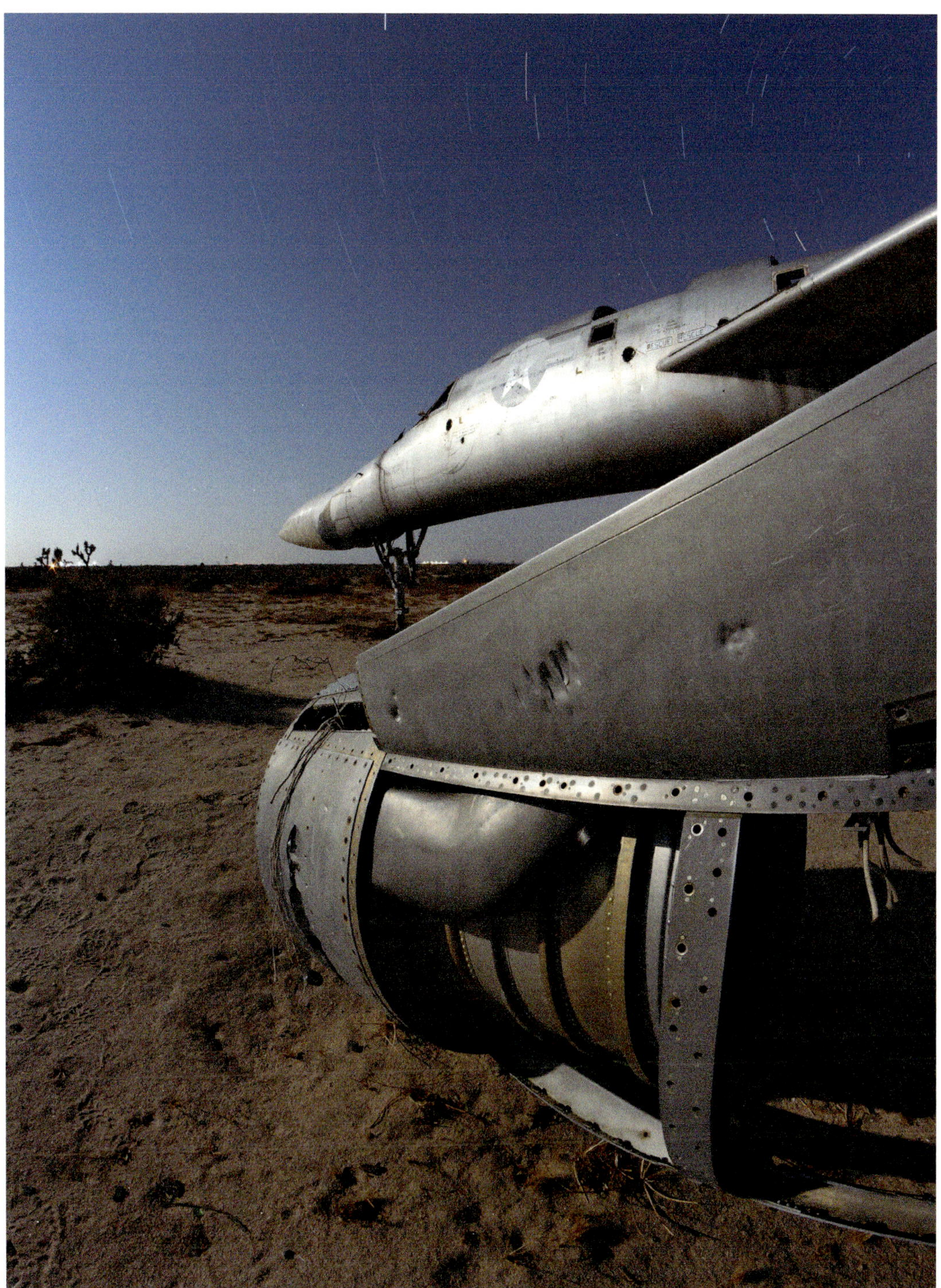

Flintfinity

The Mojave. 8/8/2014, 12:07 AM.

Canon 60D, f/8, ISO 200. 30 minutes, 3800K WB.

Full moon.

Convair B-58 Hustler.

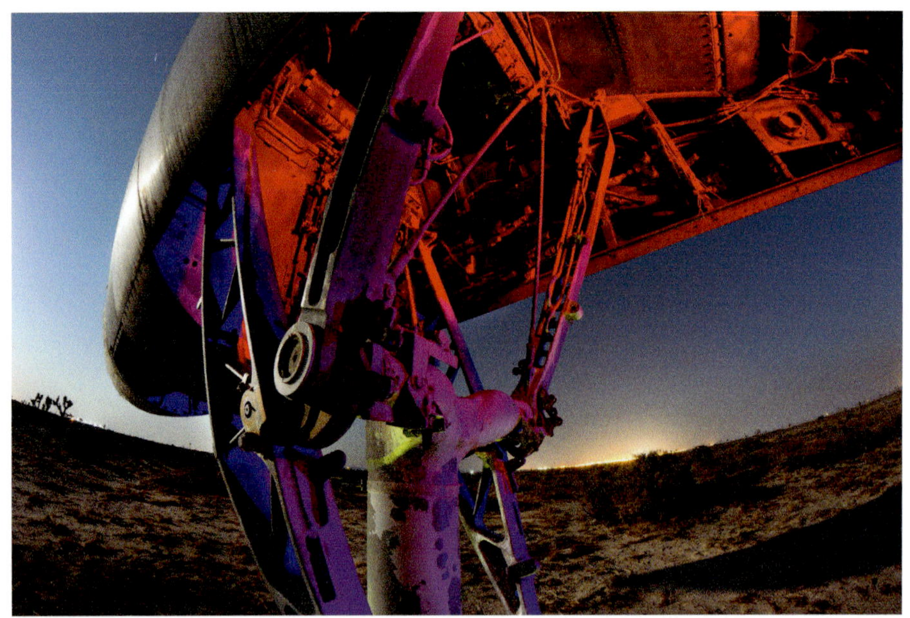

To the 10,000th
The Mojave. 8/8/2014, 12:07 AM.
Canon 60D, f/8, ISO 200. 249 seconds, 5000K WB.
Full moon / purple and red Protomachines flashlight.
Convair B-58 Hustler.

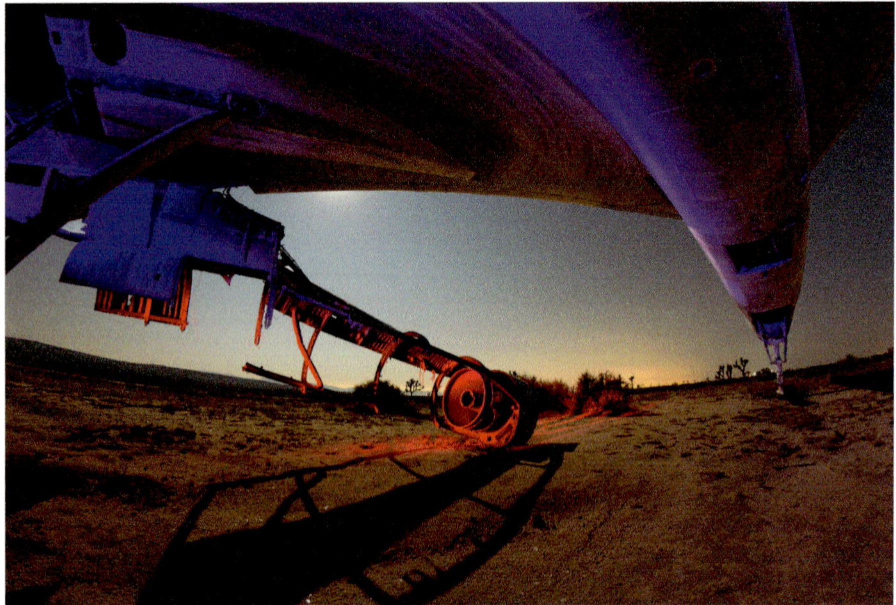

Roger Ramjet
The Mojave. 8/7/2014, 10:58 PM.
Canon 60D, f/8, ISO 200. 95 seconds, 5000K WB.
Full moon / purple and red Protomachines flashlight.
Convair B-58 Hustler.

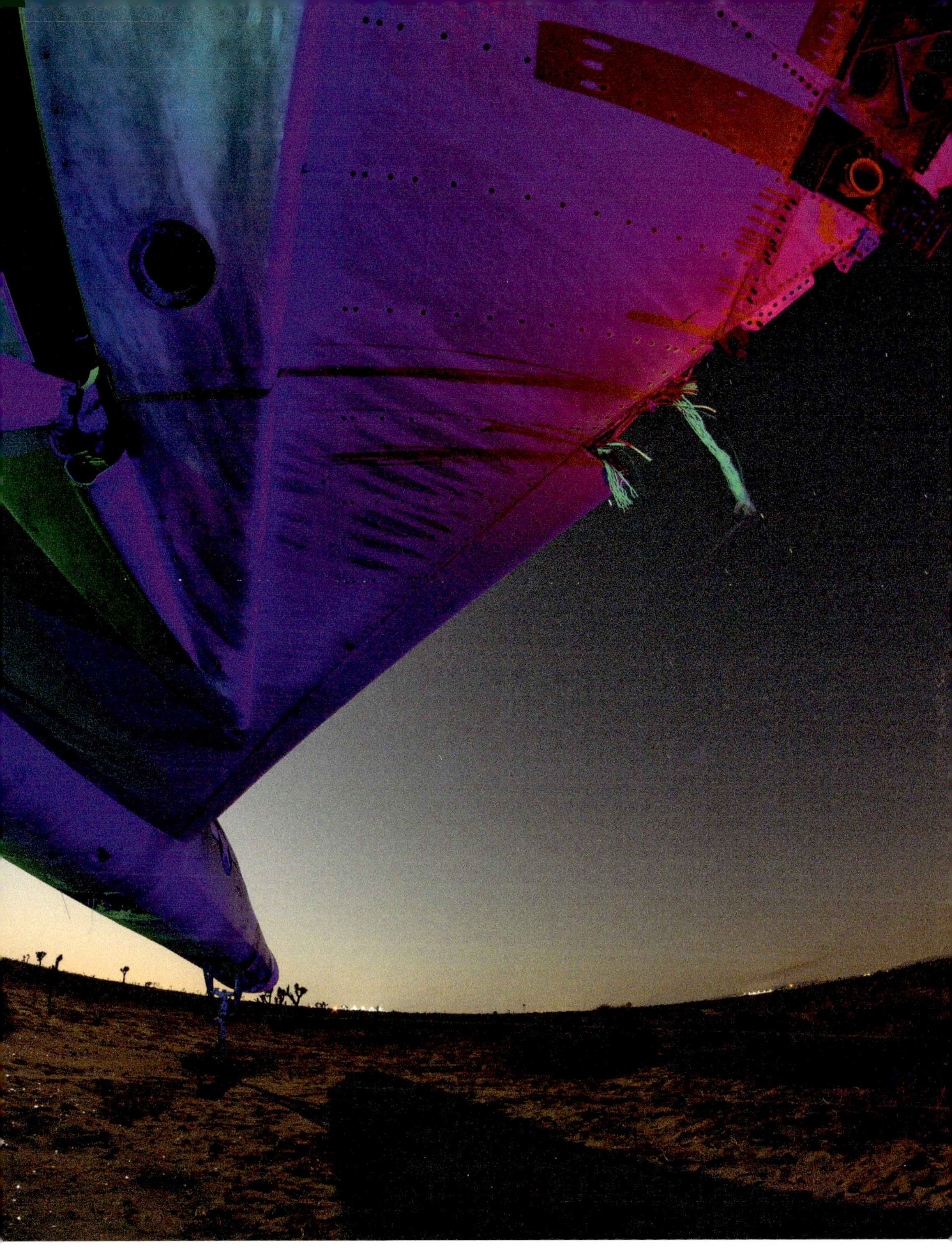

Pink Mercury
The Mojave. 8/8/2014, 1:07 AM.
Canon 60D, f/8, ISO 200. 150 seconds, 5200K WB.
Full moon / purple, green and red Protomachines flashlight.
Convair B-58 Hustler.

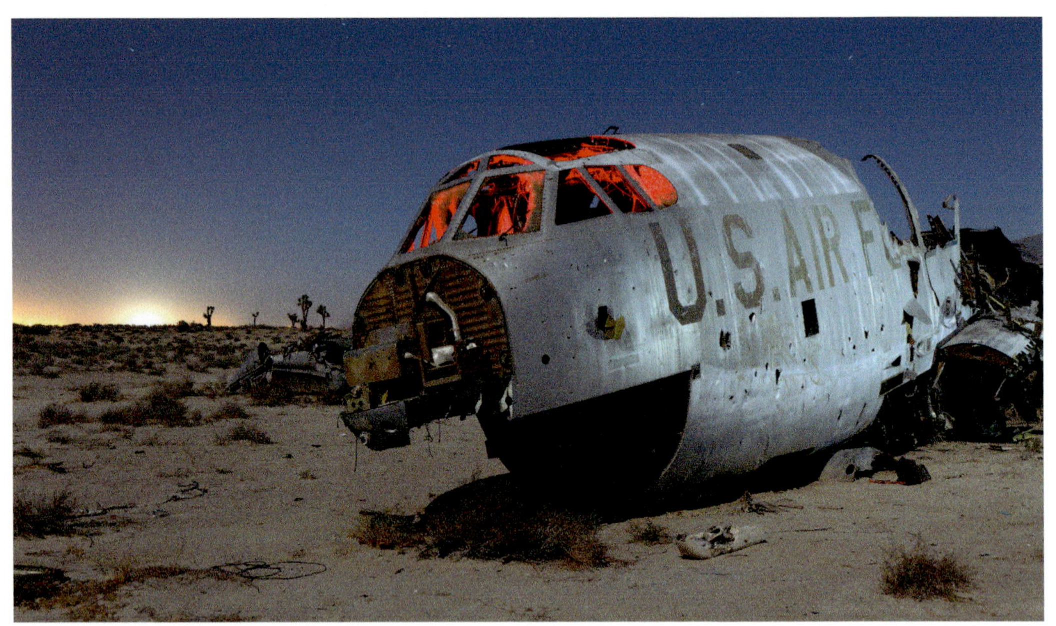

Spacewreck
The Mojave. 9/15/2016, 12:59 AM.
Canon 60D, f/8, ISO 200. 88 seconds, 3800K WB.
Full moon / white and red Protomachines flashlight.
Boeing B-52 Stratofortress.

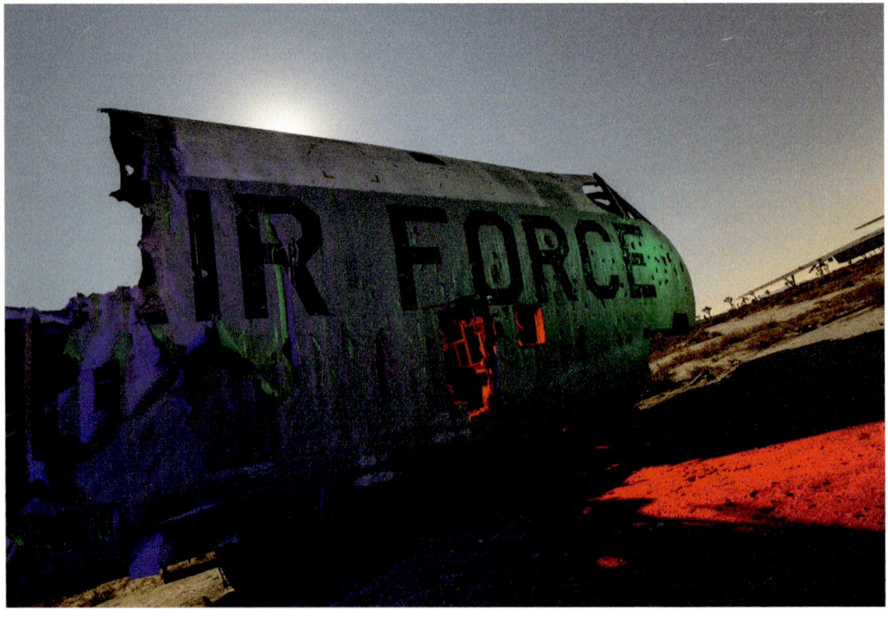

Starship Troopers
The Mojave. 8/8/2014, 9:10 PM.
Canon 60D, f/8, ISO 200. 205 seconds, 5000K WB.
Full moon / purple, green and red Protomachines flashlight.
Boeing B-52 Stratofortress.

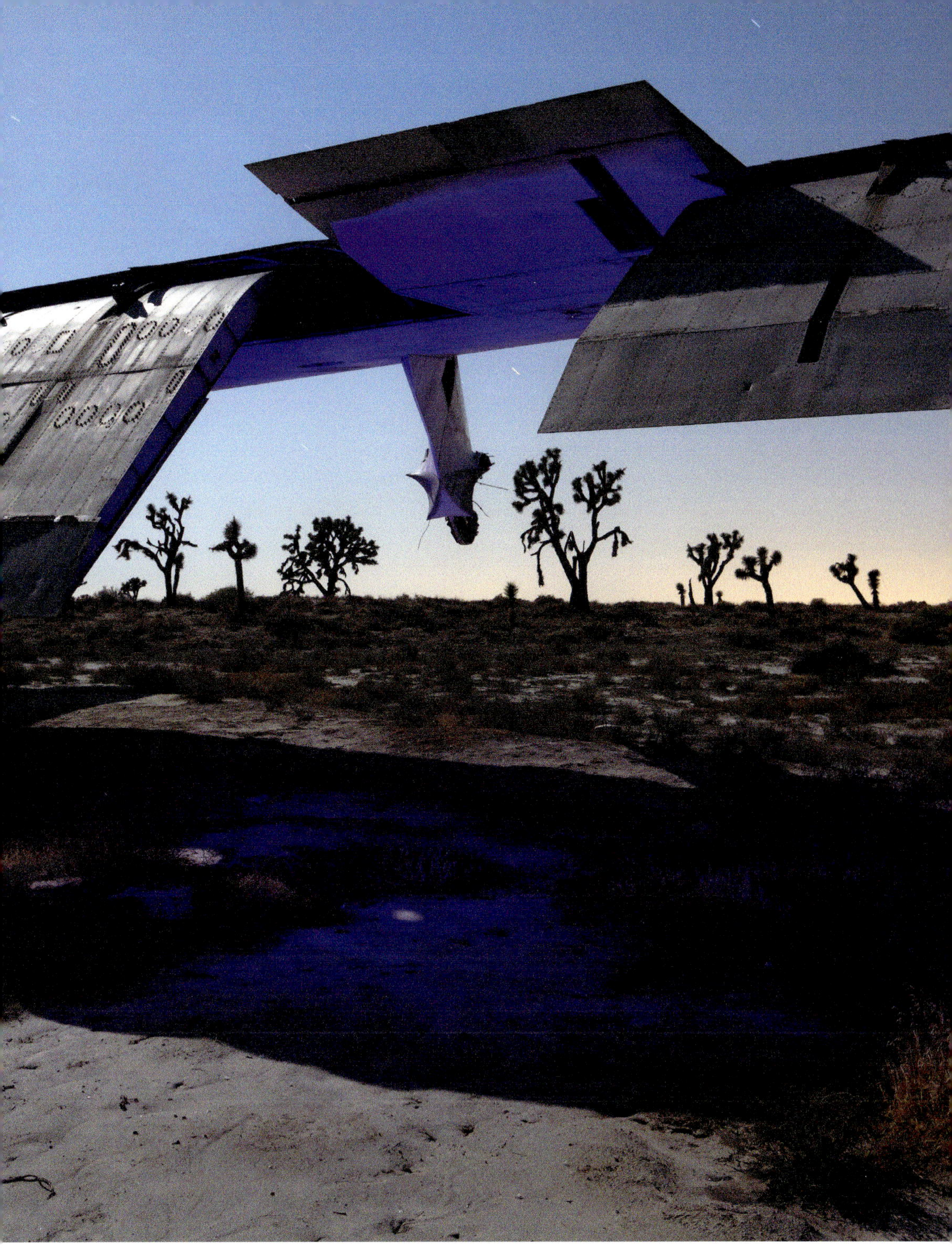

Flaps Down
The Mojave. 8/8/2014, 11:01 PM.
Canon 60D, f/8, ISO 200. 101 seconds, 3800K WB.
Full moon / purple Protomachines flashlight.
Boeing B-52 Stratofortress.

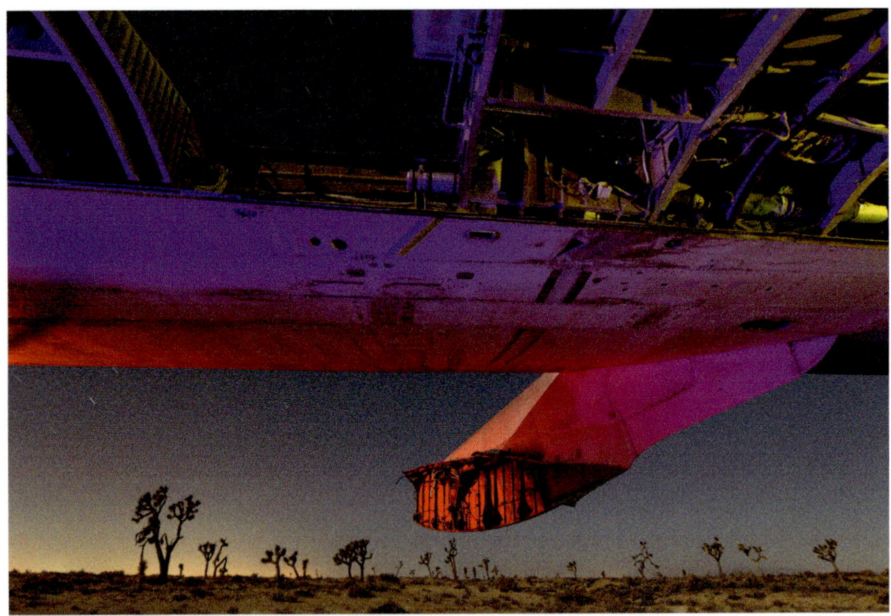

A Hole in the Wing
The Mojave. 9/14/2016, 8:28 PM.
Canon 60D, f/8, ISO 200. 180 seconds, 5000K WB.
Full moon / white, purple and red Protomachines flashlight.
Boeing B-52 Stratofortress.

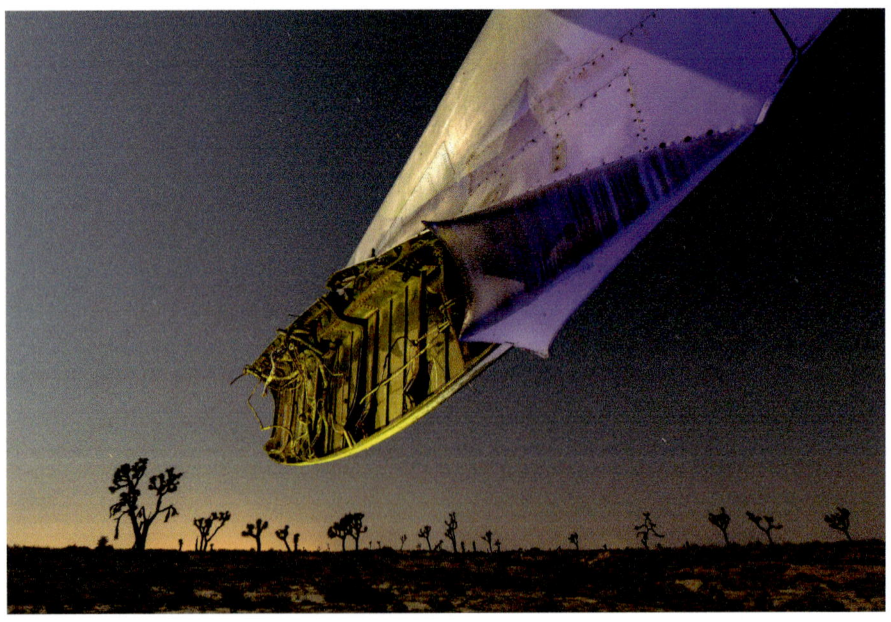

Merlin's Hat
The Mojave. 8/8/2014, 11:11 PM.
Canon 60D, f/8, ISO 200. 102 seconds, 5000K WB.
Full moon / purple and lime Protomachines flashlight.
Boeing B-52 Stratofortress.

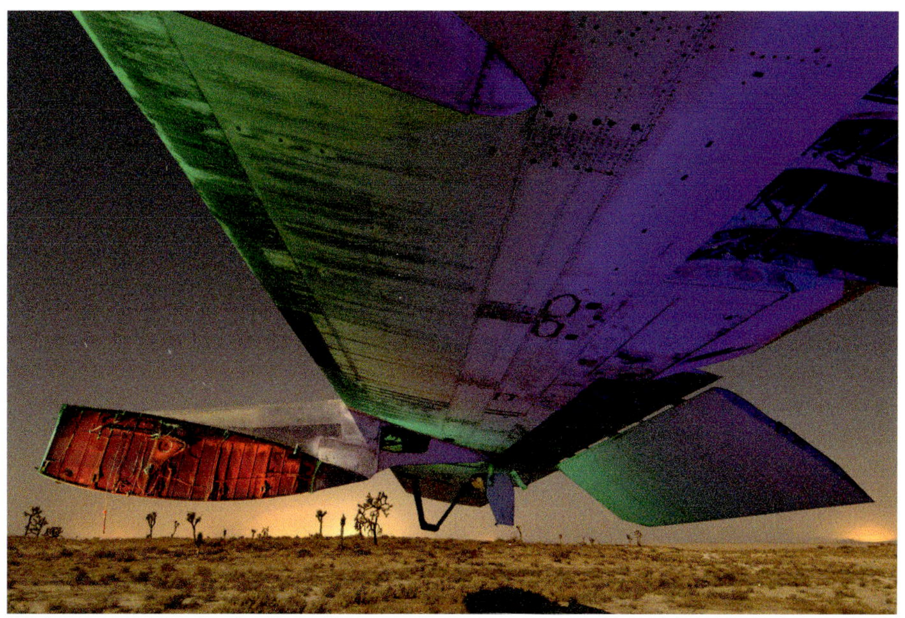

King Kong's Armpit
The Mojave. 8/8/2014, 11:50 PM.
Canon 60D, f/8, ISO 200. 153 seconds, 6200K WB.
Full moon / red, purple and green Protomachines flashlight.
Boeing B-52 Stratofortress.

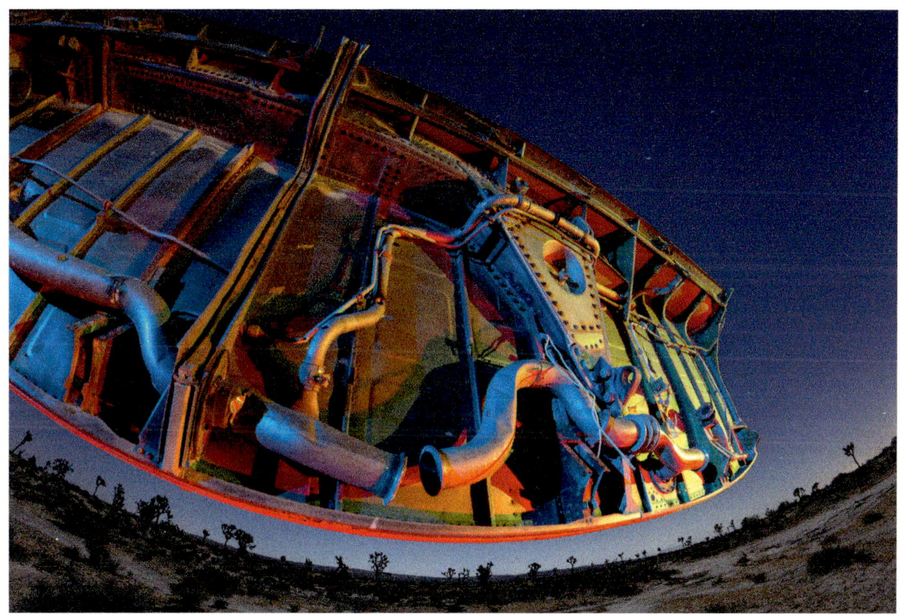

World Bender
The Mojave. 9/14/2016, 10:57 PM.
Canon 60D, f/8, ISO 200. 88 seconds, 3800K WB.
Full moon / red, blue and lime Protomachines flashlight.
Boeing B-52 Stratofortress.

Marooned

The Mojave. 9/14/2016, 9:10 PM.
Canon 60D, f/8, ISO 200. 180 seconds, 5000K WB.
Full moon / white Protomachines flashlight.
Boeing B-52 Stratofortress.

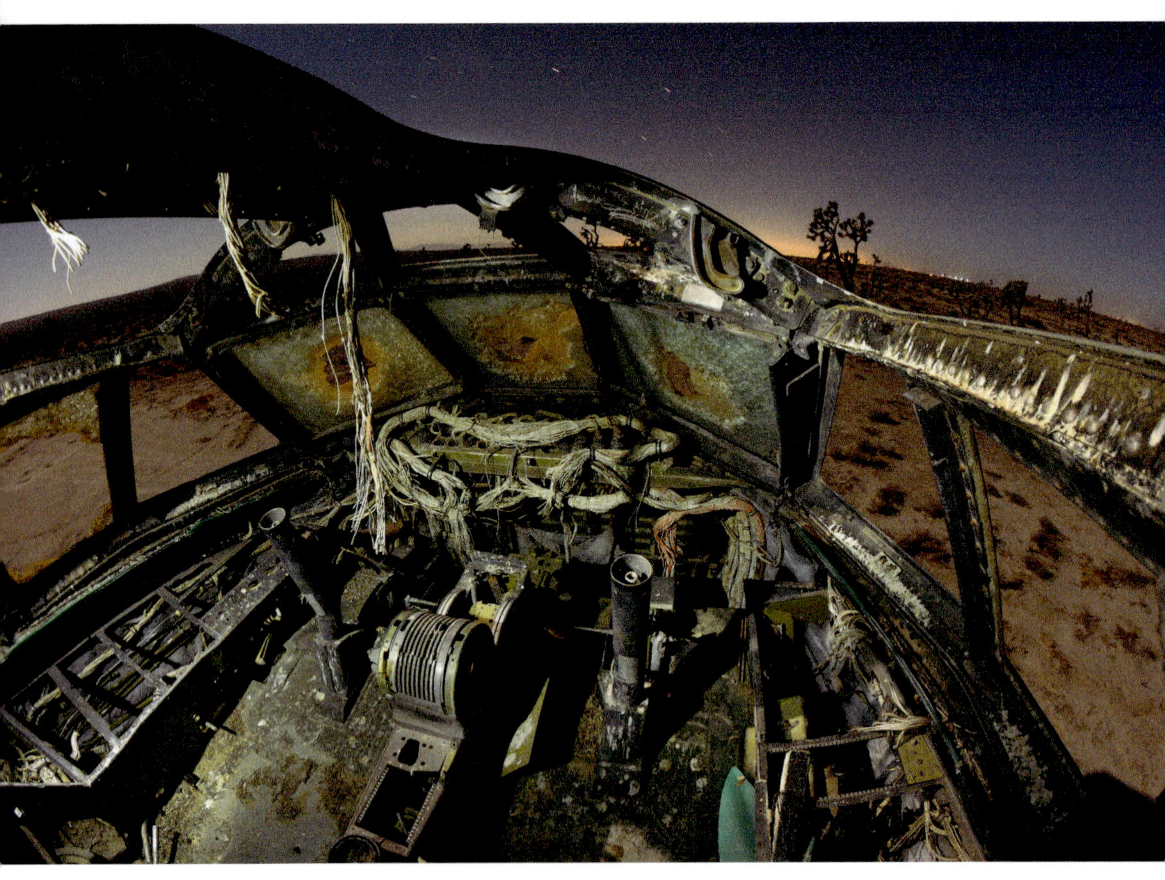

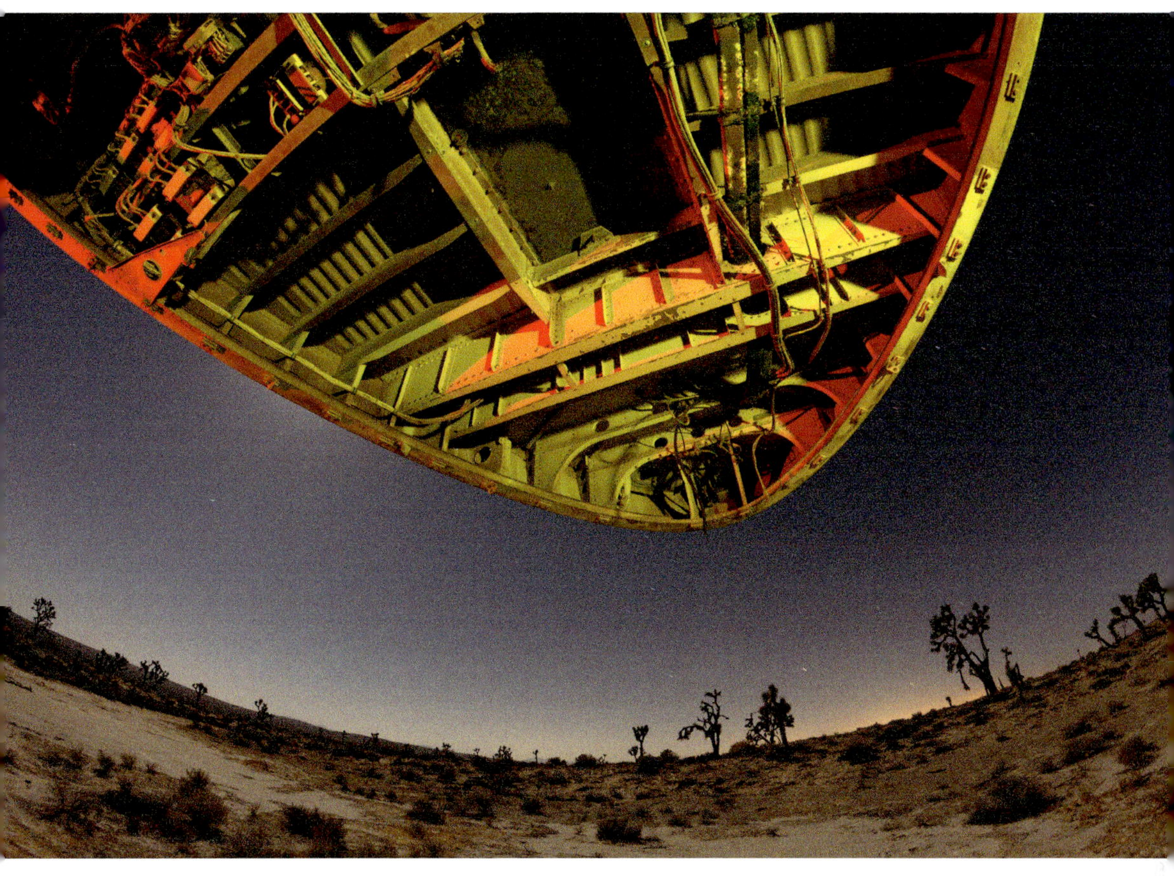

The Mother Ship

The Mojave. 9/14/2016, 10:22 PM.
Canon 60D, f/8, ISO 200. 123 seconds, 5500K WB.
Full moon / lime and red Protomachines flashlight.
Boeing B-52 Stratofortress.

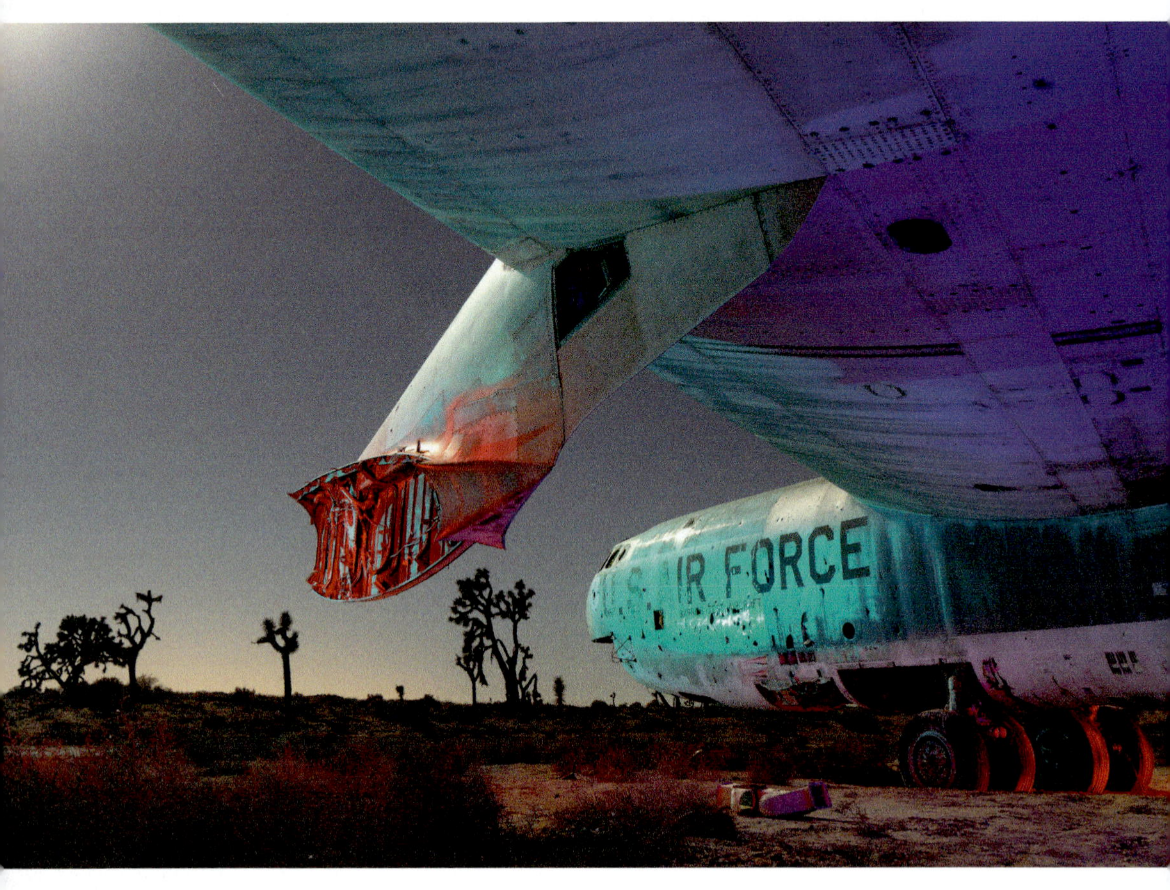

Testing Barriers
The Mojave. 9/15/2016, 2:05 AM.
Canon 60D, f/8, ISO 200. 180 seconds, 5000K WB.
Full moon / turquoise, purple and red Protomachines flashlight.
Boeing B-52 Stratofortress.

Arc Light ►
The Mojave. 9/15/2016, 12:48 AM.
Canon 60D, f/8, ISO 200. 180 seconds, 5500K WB.
Full moon / purple and red Protomachines flashlight.
Boeing B-52 Stratofortress.

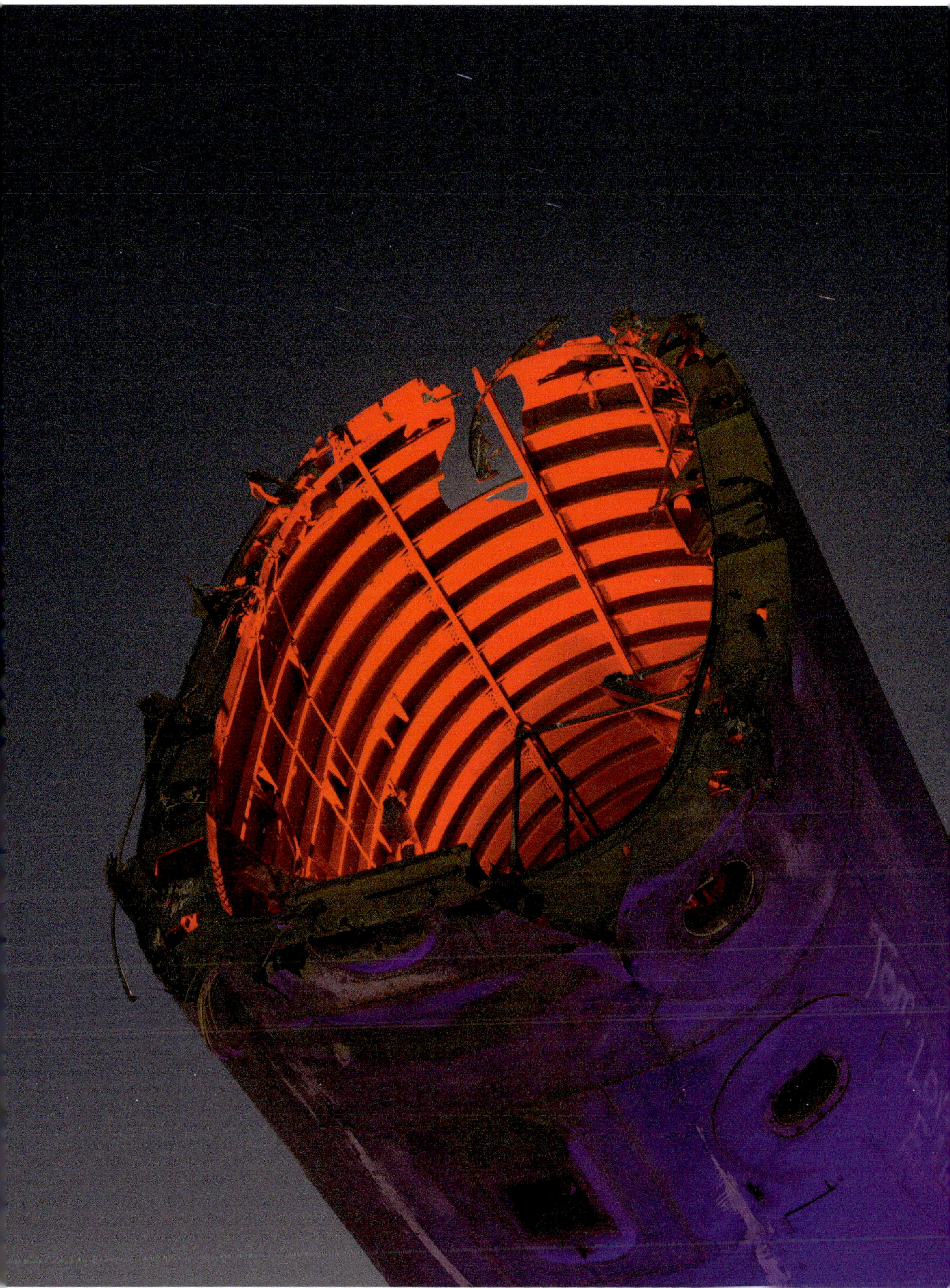

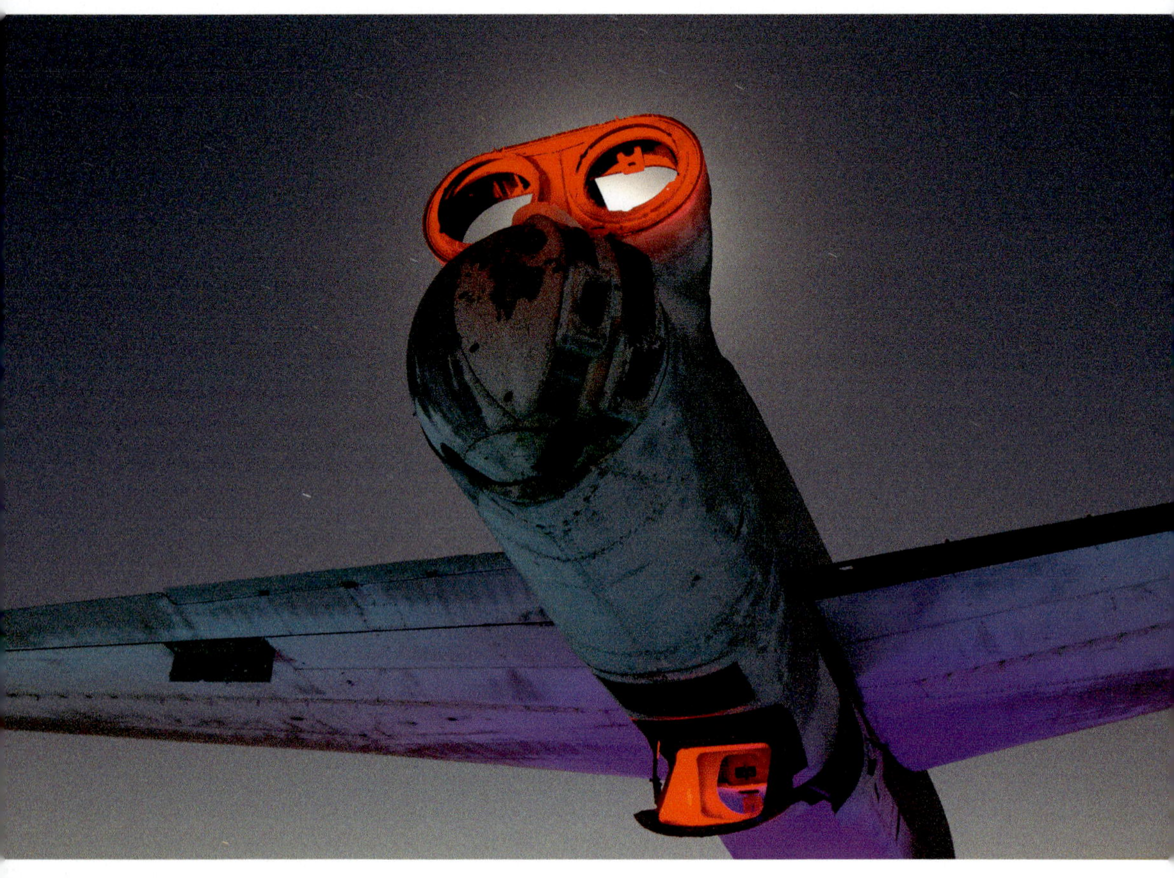

Frog Eyes
The Mojave. 9/15/2016, 1:18 AM.
Canon 60D, f/8, ISO 200. 116 seconds, 5000K WB.
Full moon / blue, purple and red Protomachines flashlight.
Boeing B-52 Stratofortress.

Buff Gear ►
The Mojave. 9/15/2016, 1:39 AM.
Canon 60D, f/8, ISO 200. 107 seconds, 3800K WB.
Full moon / white and red Protomachines flashlight.
Boeing B-52 Stratofortress.

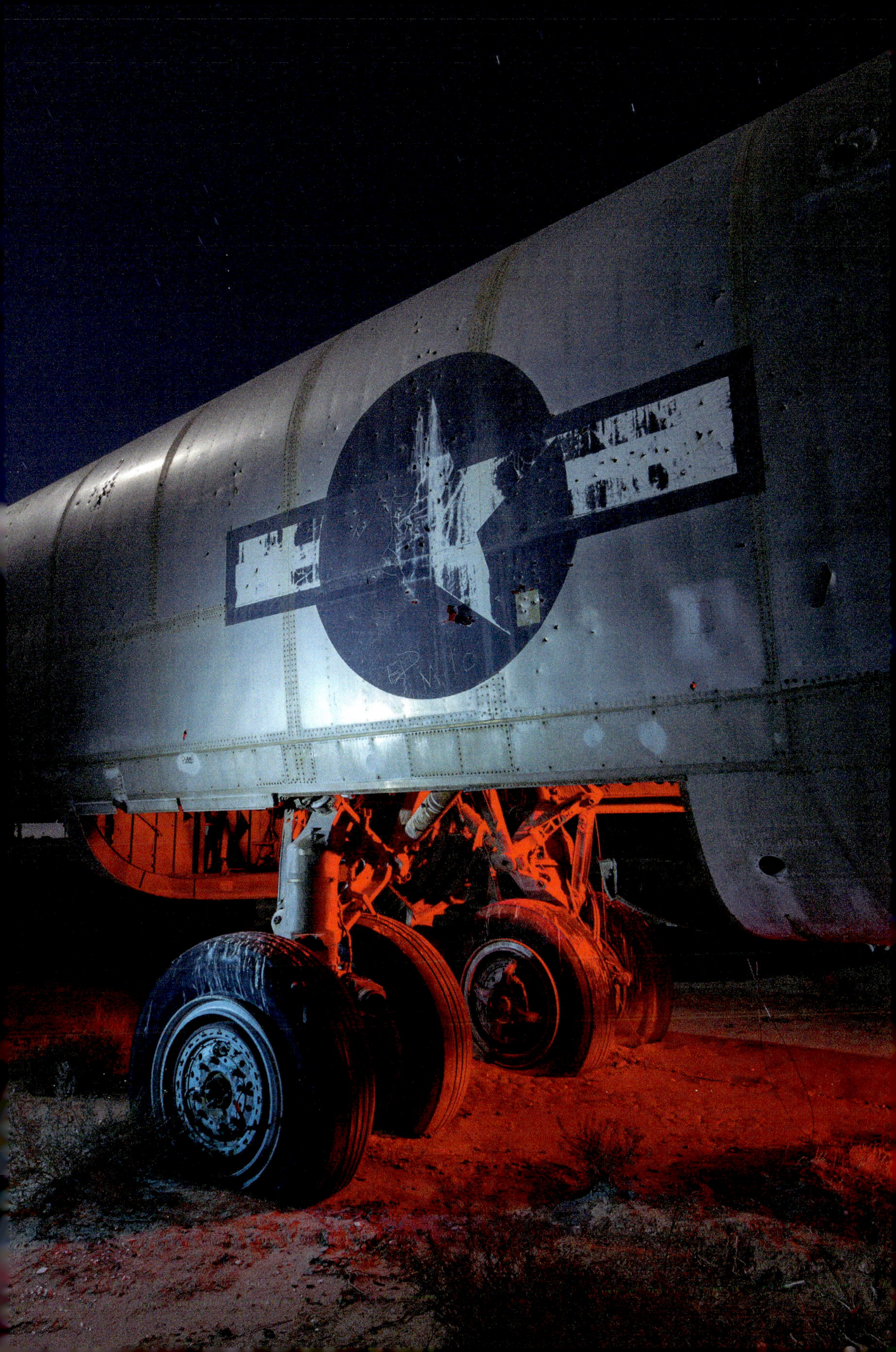

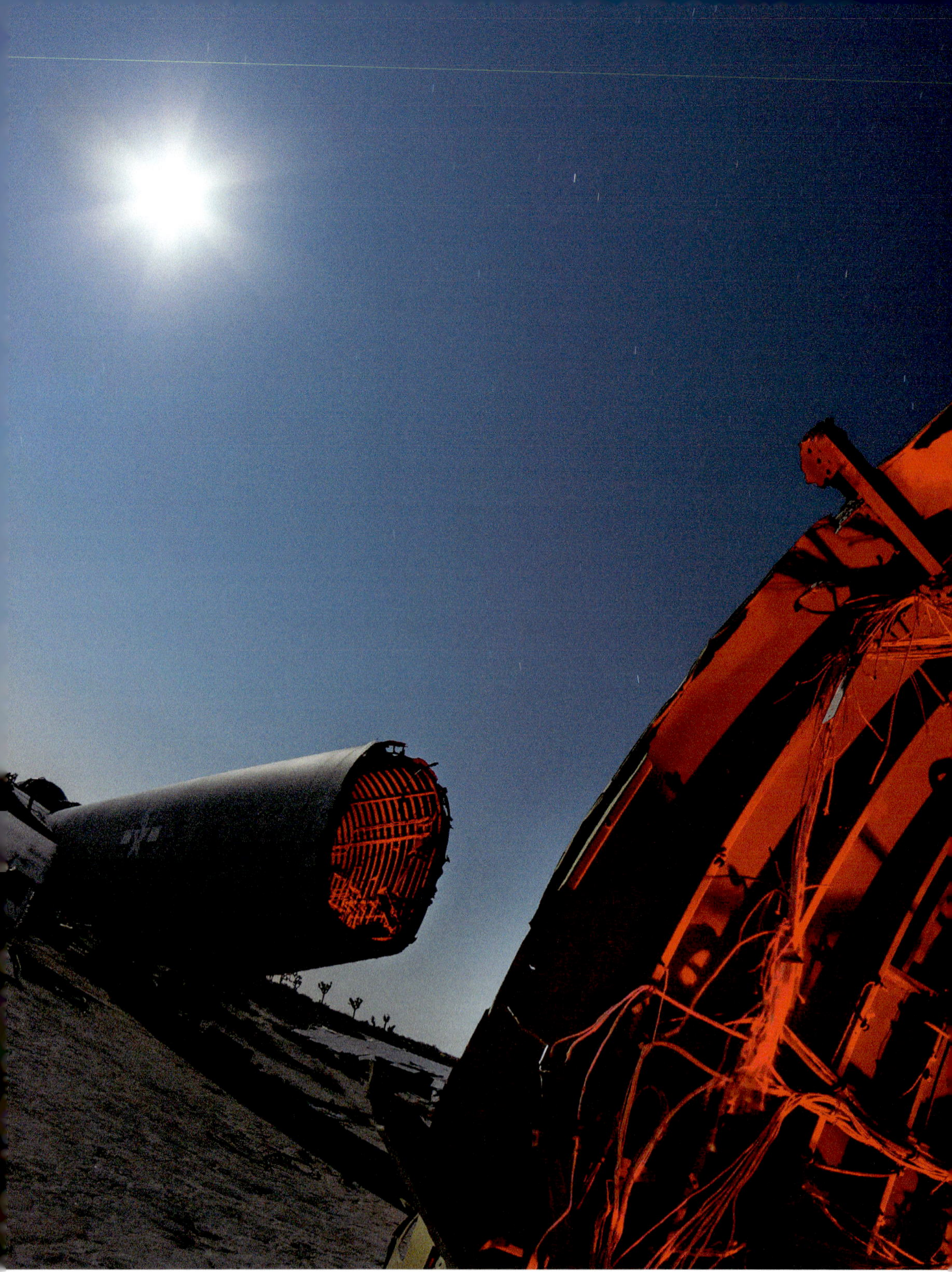

Gorilla Skull
The Mojave. 8/9/2014, 12:43 AM.
Canon 60D, f/8, ISO 200. 125 seconds, 3800K WB.

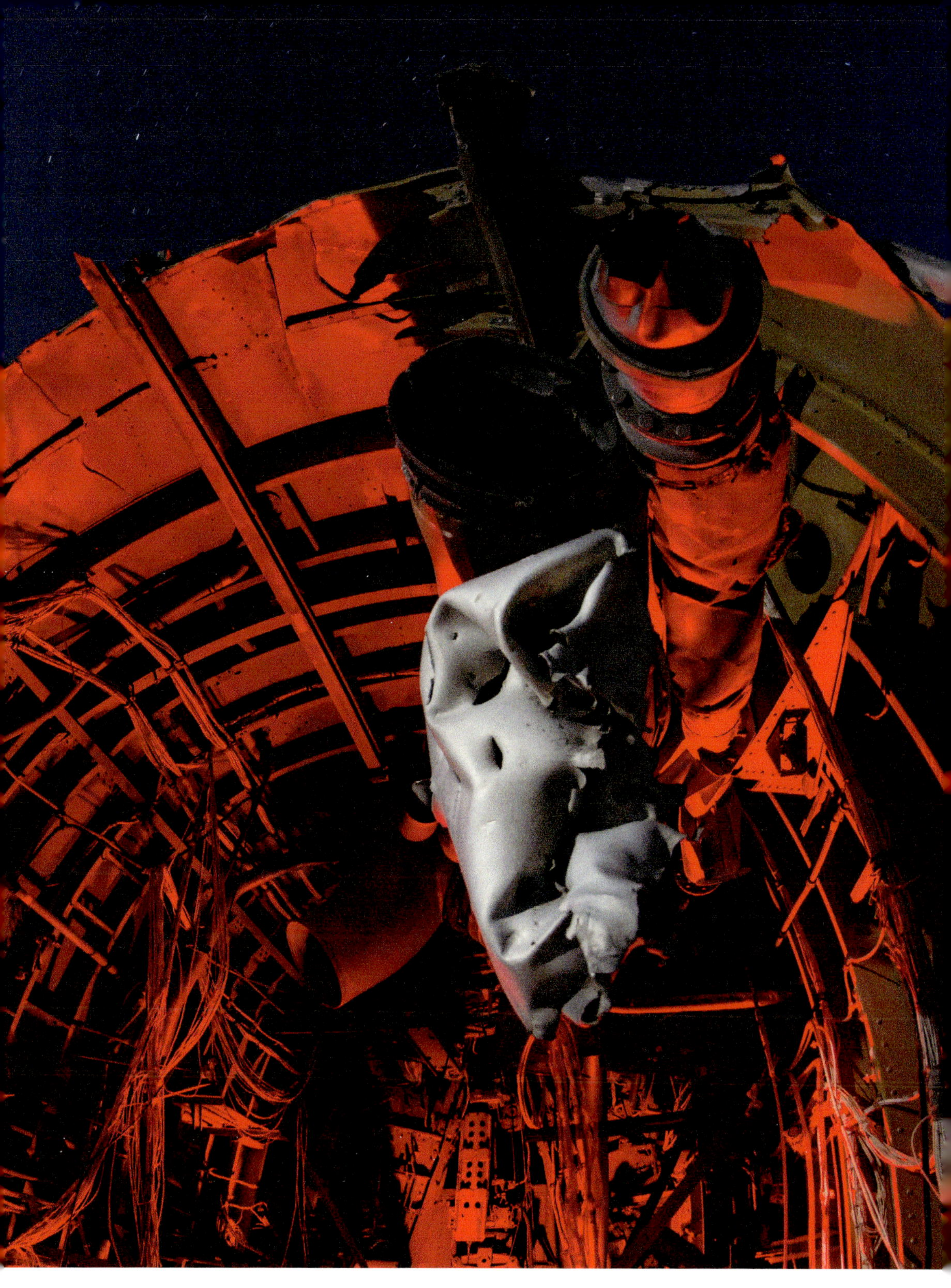

Full moon / white and red Protomachines flashlight.
Boeing B-52 Stratofortress.

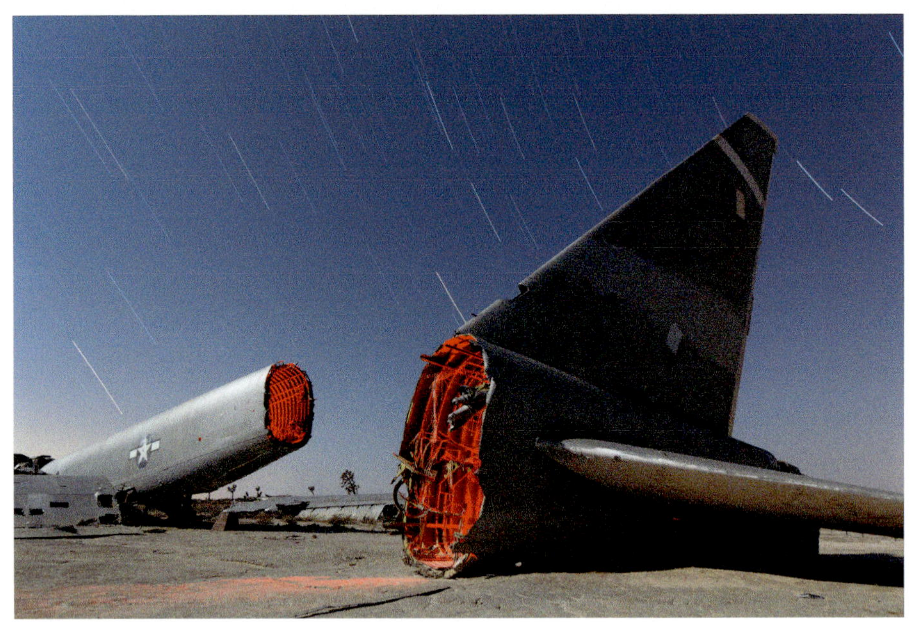

Planet Claire
The Mojave. 8/8/2014, 9:51 PM.
Canon 60D, f/8, ISO 200. 45 minutes, 3800K WB.
Full moon / red Protomachines flashlight.
Boeing B-52 Stratofortress.

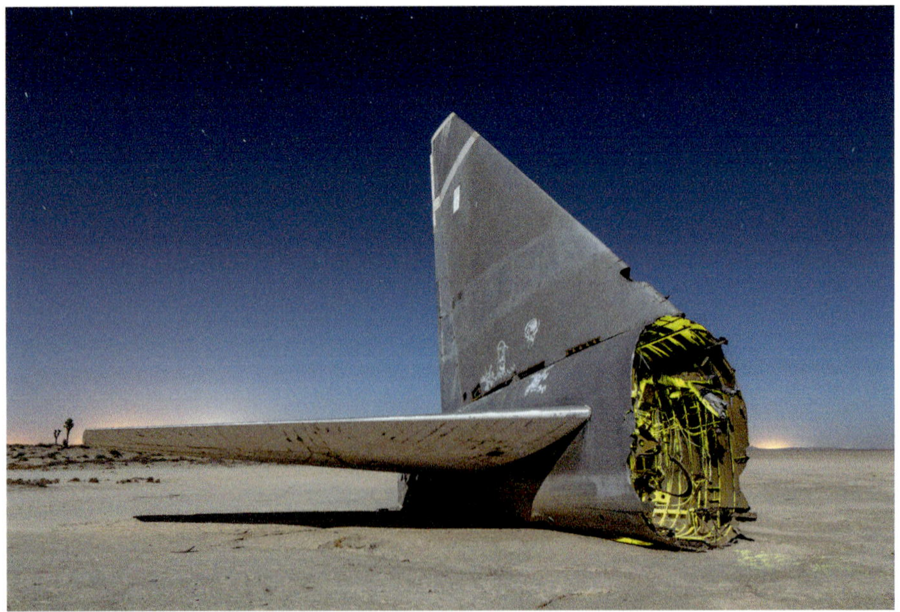

Tail Marrow
The Mojave. 9/15/2016, 12:33 AM.
Canon 60D, f/8, ISO 200. 134 seconds, 3800K WB.
Full moon / lime Protomachines flashlight.
Boeing B-52 Stratofortress.

3

AVIATION WAREHOUSE

The Aviation Warehouse boneyard is ten otherworldly acres of parted-out, crashed and smashed aircraft of every size and description, a fenced and patrolled compound on the edge of a dry lake, deep in the Mojave Desert.

The place was a tough nut to crack: I'd been stalking it for years. If I was in the area I'd drop by, but every stop at the office was met with, "No, the owner's not here. No, you can't just wander around and take pictures."

Finally, in the summer of 2006, owner Mark Thomson happened to be there. Here was my big chance to sell him on the idea. Shown into his cool dark office, I laid a copy of my first book, *Lost America*, on his desk, to show him that I was granted permission to shoot at the Mojave Airport boneyard back in 1990. He pointed at one of the pages and looked at me sternly. "This is *my* plane. Who gave you permission to take this picture of *my* plane?" I began deflating. Then he flipped through a few more pages, smiled, looked me in the eye and quietly asked, "*How* did you do these?"

From that day on, I found a new patron. Mark gave me free rein to night shoot in the yard whenever I asked. I was lucky he just "got it." I've always felt privileged, especially when you consider he rented out his yard to film and television crews for thousands a day. Sadly, Mark passed away in 2017, although the family continues on with the business and honors our friendship.

I like to get down there once every year or so to shoot during the full moon. Like any other junk/storage yard, things come and go. Pieces get moved around, opening up possibilities to see favorite objects in new ways. I've spent eighteen nights at Aviation Warehouse now, but with spaced visits, it always feels fresh.

All the images in this section were shot between 2006 and 2018. I like to visit year-round, even in the middle of summer. It is only 105 degrees during the day, but the humidity can make it nearly intolerable to be outside. I spend as many of the daylight hours as I can, restlessly dozing like a vampire, in my cool, dark motel room, waiting for the night. Winters can be a whole different kind of fun: temperatures into the twenties, with an endless, howling, sand-filled wind that scours your frozen

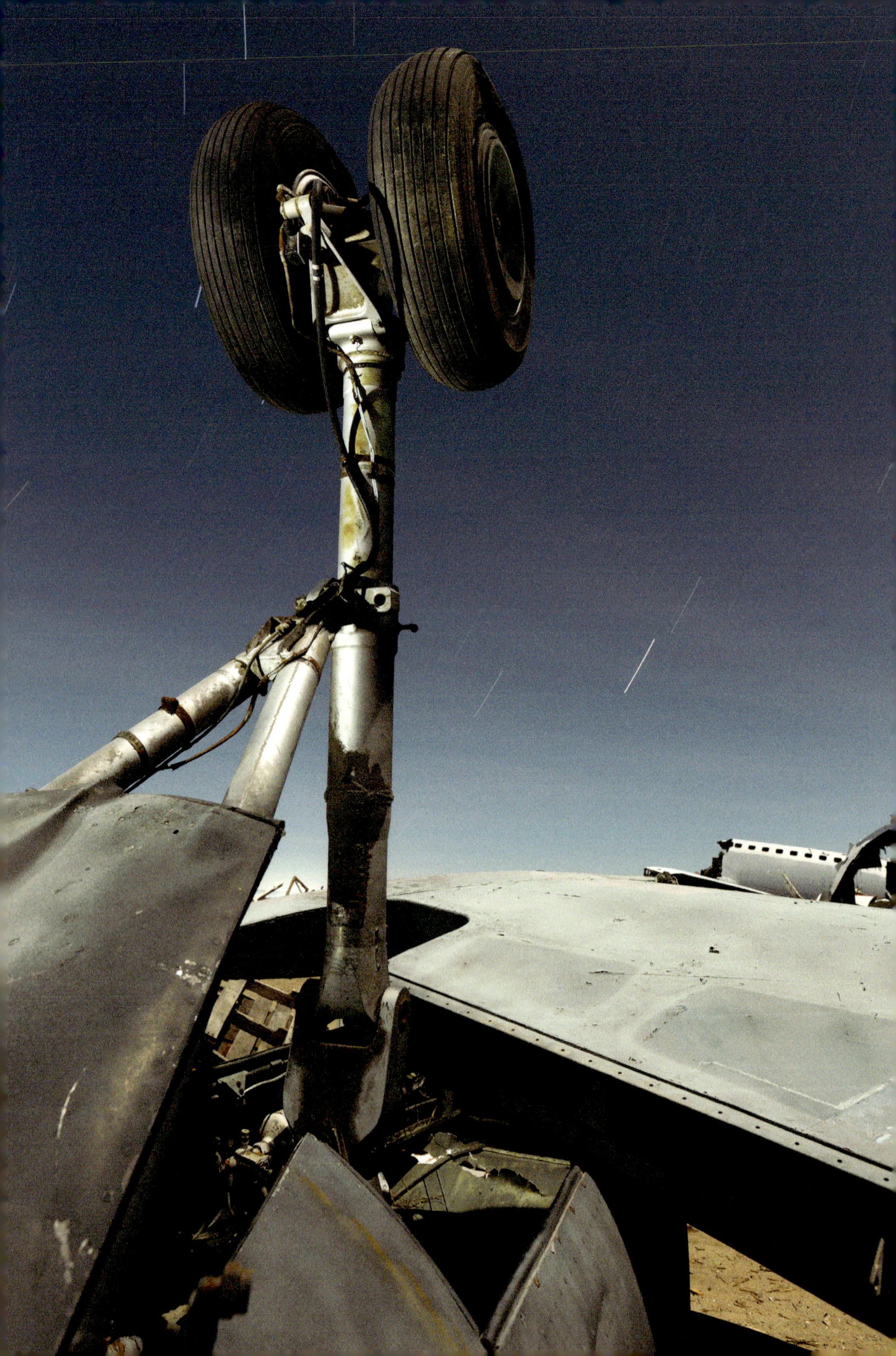

eyeballs, while your fingers turn to glass, break and fall off. Three pairs of long johns aren't enough.

Arriving at dusk, you usually won't see a soul all night, except the airport patrol jeeps that periodically cruise the fence. It often seems as if no one has been in the yard for weeks. Rippled dunes, spotted with animal tracks, drift up every windward surface. Fresh forklift tracks, snaking their way through the yard, look blurry and old in just a few hours.

At night, it's another world, a different state of being. After dark, the Joshua trees seem to come alive, as their twisted limbs wave in welcome, beckoning you into their weird embrace. They always remind me of Morticia, from *The Addams Family*, spoon-feeding raw hamburger to her carnivorous plants.

A few hours after dark, things really quiet down. You can't walk twenty-five feet without making a jackrabbit sprint from the shadows, just a flicker out of the corner of your eye. Feral creatures rustle through the debris fields. The enormous beehive hanging out of a decapitated 737 flight deck softly hums itself to sleep in the cooling air. Heavy monsoon clouds roll in as the evening progresses. The smells of hydraulic fluid and sage, of benzene and a hint of rain, waft in the breeze. The thunderheads flow into some amazing formations, so I shift gears, composing for the clouds. Hours pass like minutes.

This place affects me deeply. Its haunting strangeness can't be overstated. Simulated plane crashes dot the yard, their jagged shapes tearing at the clouds. They tower twenty feet overhead in monumental sculptures. Exotic materials and futuristic shapes formed and milled to the ten-thousandth of an inch are crushed and bent and left exposed for years to be brutally baked and sandblasted. The most advanced space-age technology the world had ever seen, now rendered mute and inert, meaningless and inscrutable.

This goes beyond simple plane spotting and into the realm of contemplating mankind's place in the universe. With the end of the Concorde and space shuttle programs, when will we reach for these heights again? Taken in this context, it's one small step into a surreal emotional state that's both heartbreaking and thrilling at the same time.

◀ **Of Metal and Light**
Aviation Warehouse. 2/3/2015, 11:28 PM.
Canon 5D MkIII, f/8, ISO 200. 17 minutes, 5000K WB.
Full moon.

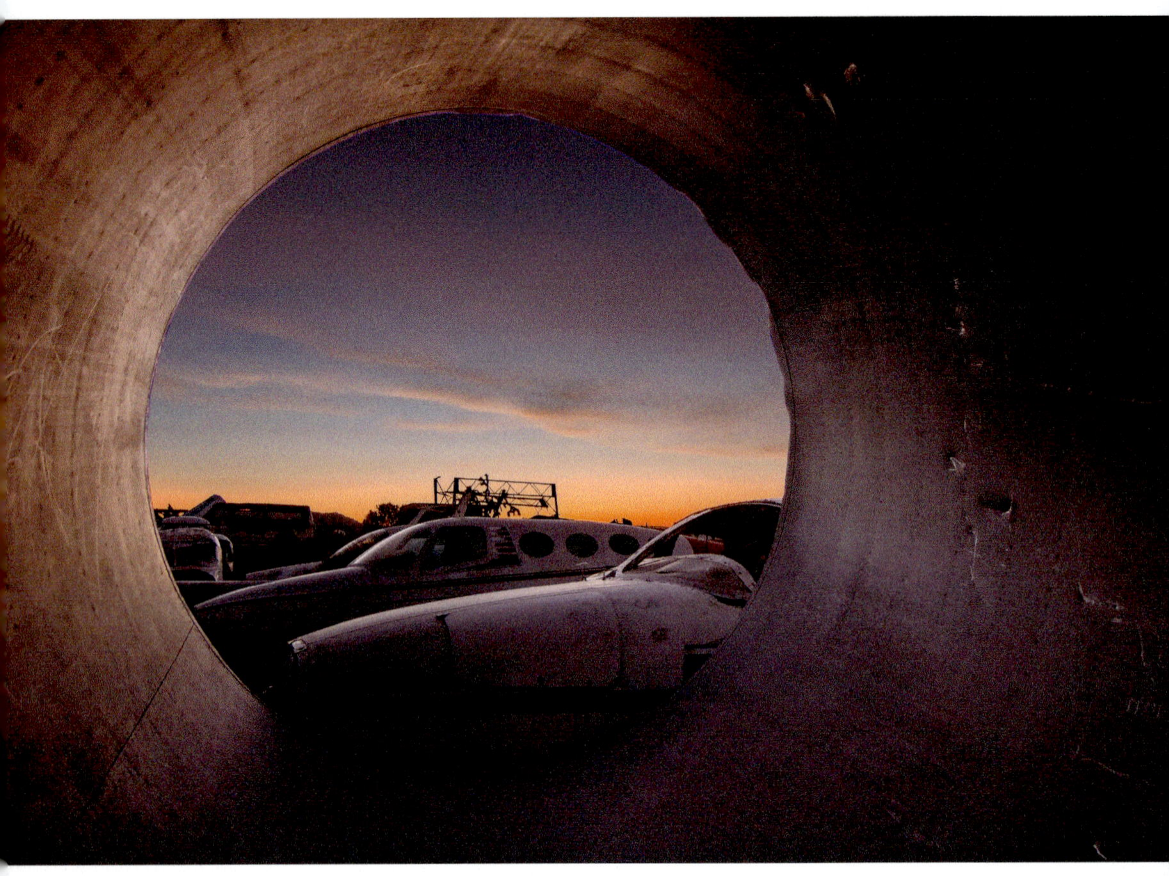

Aluminum Sunset
Aviation Warehouse. 7/30/2012, 8:30 PM.
Canon 60D, f/8, ISO 200. 1.6, 6 and 20 seconds, 4700K WB.
Sunset.
DC10 Nacelle

Deep Dream Decoder Ring ▶
Aviation Warehouse. 11/27/2009, 11:10 PM.
Canon 20D, f/5.6, ISO 100. 241 seconds, 3900K WB.
Full moon / natural LED flashlight.

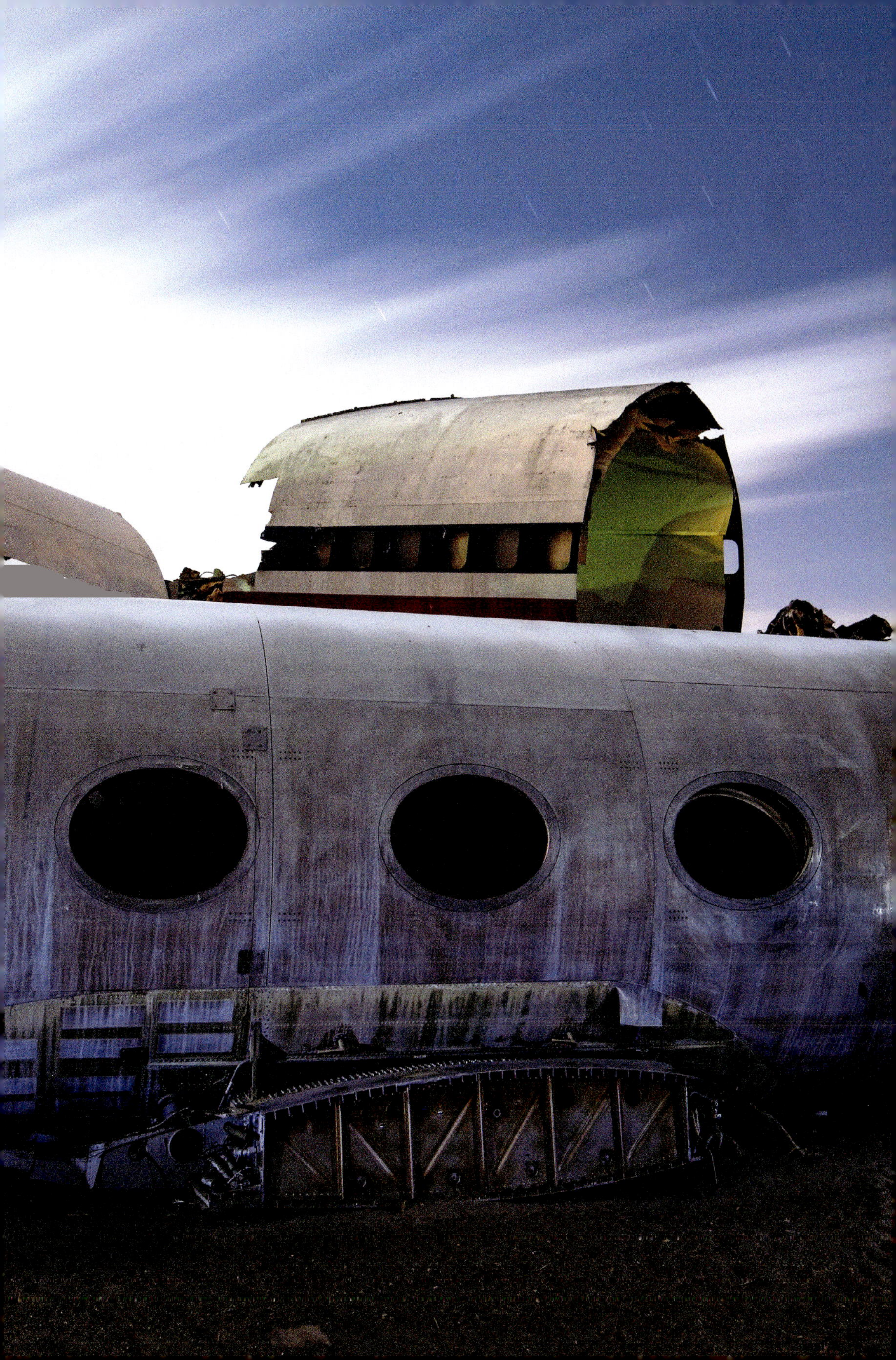

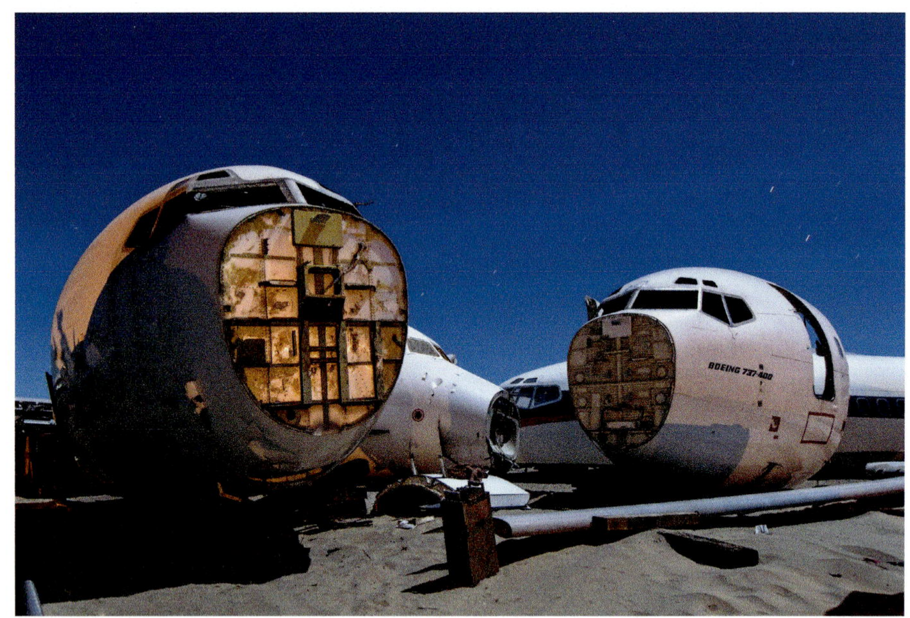

Jet Skulls
Aviation Warehouse. 11/29/2009, 10:12 PM.
Canon 20D, f/5.6, ISO 100, 120 seconds, 3300K WB.
Full moon, sodium vapor streetlights.
Boeing 727, 737 and MD-80.

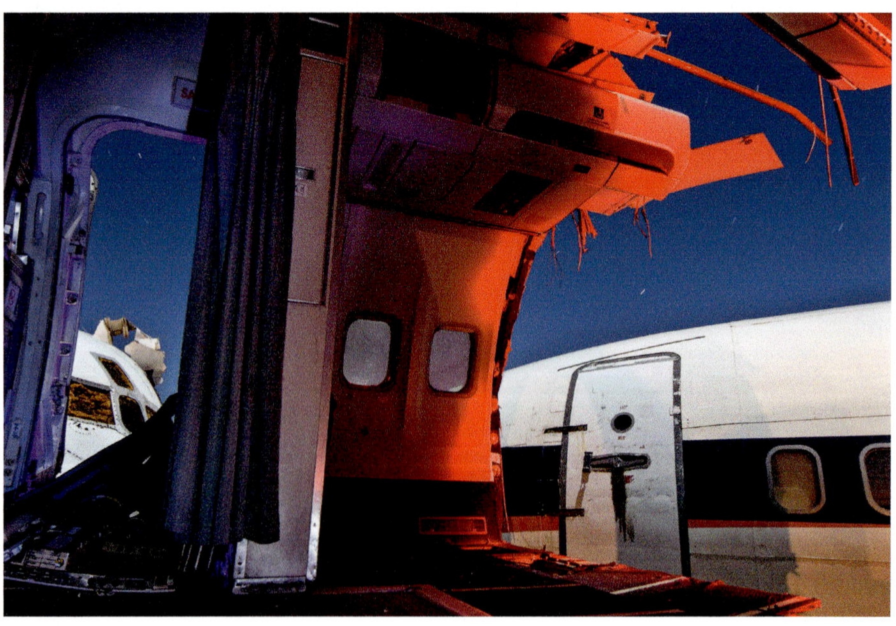

Exit Row
Aviation Warehouse. 11/29/2009, 10:45 PM
Canon 20D, f/5.6, ISO 100, 120 seconds, 3300K WB.
Full moon, sodium vapor streetlights / natural white, red and purple LED flashlight.
Boeing 727, 737 and MD-80.

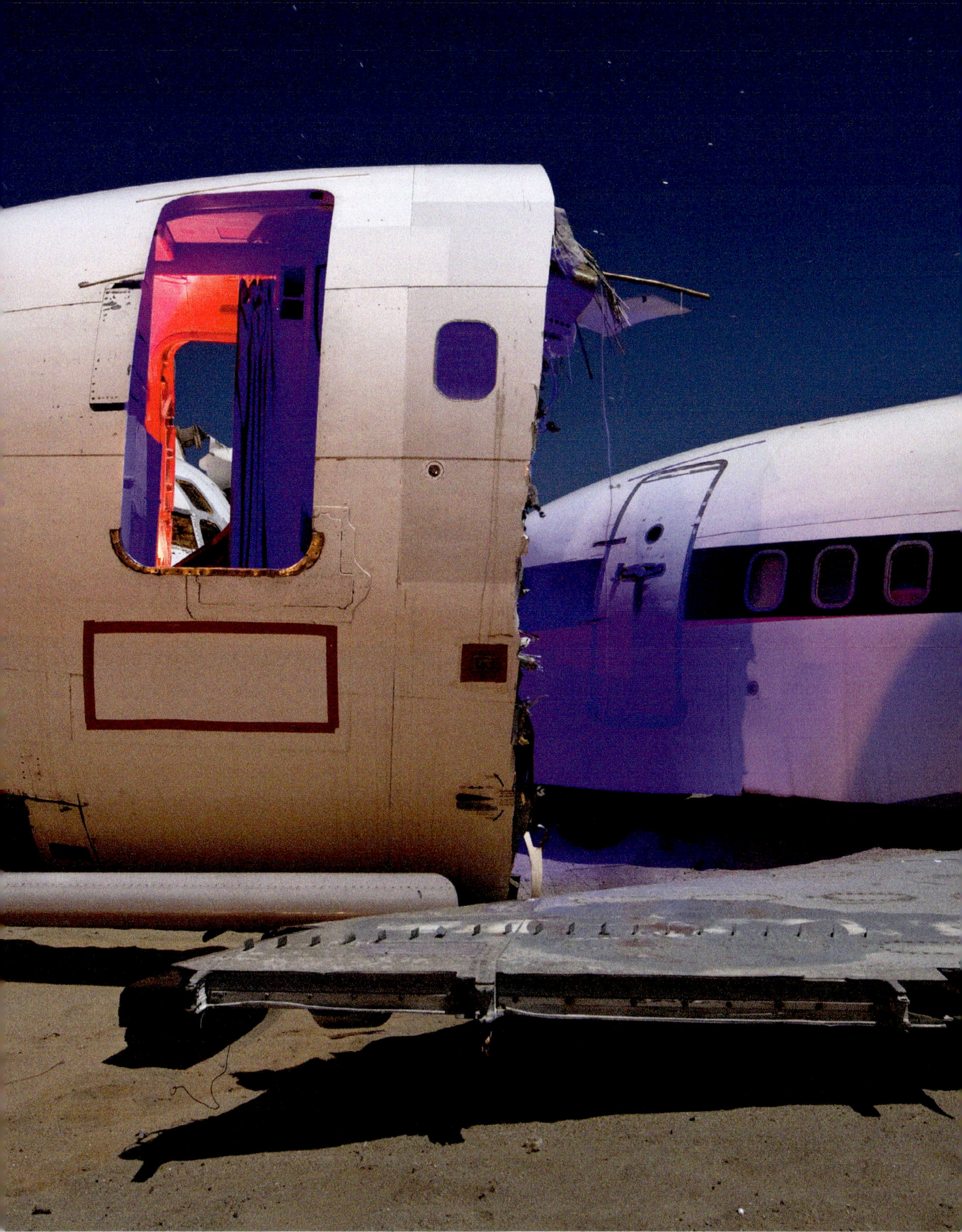

The Pink Vestibule
Aviation Warehouse. 11/29/2009, 10:28 PM.
Canon 20D, f/5.6, ISO 100, 120 seconds, 3900K WB.
Full moon / natural white, red and purple LED flashlight.
Boeing 727, 737 and MD-80.

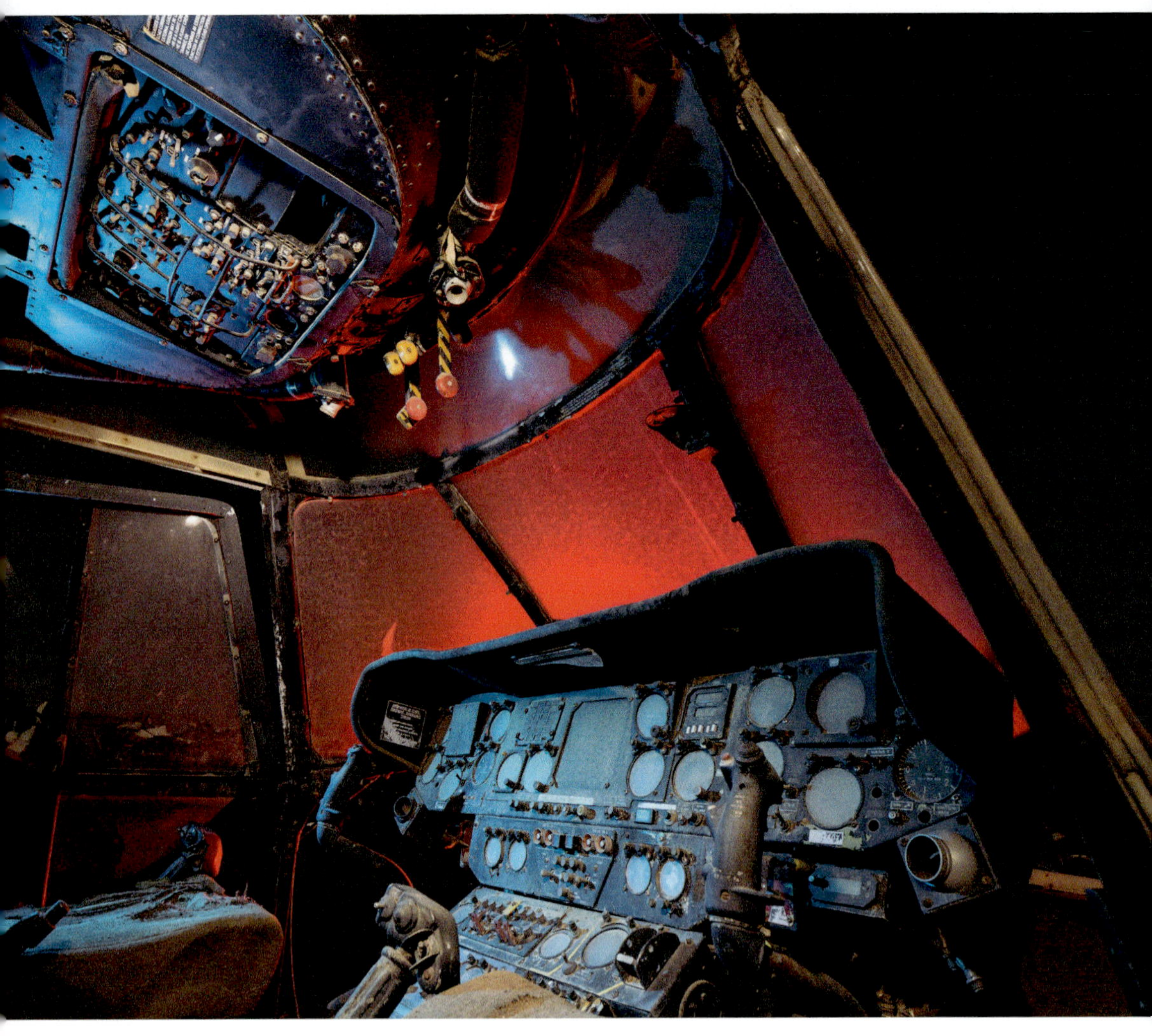

Collective Gasp 18
Aviation Warehouse. 7/25/2018, 10:53 PM.
Canon 6D MkII, f/8, ISO 200. 72 seconds, 4800K WB.
Full moon / red, white and blue Protomachines flashlight.
Helicopter Cockpit.

Keluar ►
Aviation Warehouse. 8/2/2012, 12:21 AM.
Canon 60D, f/8, ISO 200. 128 seconds, 4700K WB.
Full moon / lime and purple Protomachines flashlight.
Boeing 737.

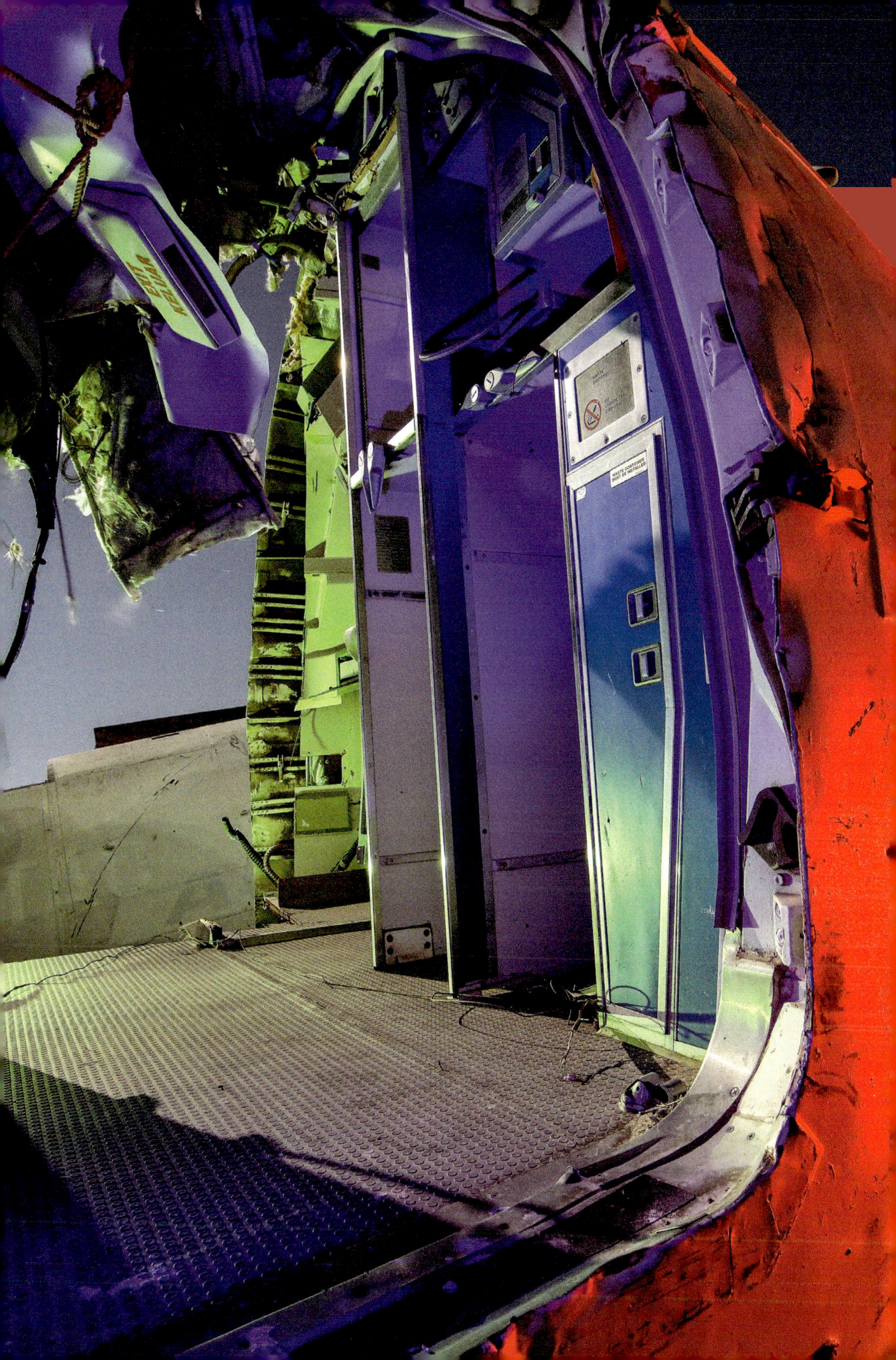
EXIT
KELUAR
WASTE CONTAINER
MUST BE INSTALLED

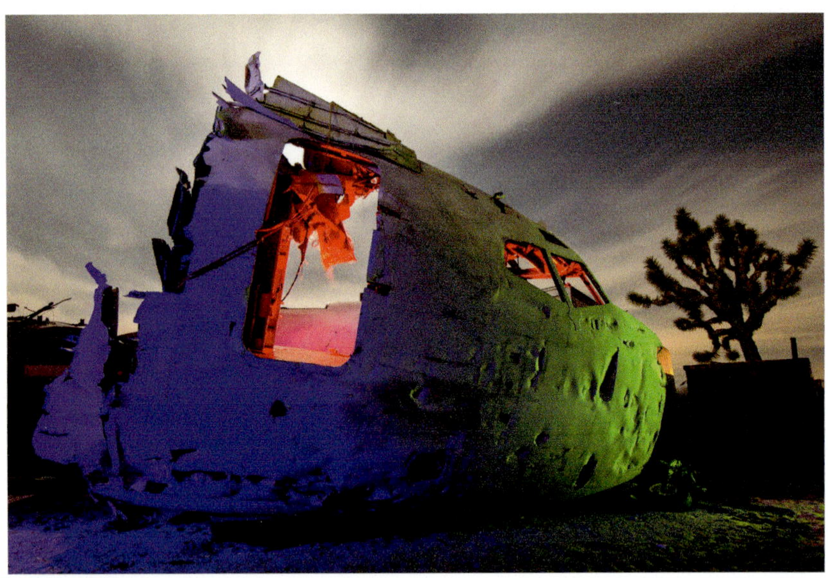

Cockpit Heater
Aviation Warehouse. 7/30/2012, 11:09 PM.
Canon 60D, f/8, ISO 200. 139 seconds, 5000K WB.
Full moon, partial cloud cover / purple, green and red Protomachine flashlight.
Boeing 737.

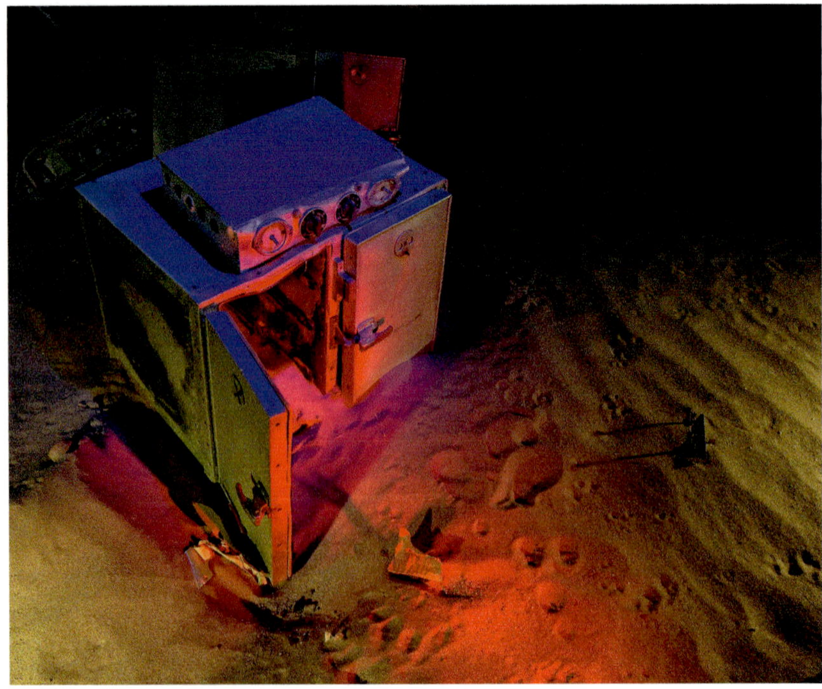

Inflight Meals for Jackalopes
Aviation Warehouse. 7/30/2012, 10:31 PM.
Canon 60D, f/8, ISO 200. 46 seconds, 3300K WB.
Full moon, partial cloud cover / yellow, red and blue Protomachine flashlight.

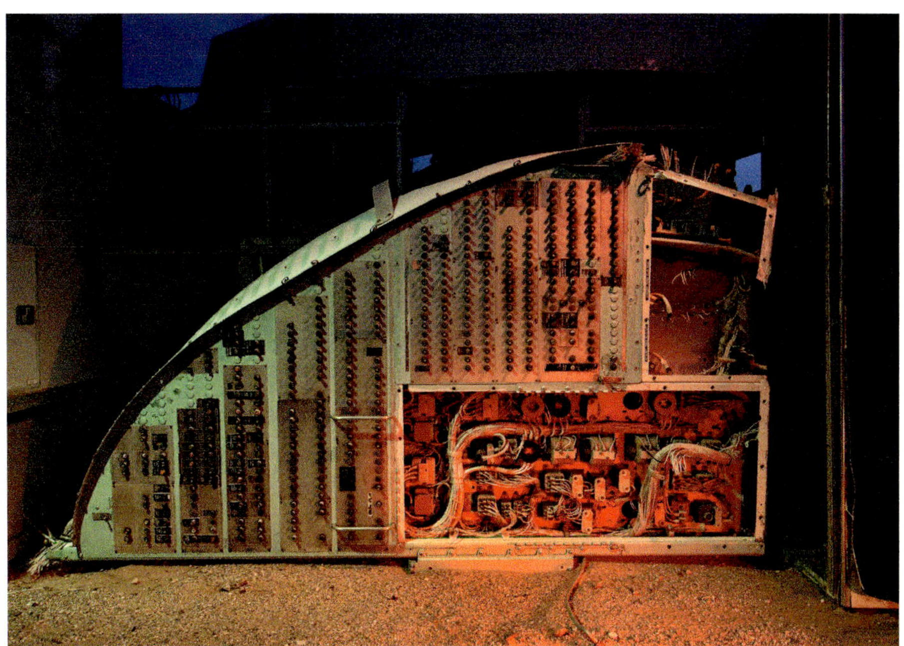

Relayer
Aviation Warehouse. 7/31/2012, 8:50 PM.
Canon 60D, f/8, ISO 200. 45 seconds, 2850K WB.
Full moon / red and white Protomachines flashlight.

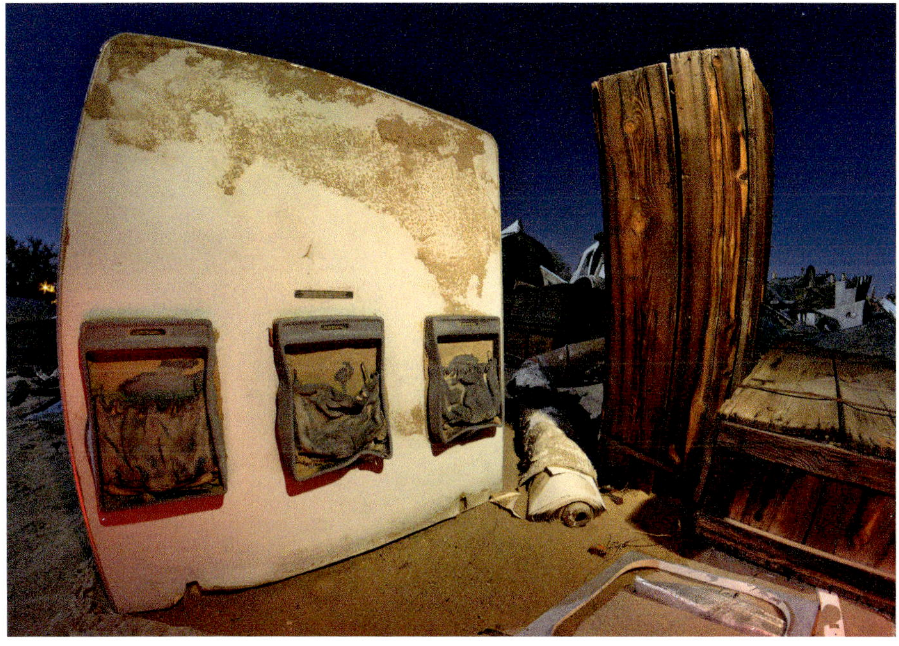

The Highly Coveted Bulkhead Row
Aviation Warehouse. 11/6/2014, 8:18 PM.
Canon 60D, f/8, ISO 200. 46 seconds, 3600K WB.
Full moon / red and white Protomachines flashlight.

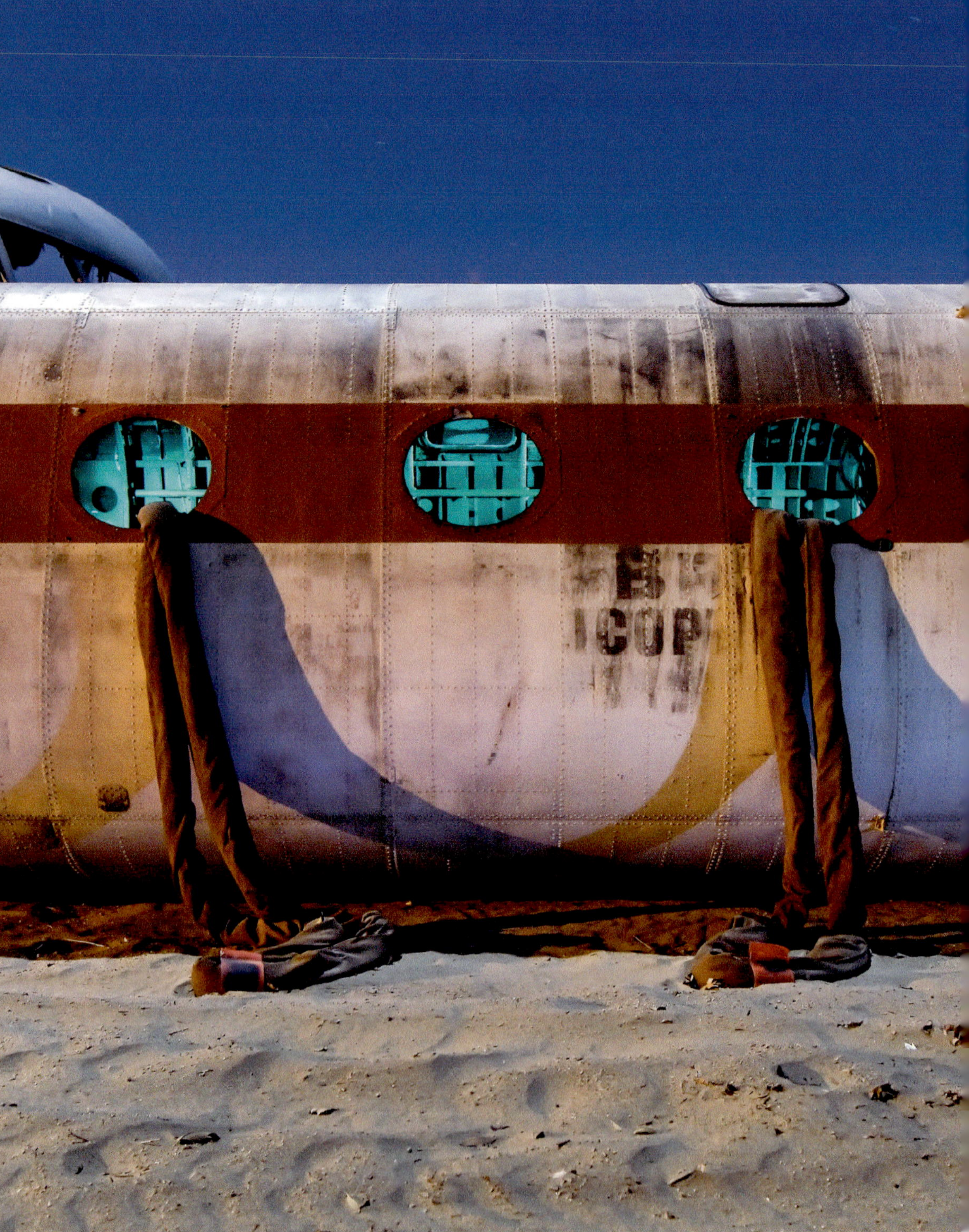

Piasnakies

Aviation Warehouse. 11/28/2009, 9:51 PM.
Canon 20D, f/5.6, ISO 100, 120 seconds, 3500K WB.
Full moon, sodium vapor streetlights / green-gelled strobe, natural white LED flashlight.
Piasecki H-21 Shawnee helicopter.

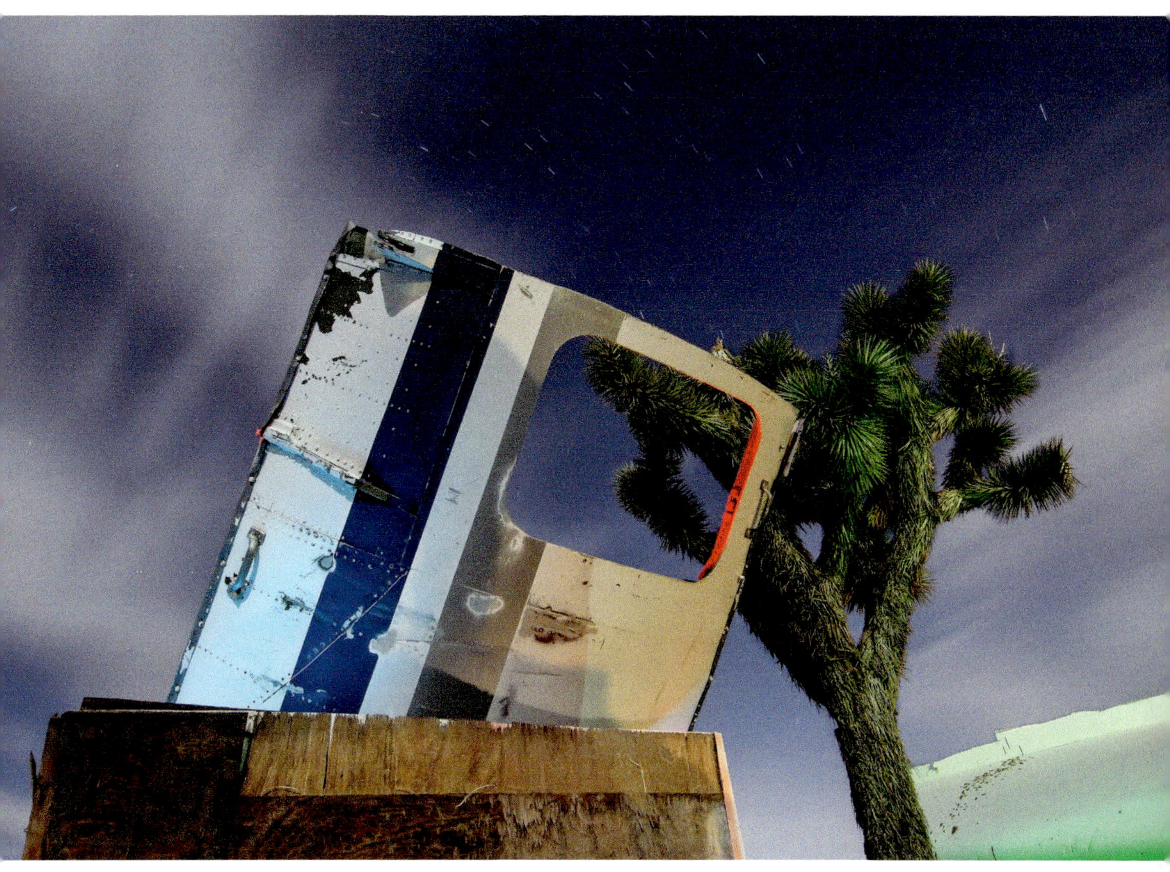

Box of Hatch
Aviation Warehouse. 7/31/2012, 1:00 AM.
Canon 60D, f/8, ISO 200. 287 seconds, 3900K WB.
Full moon, partial cloud cover, sodium vapor streetlights / blue, red and green Protomachines flashlight.

On the following page:

Charred Remains
Aviation Warehouse. 7/31/2012, 12:23 AM.
Canon 60D, f/8, ISO 200. 280 seconds, 3800K WB
Full moon, partial cloud cover / red, white and lime Protomachines flashlight.
Boeing 737 and 747.

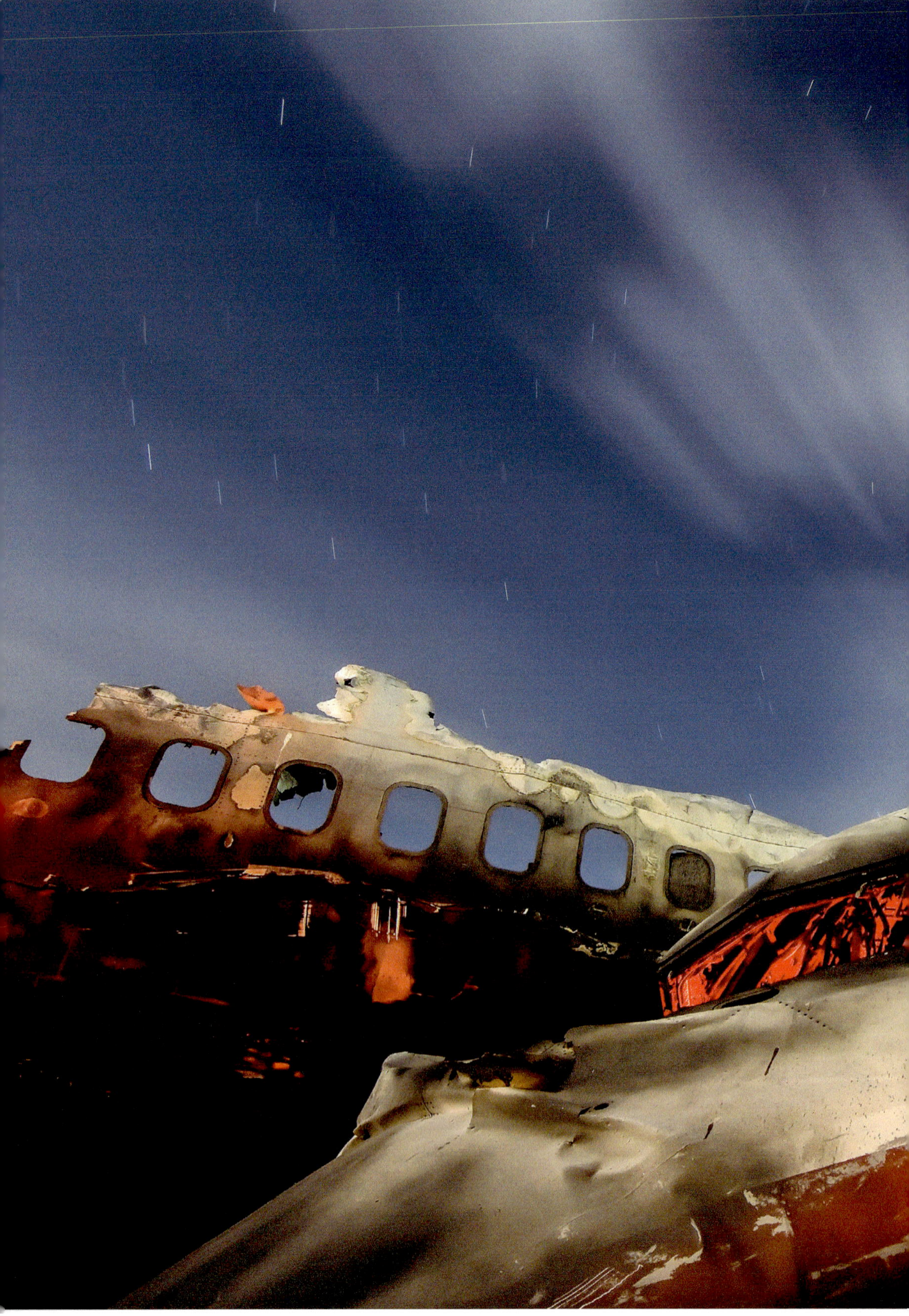

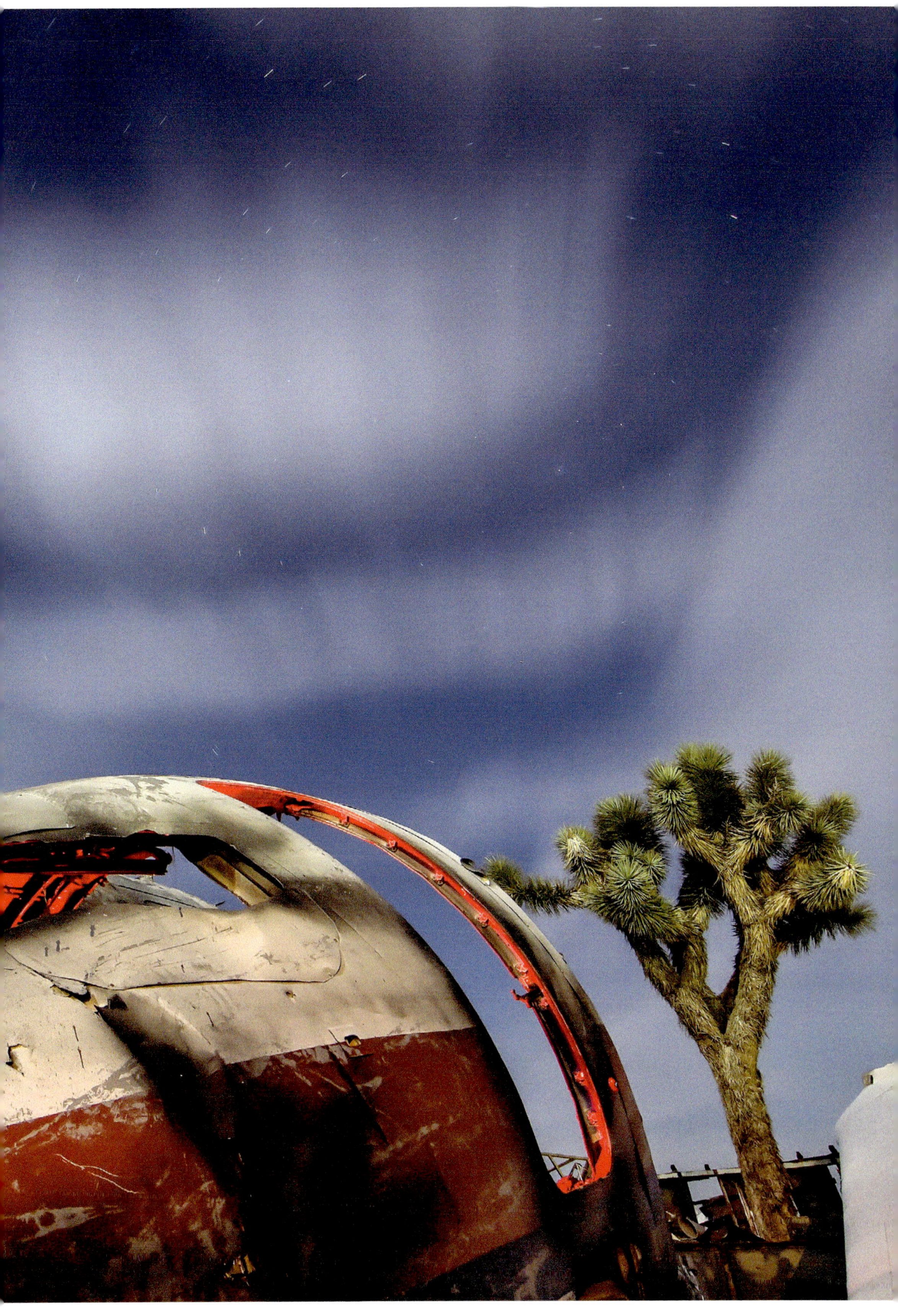

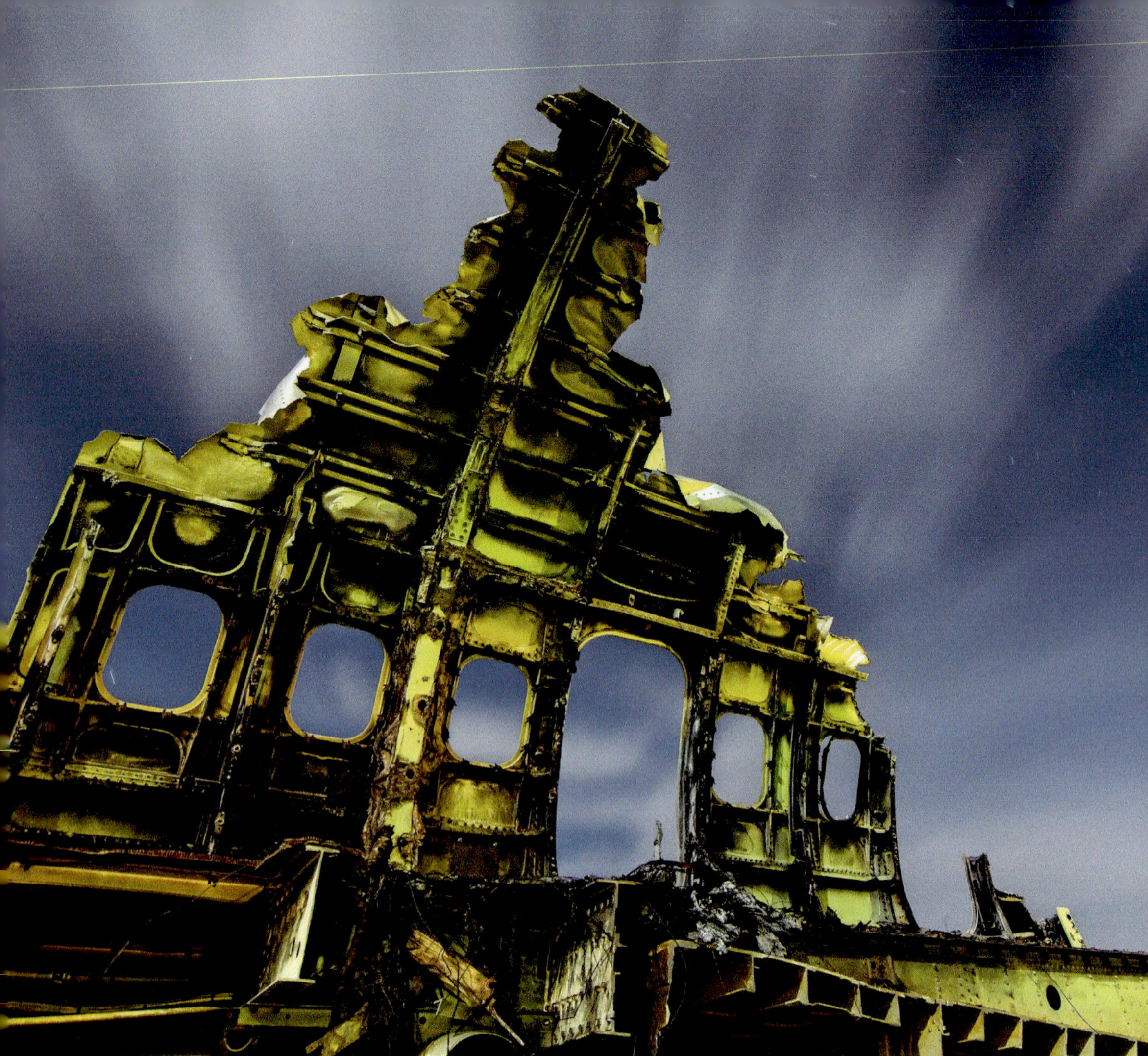

(Way Past Being an) Emergency Exit
Aviation Warehouse. 7/31/2012, 12:45 AM.
Canon 60D, f/8, ISO 200. 285 seconds, 3800K WB.
Full moon, partial cloud cover / lime Protomachines flashlight.
Boeing 747.

Test Flux Valve ►
Aviation Warehouse. 8/6/2006, 7:52 PM.
Canon 20D, f/5.6, ISO 100. 5 seconds, 3000K WB.
Full moon / natural white LED flashlight.

The Flying Crocodile ►
Aviation Warehouse. 7/26/2018, 9:21 PM.
Canon 6D MkII, f/8, ISO 200. 96 seconds, 3900K WB.
Full moon / red, white, purple and green Protomachines flashlight.
Mil Mi-24 Hind Helicopter.

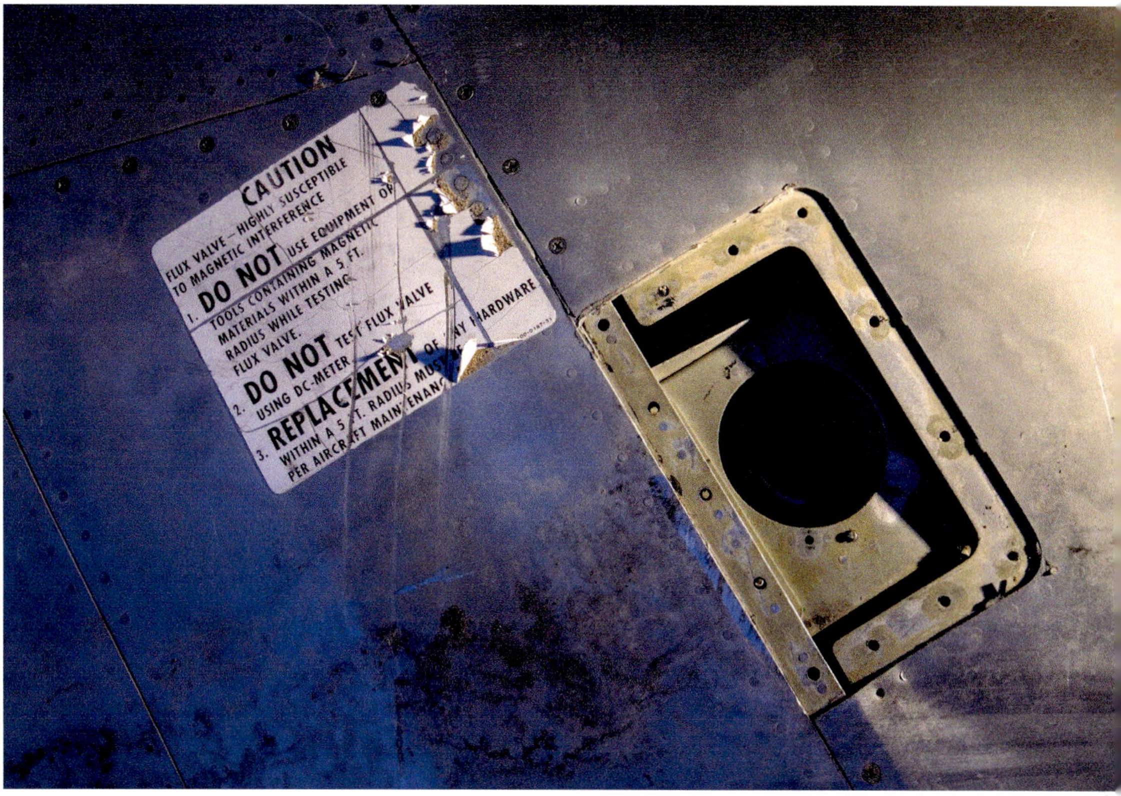

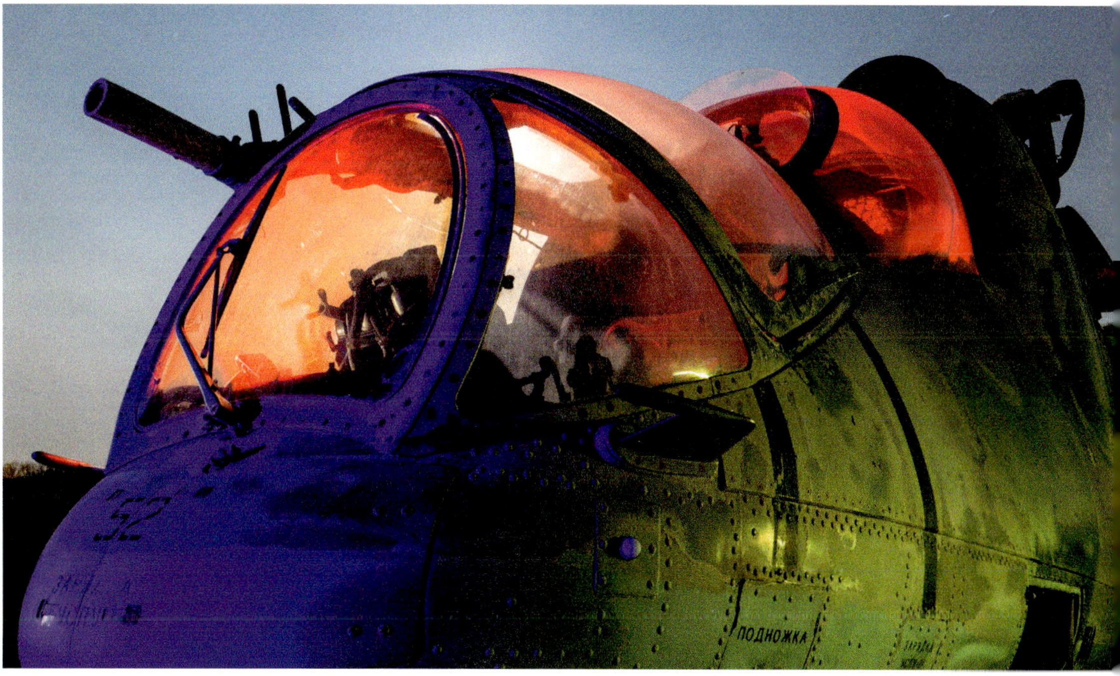

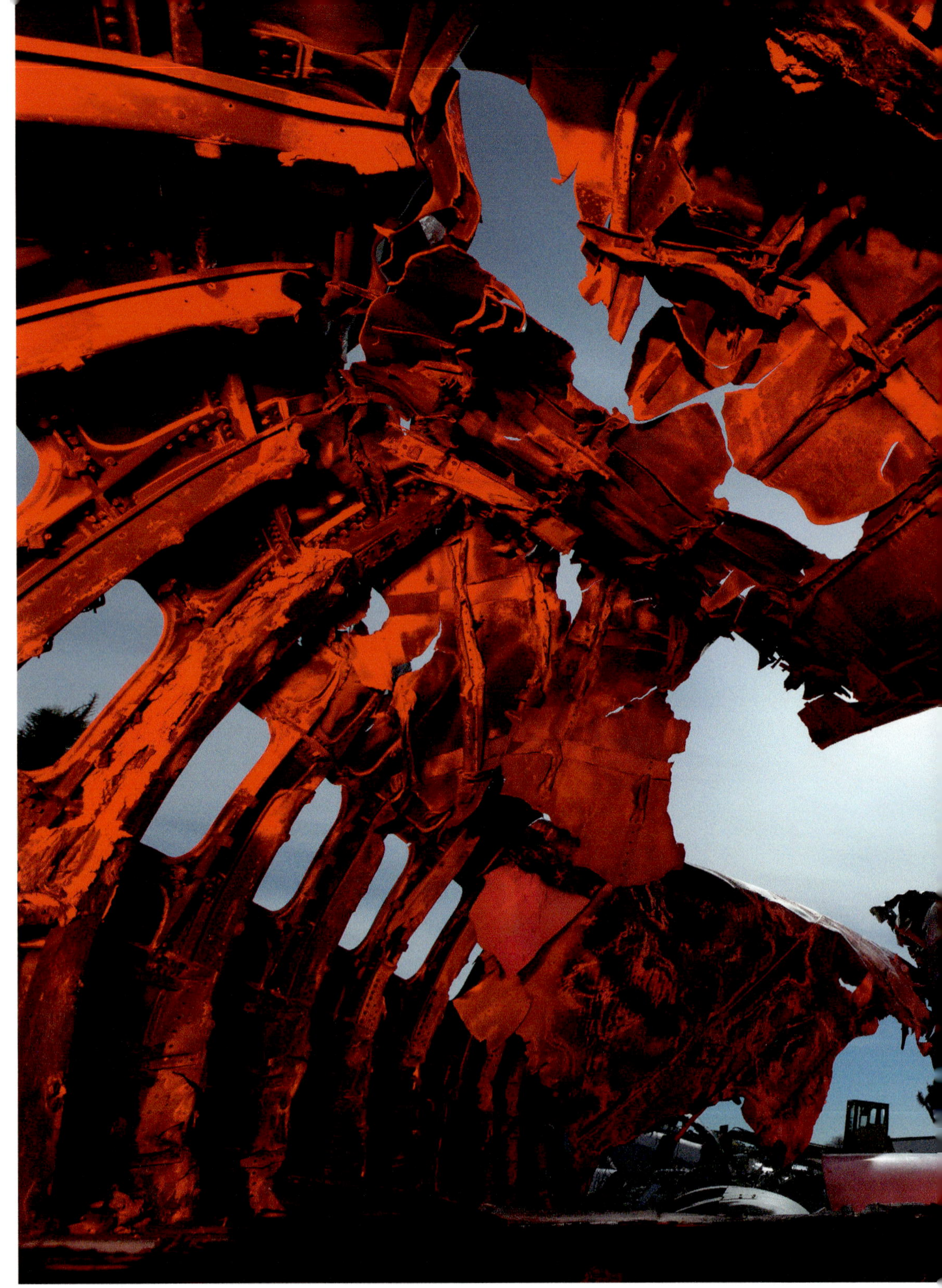

Hot Enough to Melt Aluminum
Aviation Warehouse. 2/3/2015, 8:05 PM.
Canon 5D MkIII, f/8, ISO 200. 178 seconds, 3800K WB.

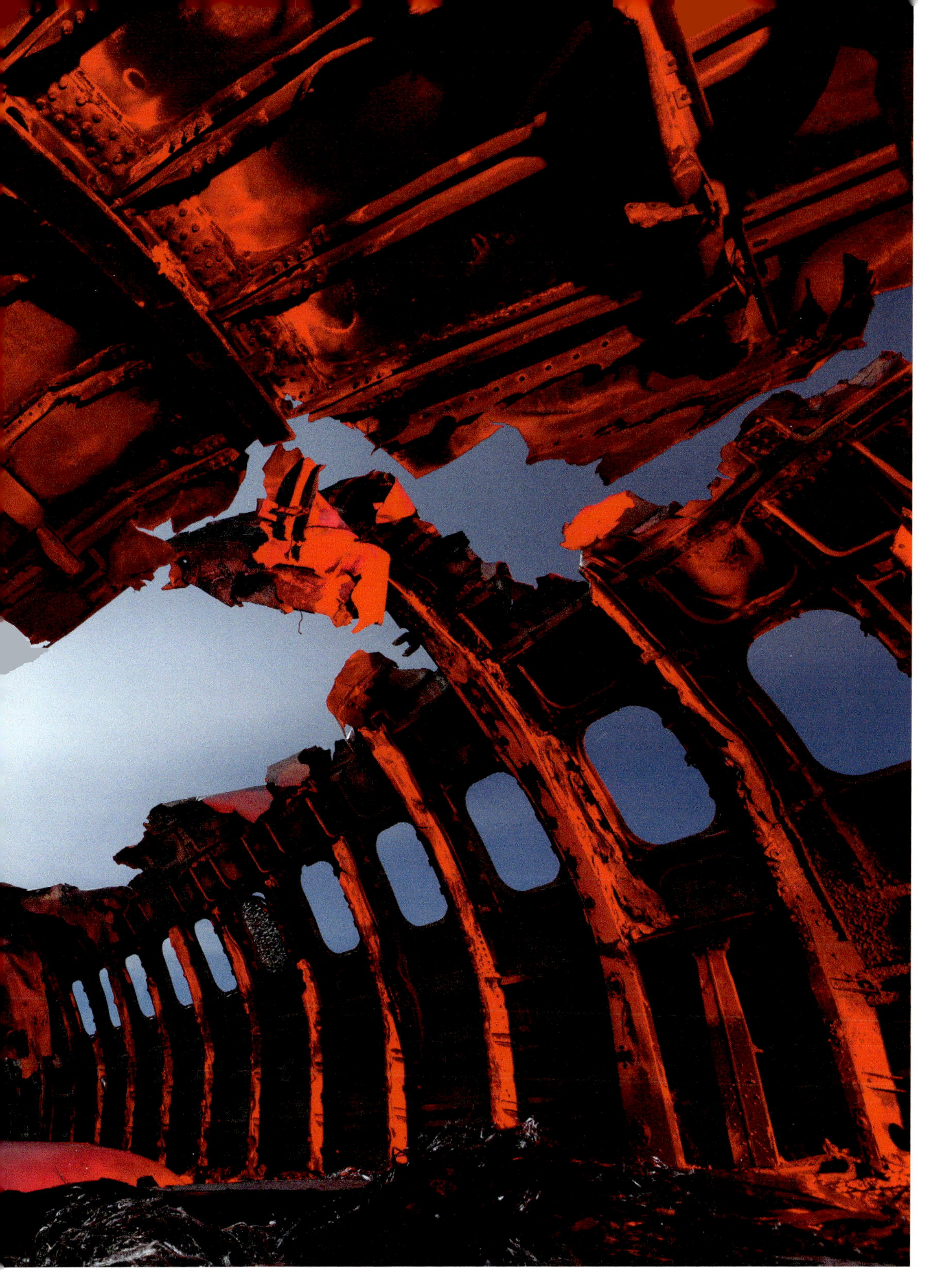

Full moon / red Protomachines flashlight.
Boeing 747.

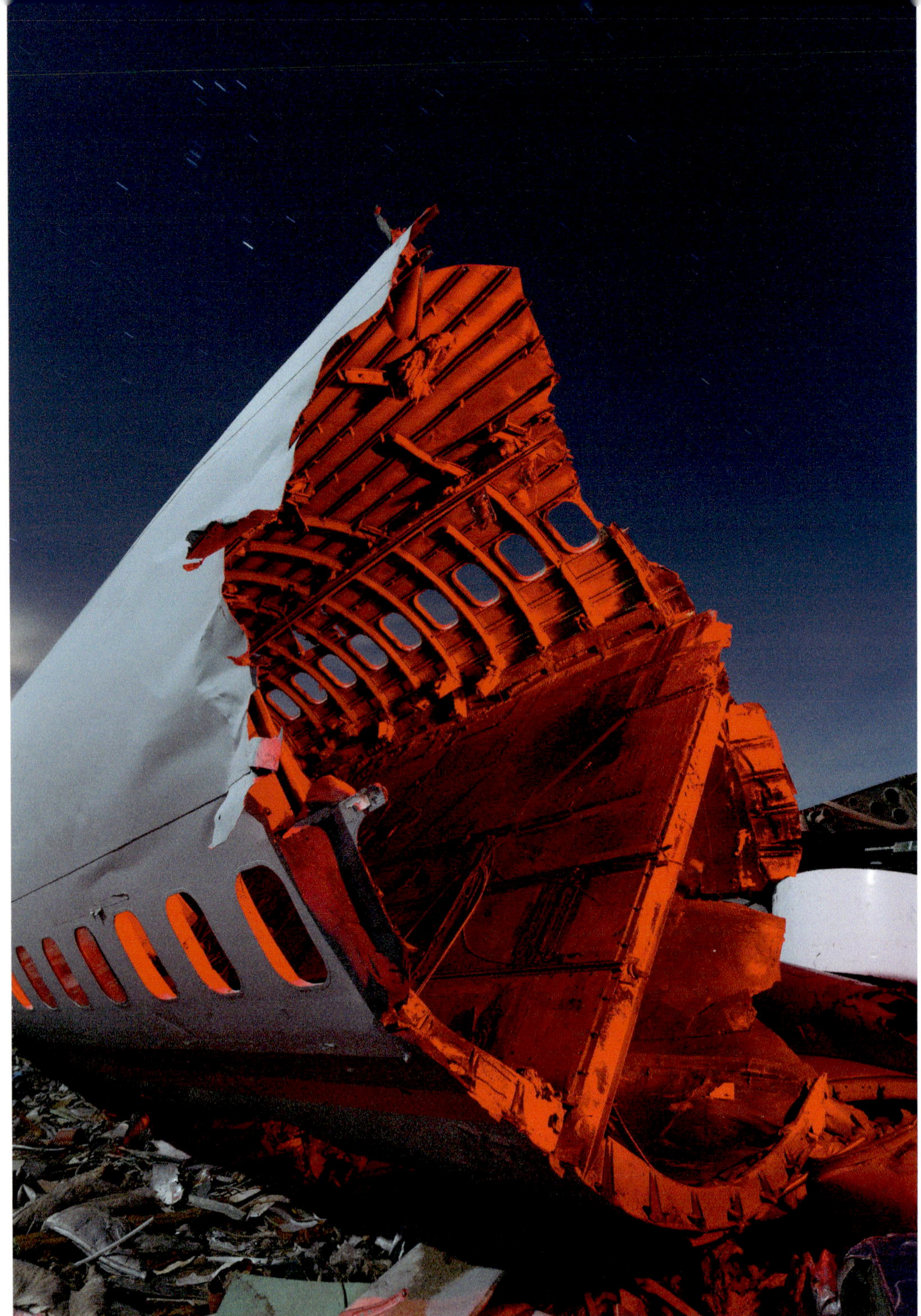

Final Boarding
Aviation Warehouse. 2/3/2015, 8:58 PM.
Canon 5D MkIII, f/8, ISO 200. 177 seconds, 3800K WB.
Full moon / red Protomachines flashlight.
Boeing 737.

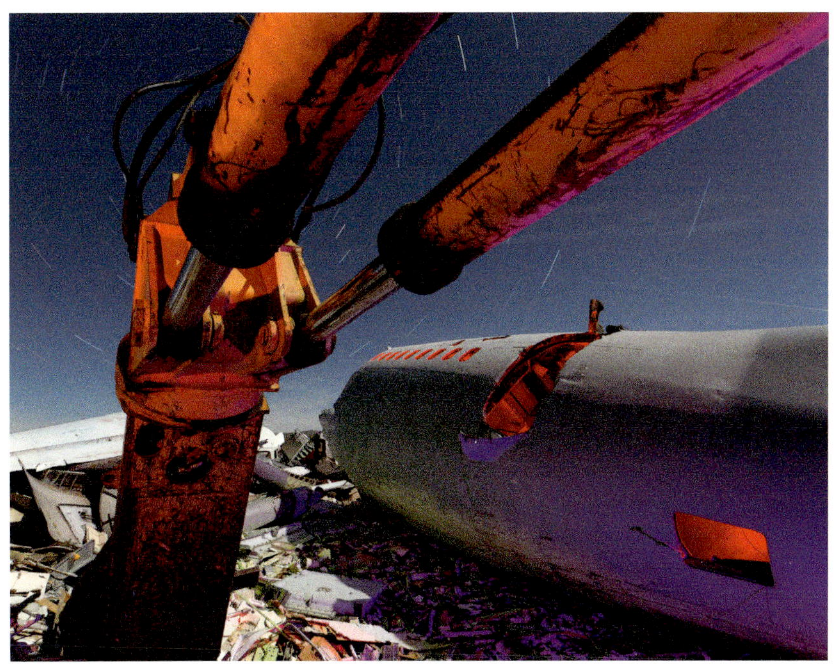

No Pressure
Aviation Warehouse. 2/3/2015, 8:39 PM.
Canon 5D MkIII, f/8, ISO 200. 45 minutes, 5000K WB.
Full moon / white, red, purple and lime Protomachines flashlight.
Boeing 737.

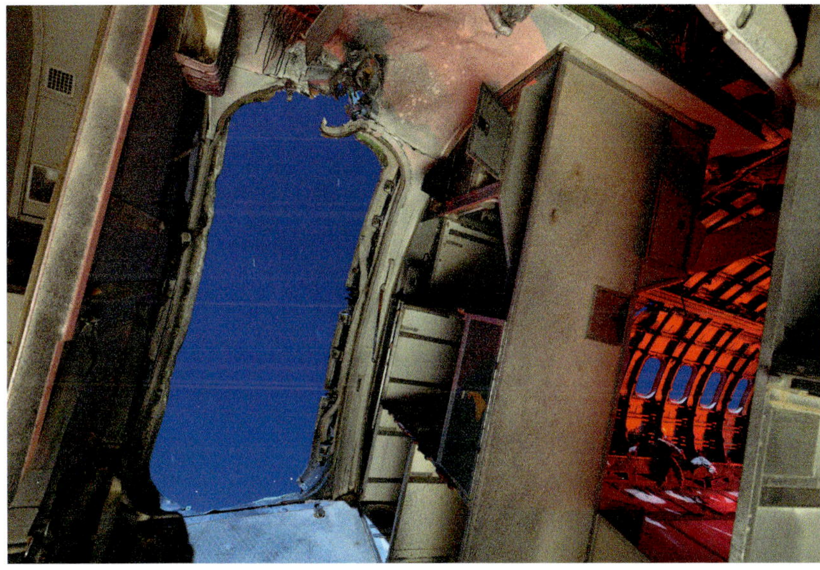

Galley Blowout
Aviation Warehouse. 2/3/2015, 10:23 PM.
Canon 5D MkIII, f/8, ISO 200. 258 seconds, 2850 WB.
Full moon / white and red Protomachines flashlight.
Boeing 737.

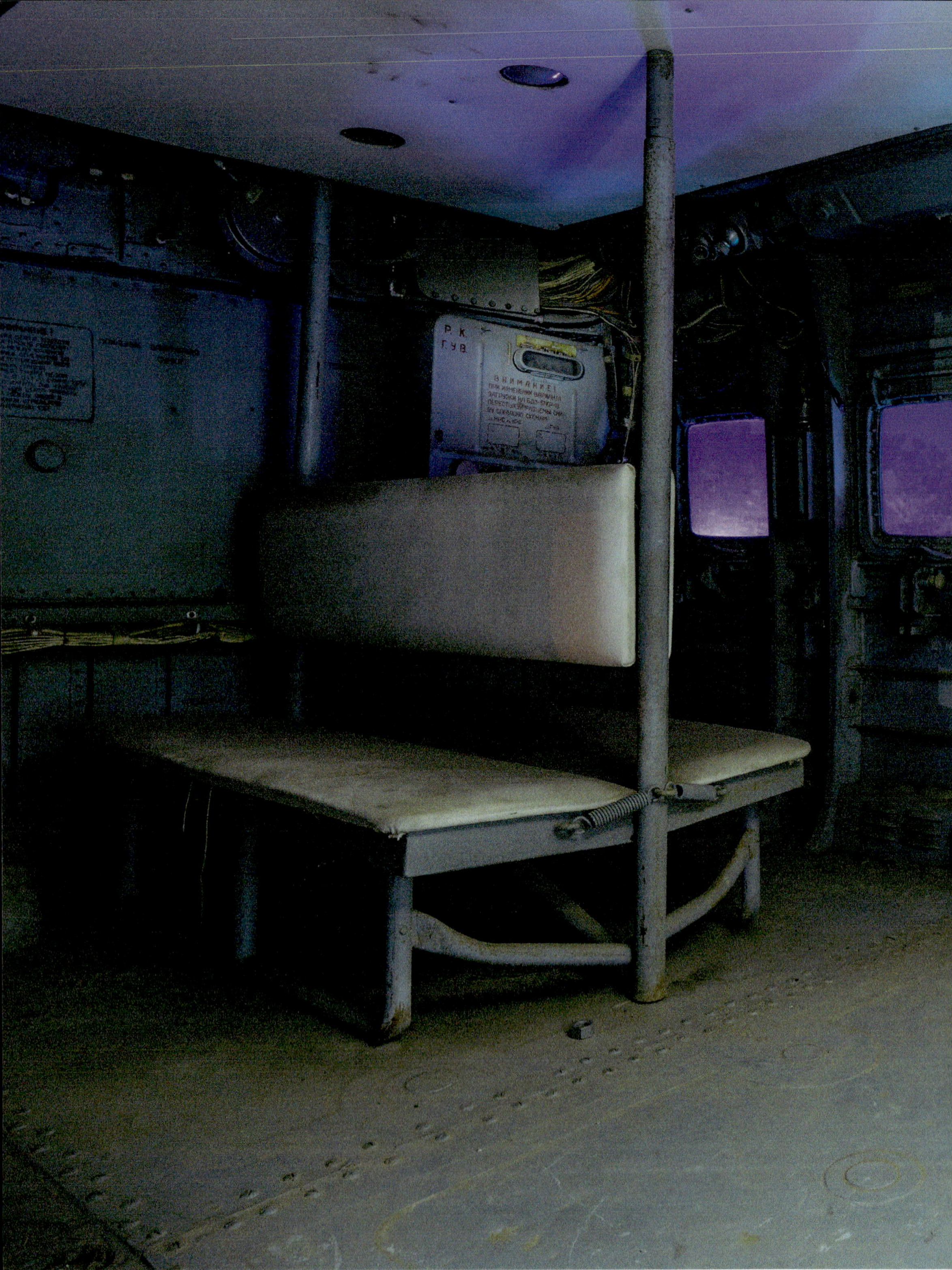

Hind Quarters
Aviation Warehouse. 7/25/2018, 10:34 PM.
Canon 6D MkII, f/8, ISO 200. 96 seconds, 3800K WB.

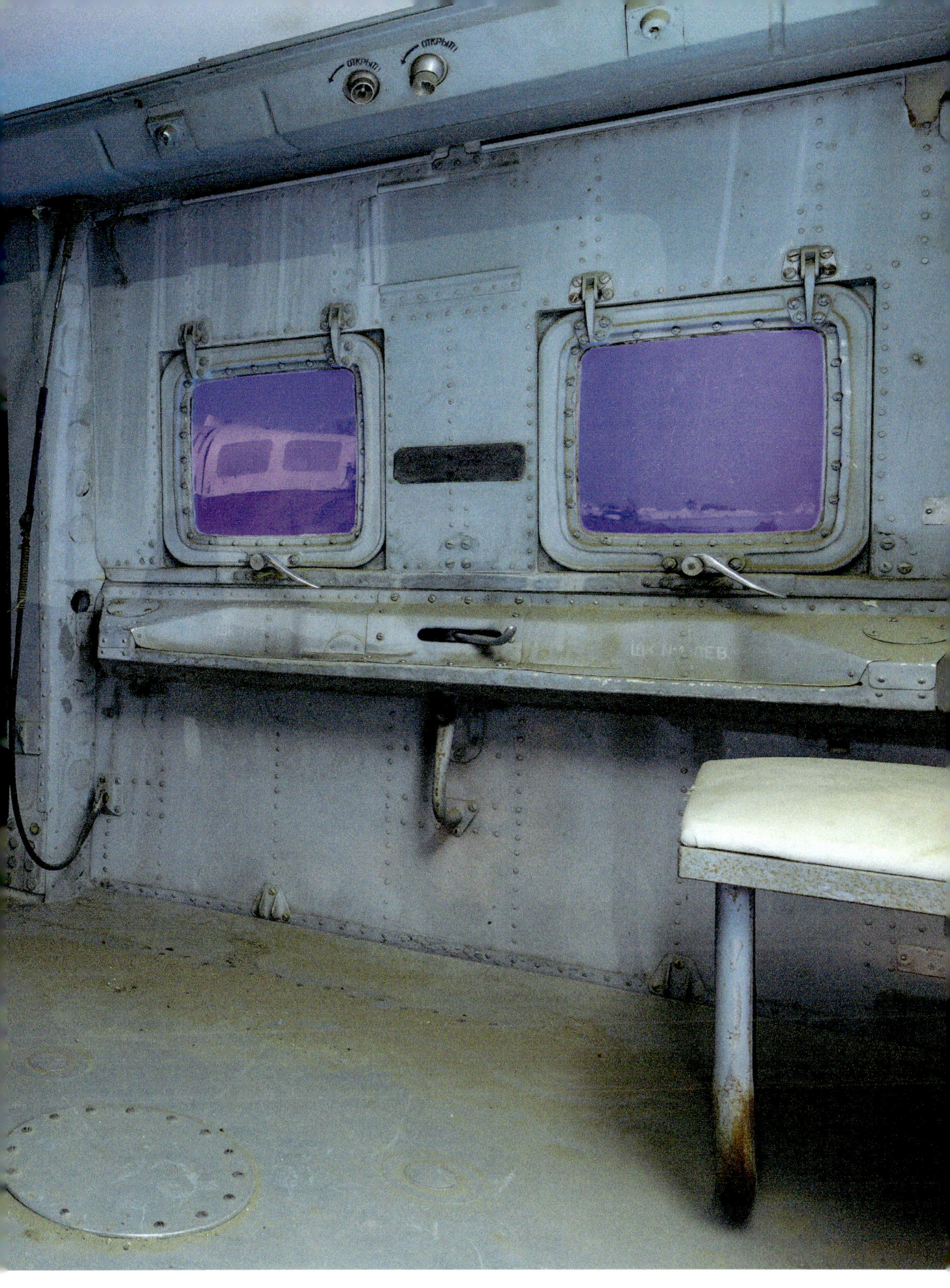

Total darkness / white and purple Protomachines flashlight.
Mil Mi-24 Hind Helicopter.

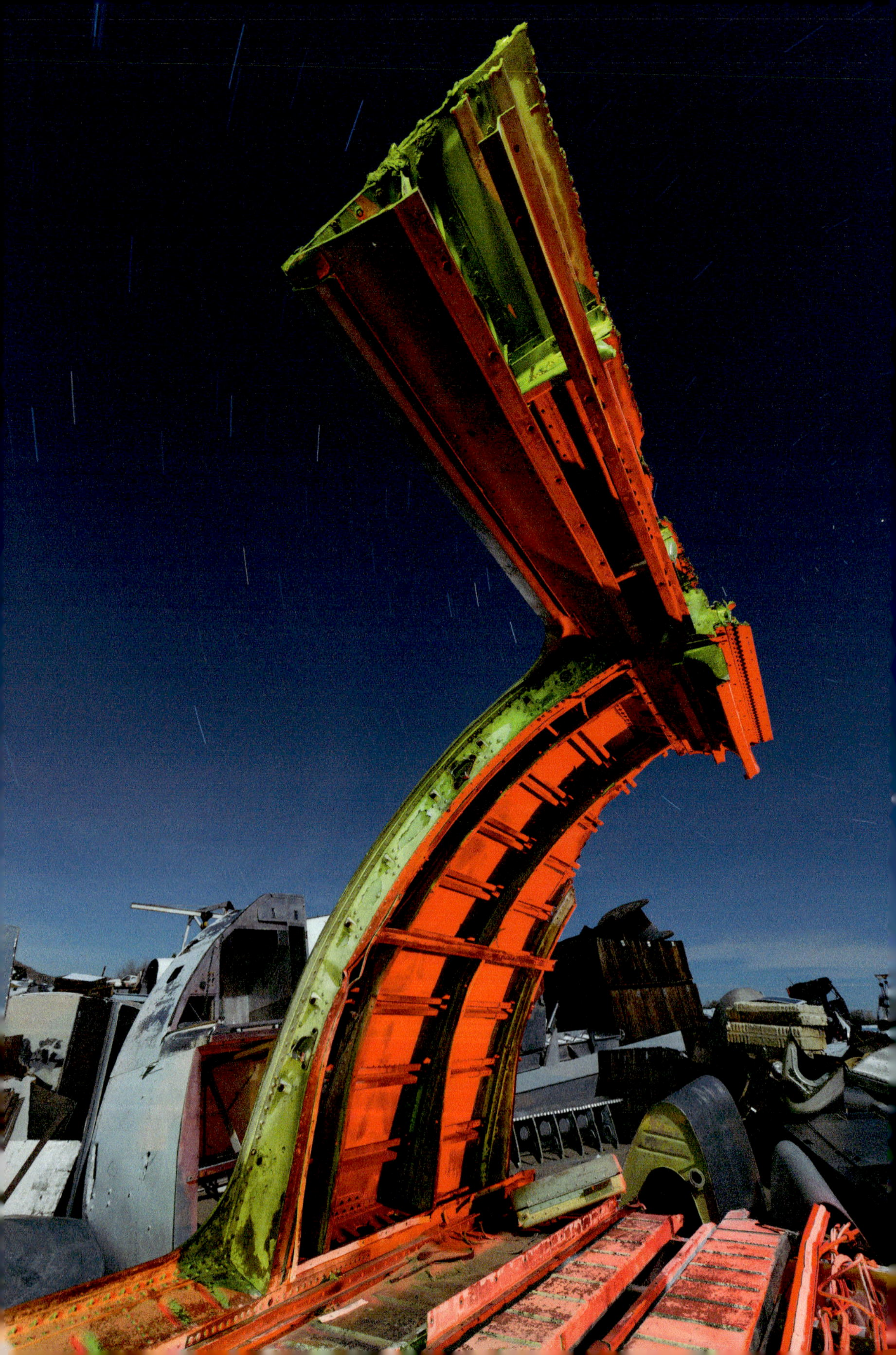

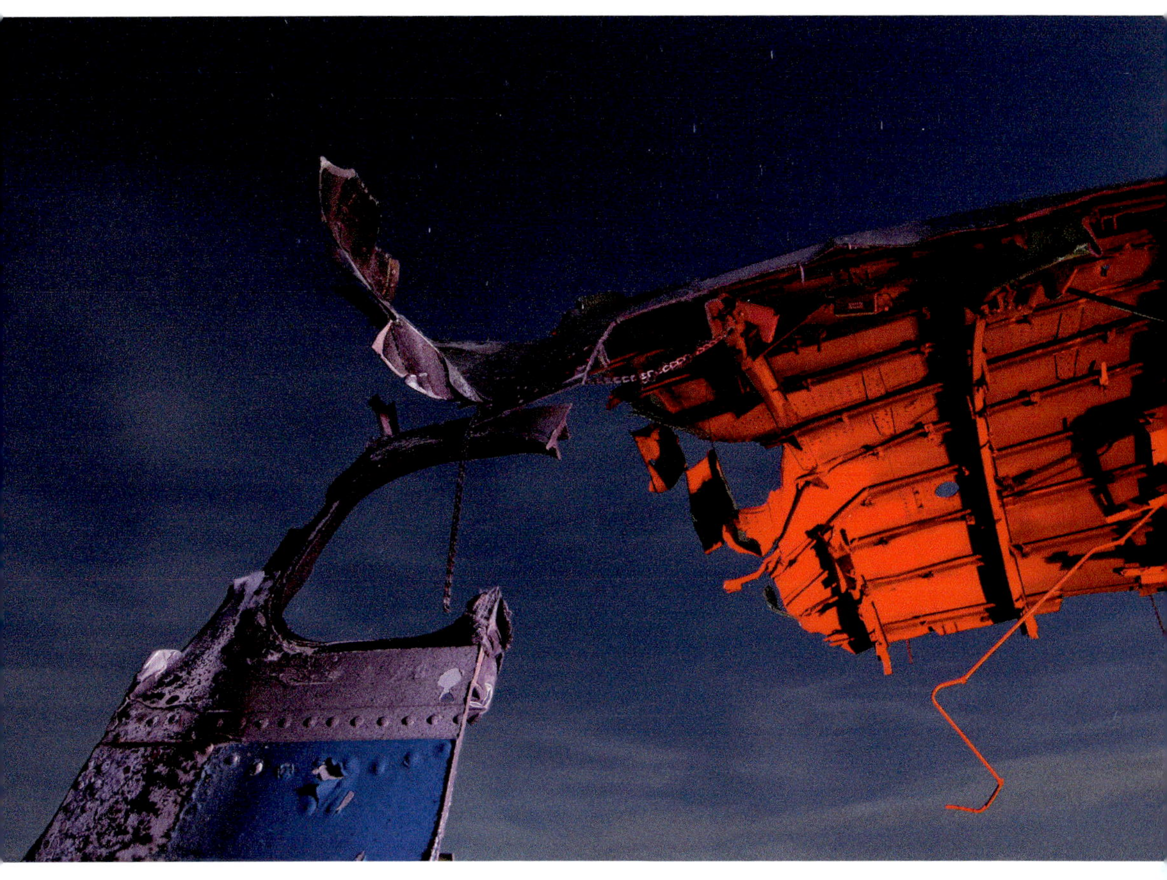

Starship Implosion
Aviation Warehouse. 7/31/2012, 9:43 PM.
Canon 60D, f/8, ISO 200. 129 seconds, 3500K WB.
Full moon, partial cloud cover / red and purple Protomachines flashlight.
Boeing 737.

◀ **Red 7**
Aviation Warehouse. 2/2/2015, 8:35 PM.
Canon 5D MkIII, f/8, ISO 200. 11 minutes, 3800K WB.
Full moon / red and lime Protomachines flashlight.

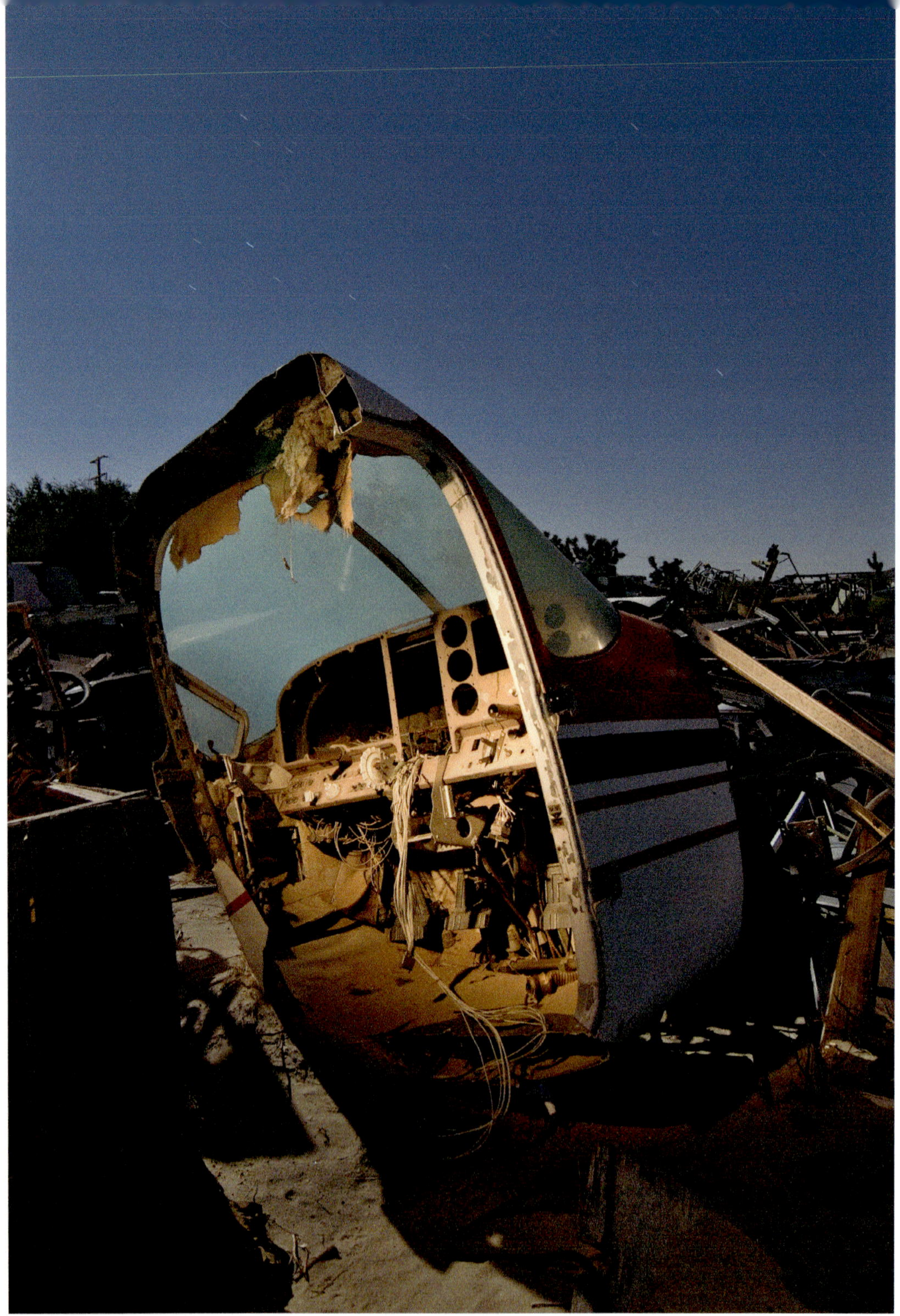

Sandy Cessna
Aviation Warehouse. 8/8/2006, 1:32 AM.
Canon 20D, f/5.6, ISO 100. 118 seconds, 3900K WB.
Full moon / natural white xenon flashlight.

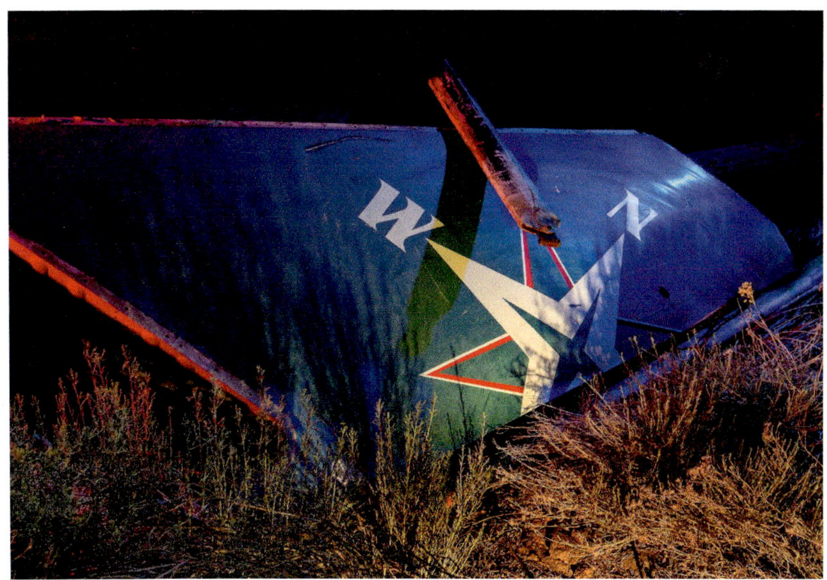

North By Northwest
Aviation Warehouse. 8/1/2012, 11:44 PM.
Canon 60D, f/8, ISO 200. 59 seconds, 3850K WB.
Full moon / red, white and lime Protomachines flashlight.

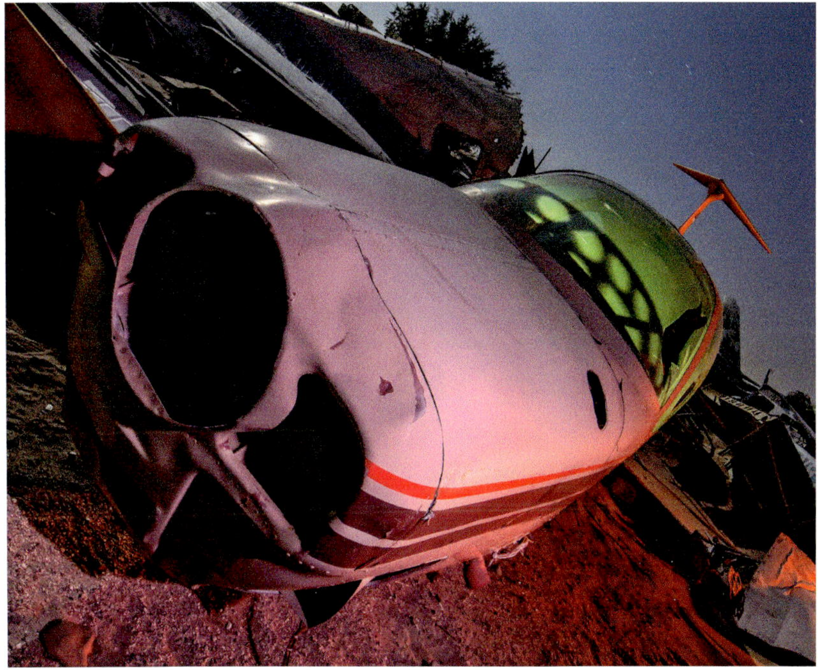

Rooftop Boomerang
Aviation Warehouse. 7/31/2012, 10:08 PM.
Canon 60D, f/8, ISO 200. 97 seconds, 3800K WB.
Full moon / green and red Protomachines flashlight.
Beechcraft Bonanza.

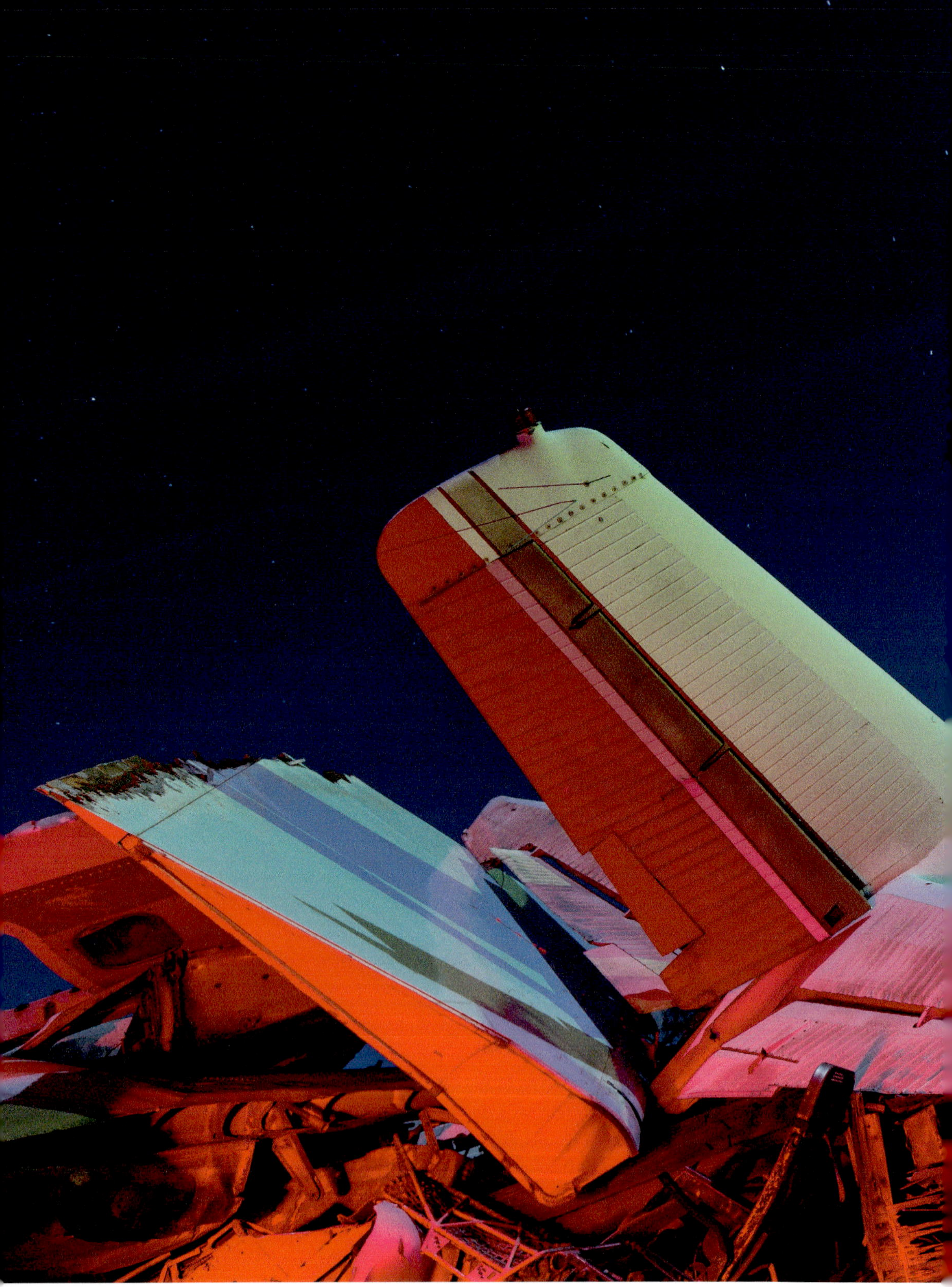

On Alien Fields
Aviation Warehouse. 2/2/2015, 10:08 PM.

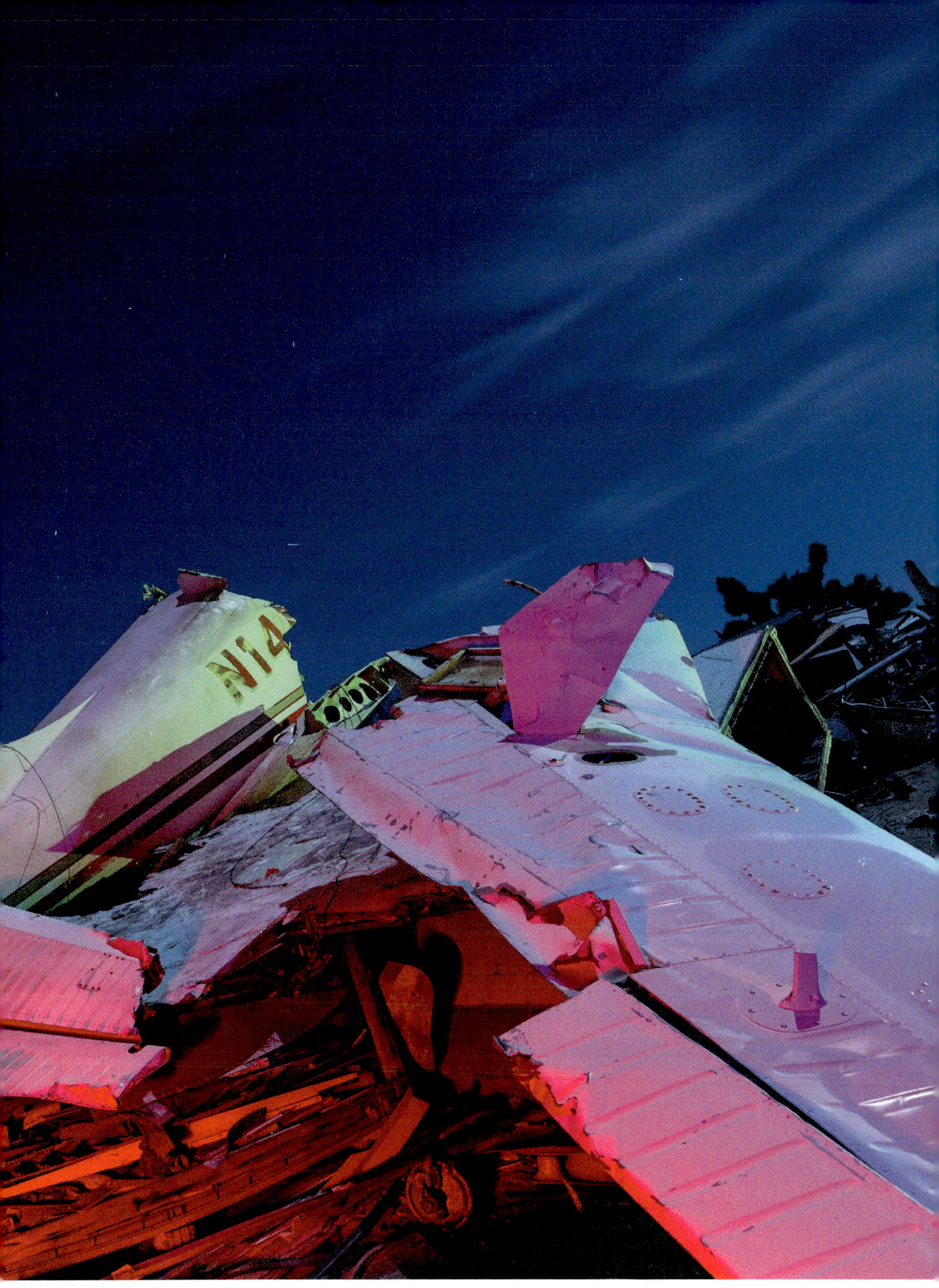

Canon 5D MkIII, f/8, ISO 200. 60 seconds, 2850K WB.
Full moon / green, red and purple Protomachines flashlight.

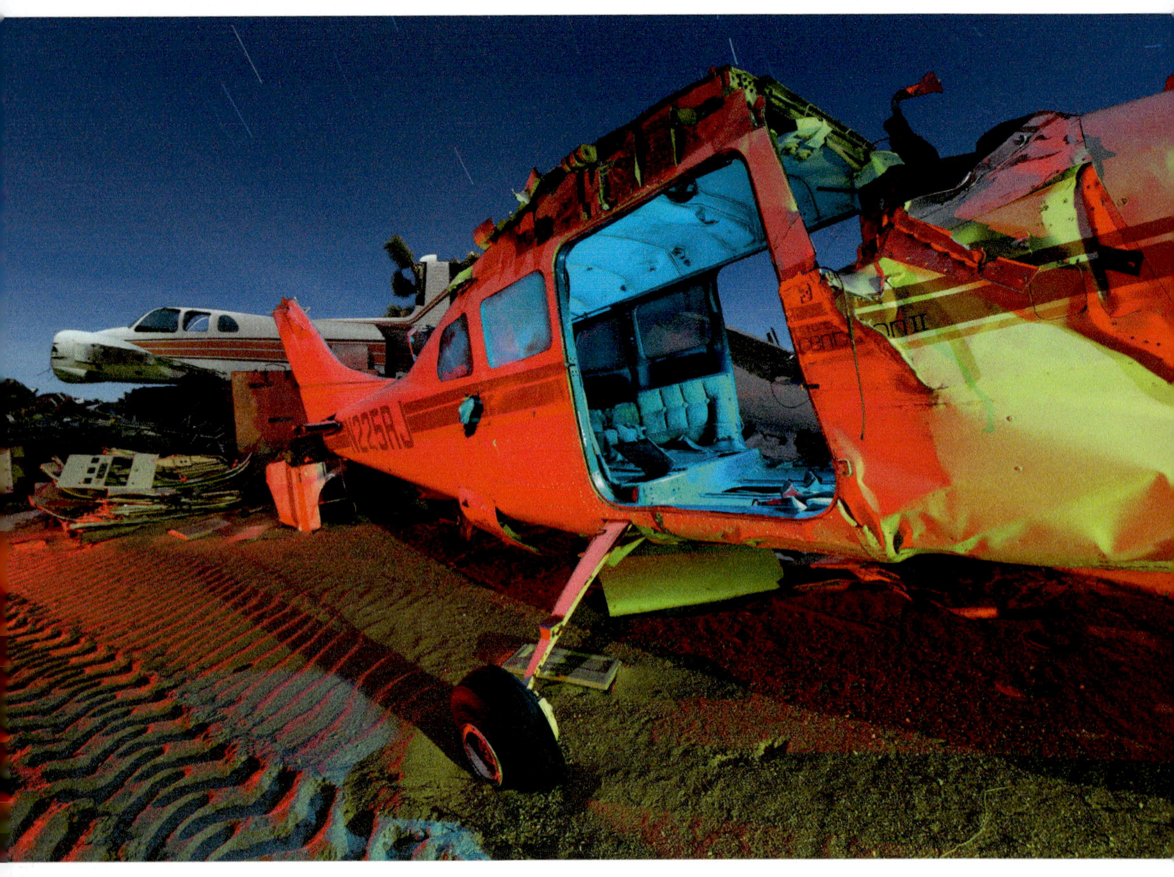

Centurion 2
Aviation Warehouse. 2/2/2015, 9:30 PM.
Canon 5D MkIII, f/8, ISO 200. 16 minutes, 3800K WB.
Full moon / lime, red and blue Protomachines flashlight.
Cessna 210.

Motor Mount ►
Aviation Warehouse. 10/25/2007, 9:35 PM.
Canon 20D, f/5.6, ISO 100. 120 seconds, 3800K WB.
Full moon, mercury vapor streetlights / yellow-gelled LED flashlight.

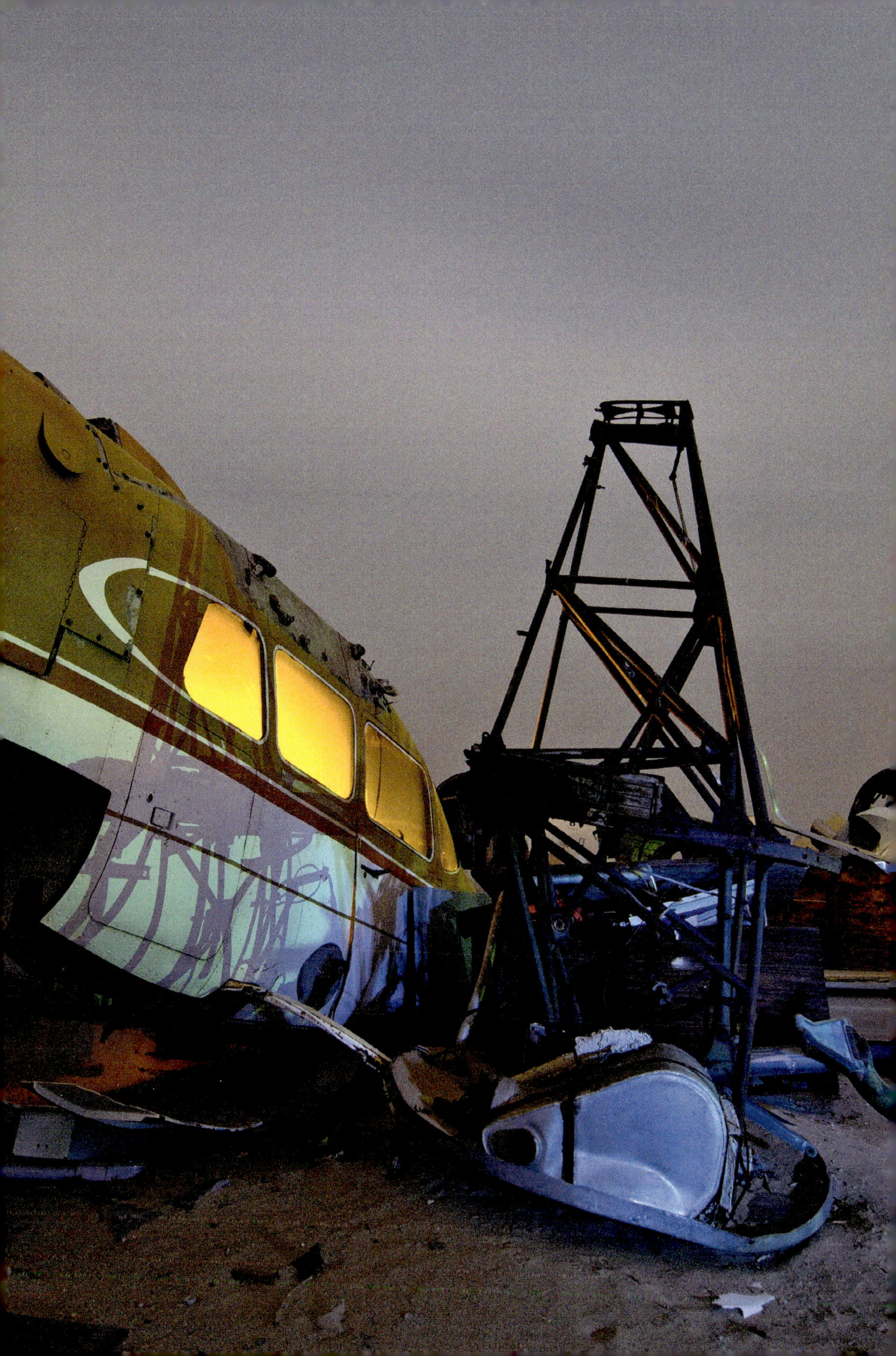

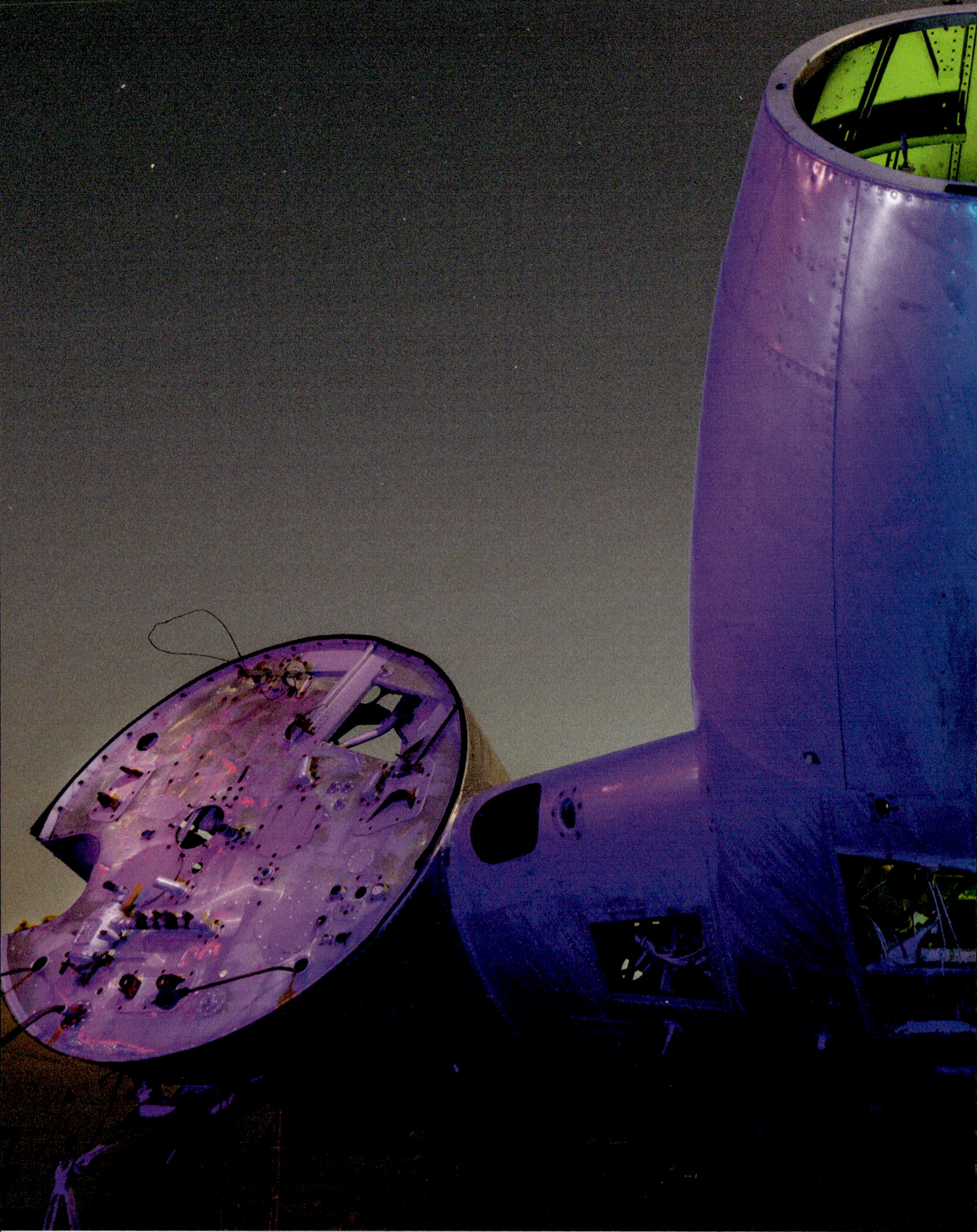

Electra Pink
Aviation Warehouse. 7/27/2018, 12:40 AM.
Canon 6D MkII, f/8, ISO 200. 123 seconds, 6000K WB.

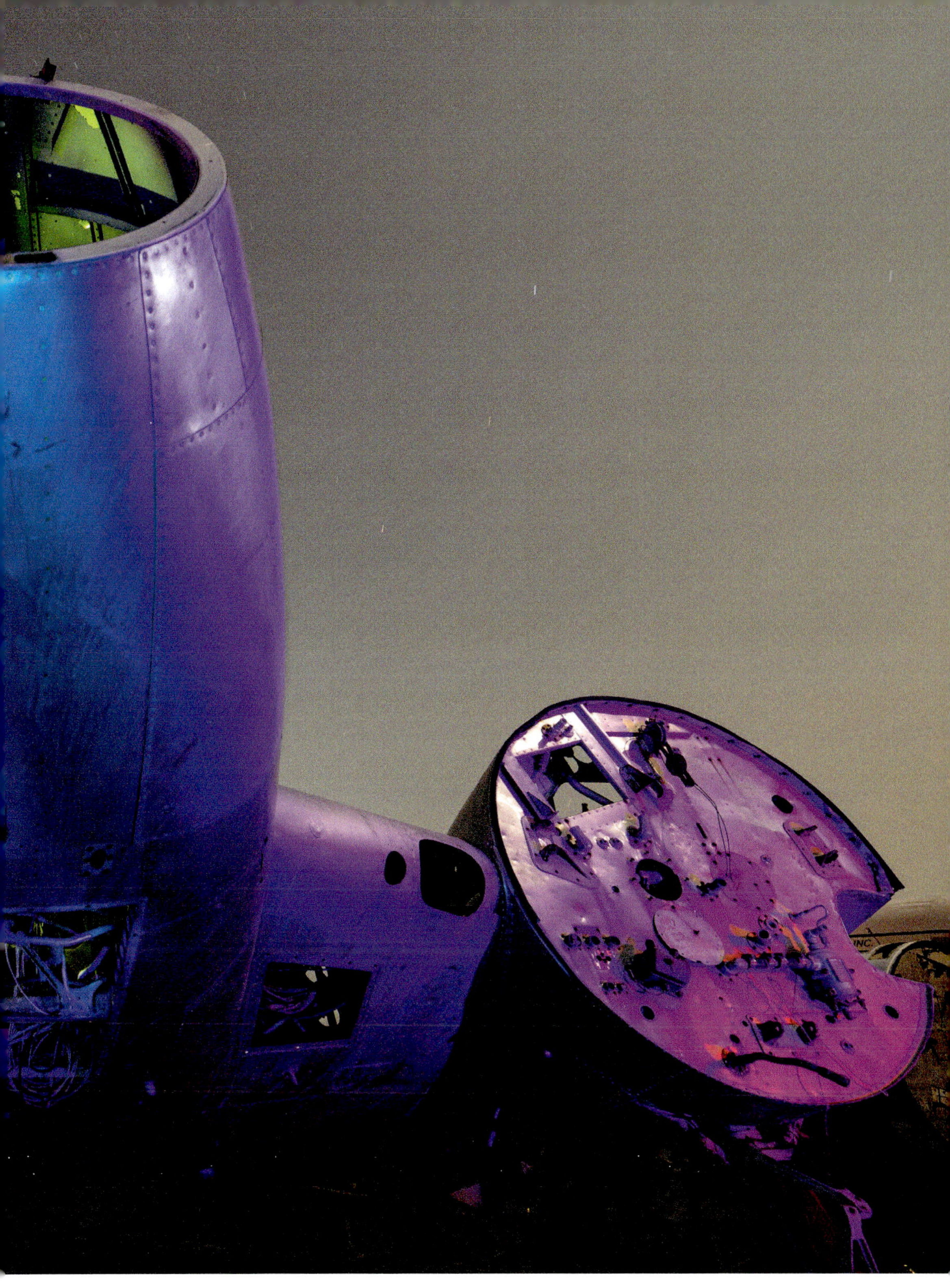

Full moon / blue, purple and green Protomachines flashlight.
Lockheed Model 10 Electra.

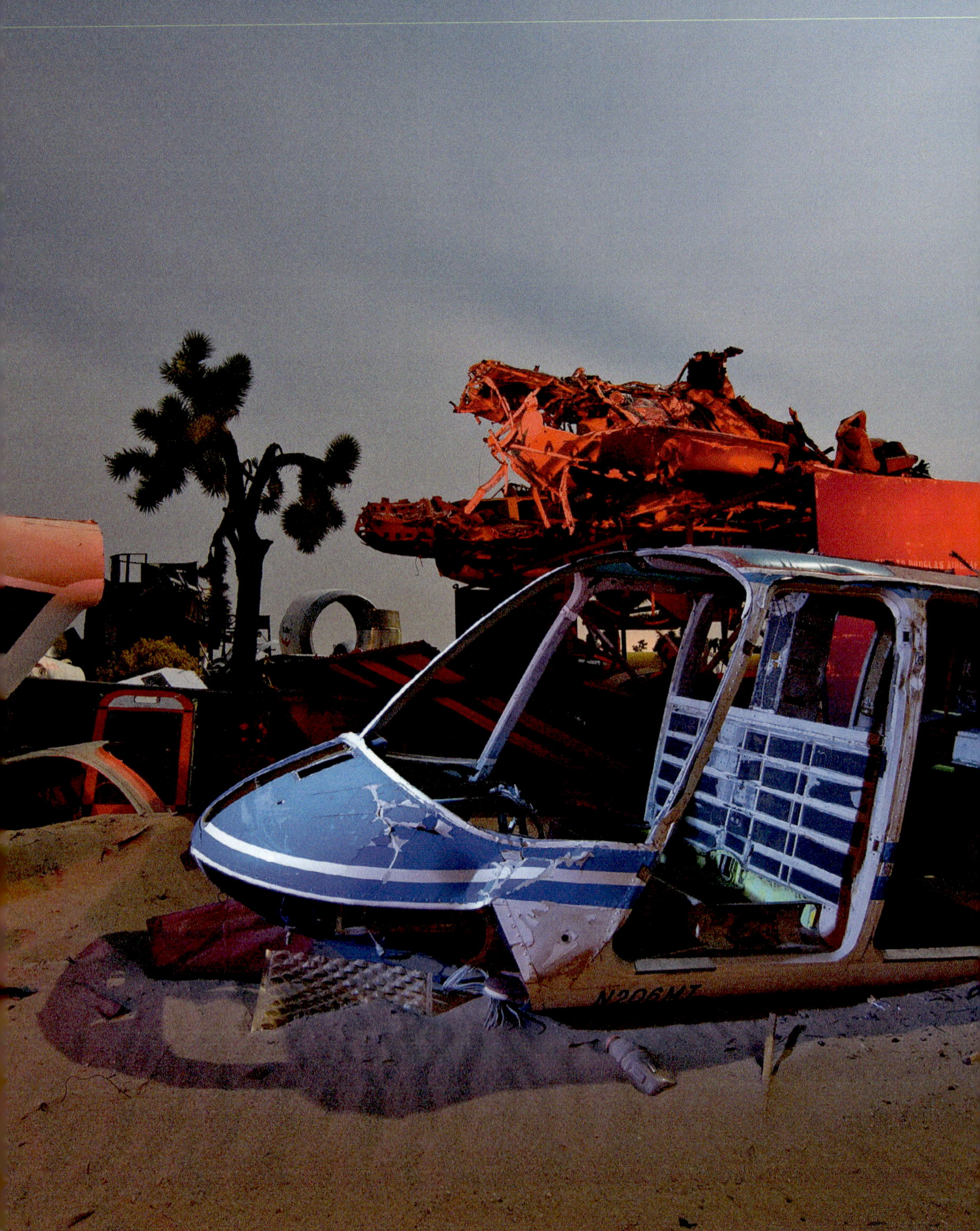

Blue Nose

Aviation Warehouse. 10/25/2007, 10:29 PM.
Canon 20D, f/5.6, ISO 100. 90 seconds, 3850K WB.
Full moon, mercury vapor streetlights / natural white and red LED flashlight.

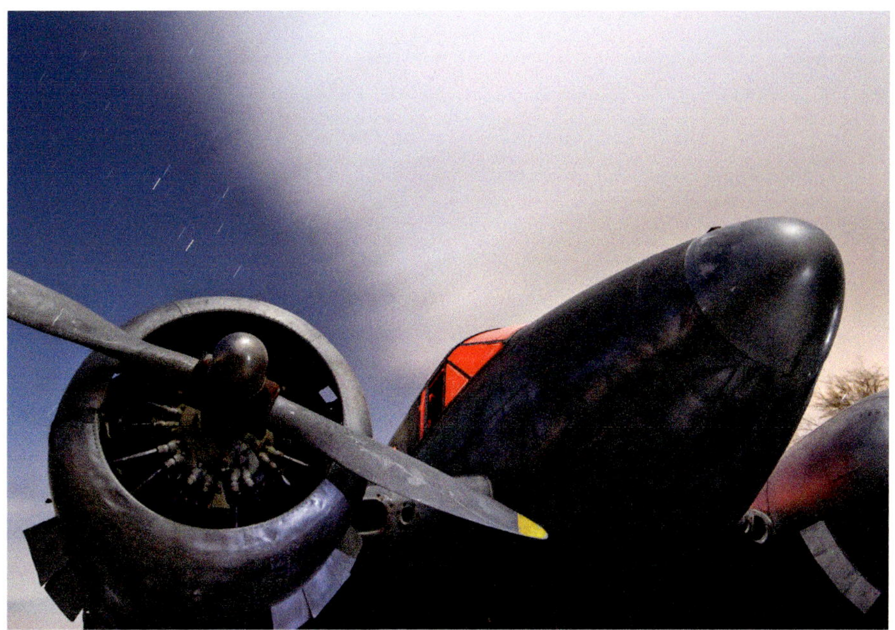

Undertow Beech
Aviation Warehouse. 11/27/2009, 11:25 PM.
Canon 20D, f/5.6, ISO 100, 241 seconds, 3950K WB.
Full moon, partial cloud cover / natural white and red LED flashlight.
Beech 18.

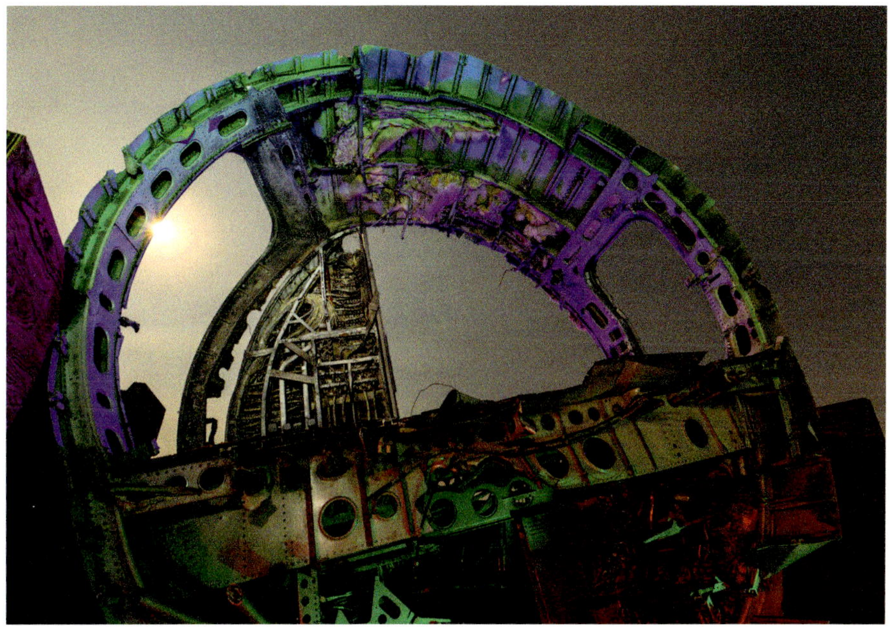

Orbital Decay 18
Aviation Warehouse. 7/25/2018, 10:36 PM.
Canon 6D MkII, f/8, ISO 200. 112 seconds, 6250K WB.
Full moon / white, red, purple and green Protomachines flashlight

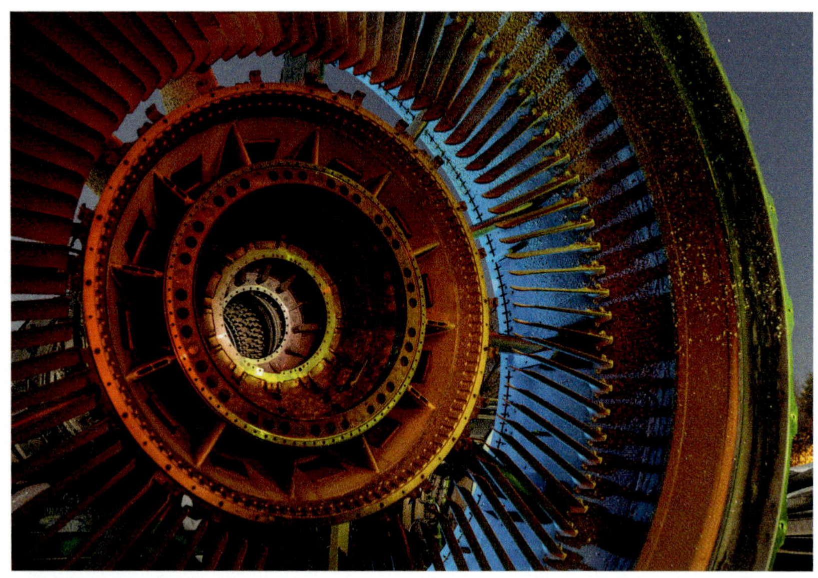

Sarlacc
Aviation Warehouse. 7/27/2018, 1:28 AM.
Canon 6D MkII, f/8, ISO 200. 83 seconds, 4500K WB.
Full moon / white, red, blue and lime Protomachines flashlight.

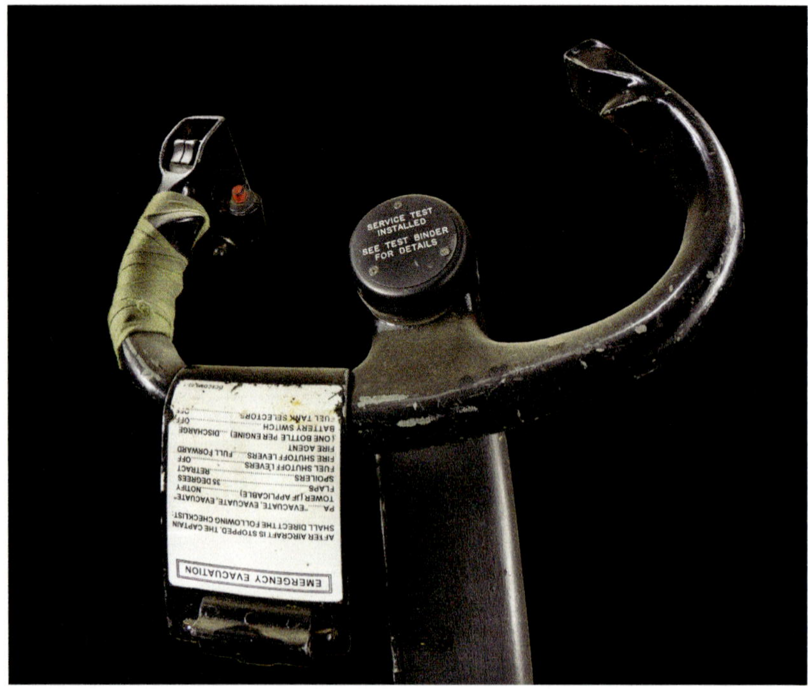

Emergency Evacuation
Aviation Warehouse. 12/7/2014, 9:08 PM.
Canon 60D, f/8, ISO 200. 21 seconds, 5400K WB.
Total darkness / white Protomachines flashlight.

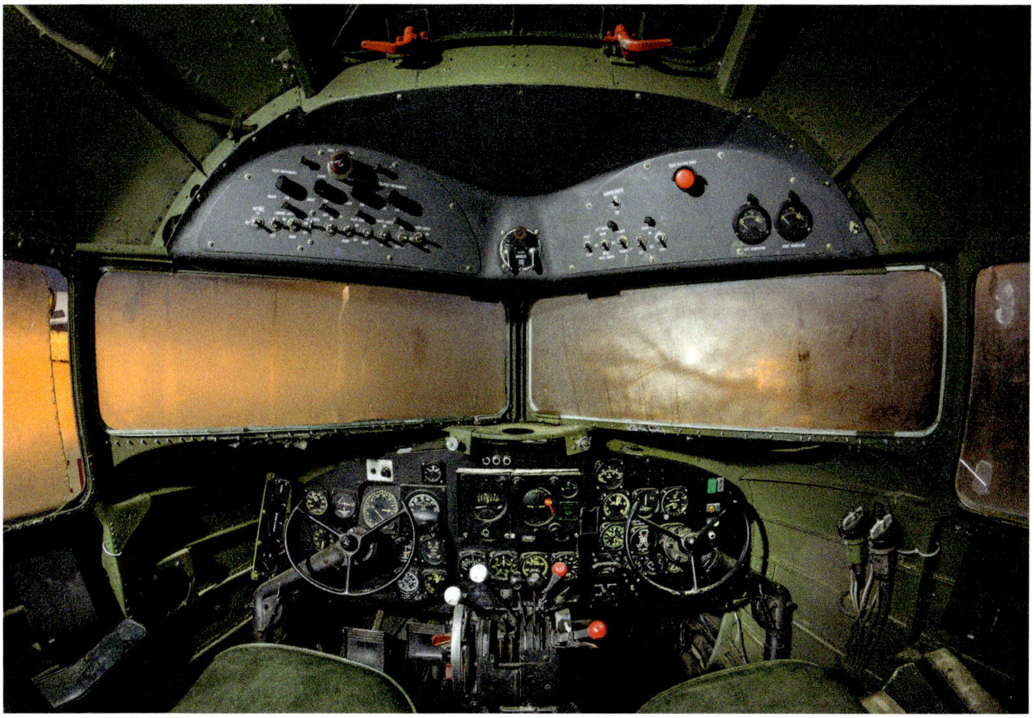

Flight to Jupiter
Aviation Warehouse. 12/6/2014, 10:06 PM.
Canon 60D, f/8, ISO 200. 121 seconds, 3600K WB.
Full moon / red and white Protomachines flashlight.
Douglas DC-3.

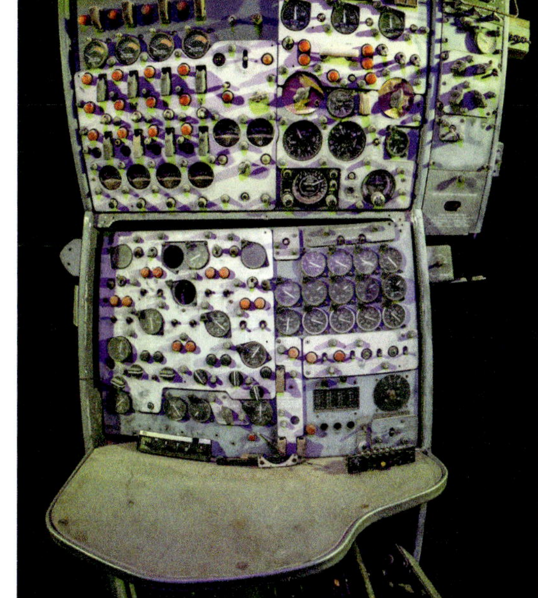

Instrumental flight
Aviation Warehouse. 12/7/2014, 6:35 PM.
Canon 60D, f/8, ISO 200. 36 seconds, 3900K WB.
Total darkness / purple, green and white Protomachines flashlight.
Boeing 707.

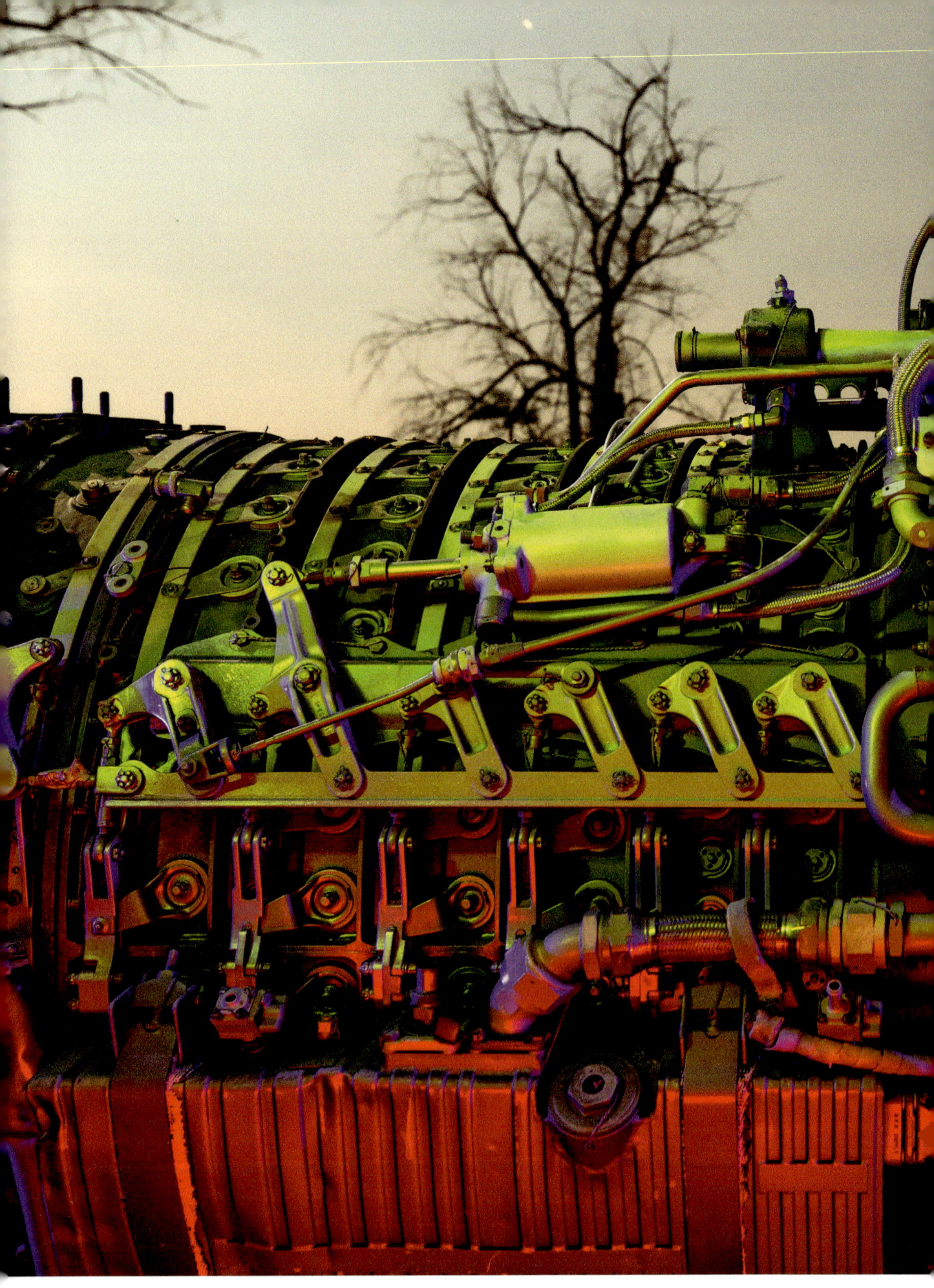

Compressor Stall
Aviation Warehouse. 7/27/2018, 1:46 AM.

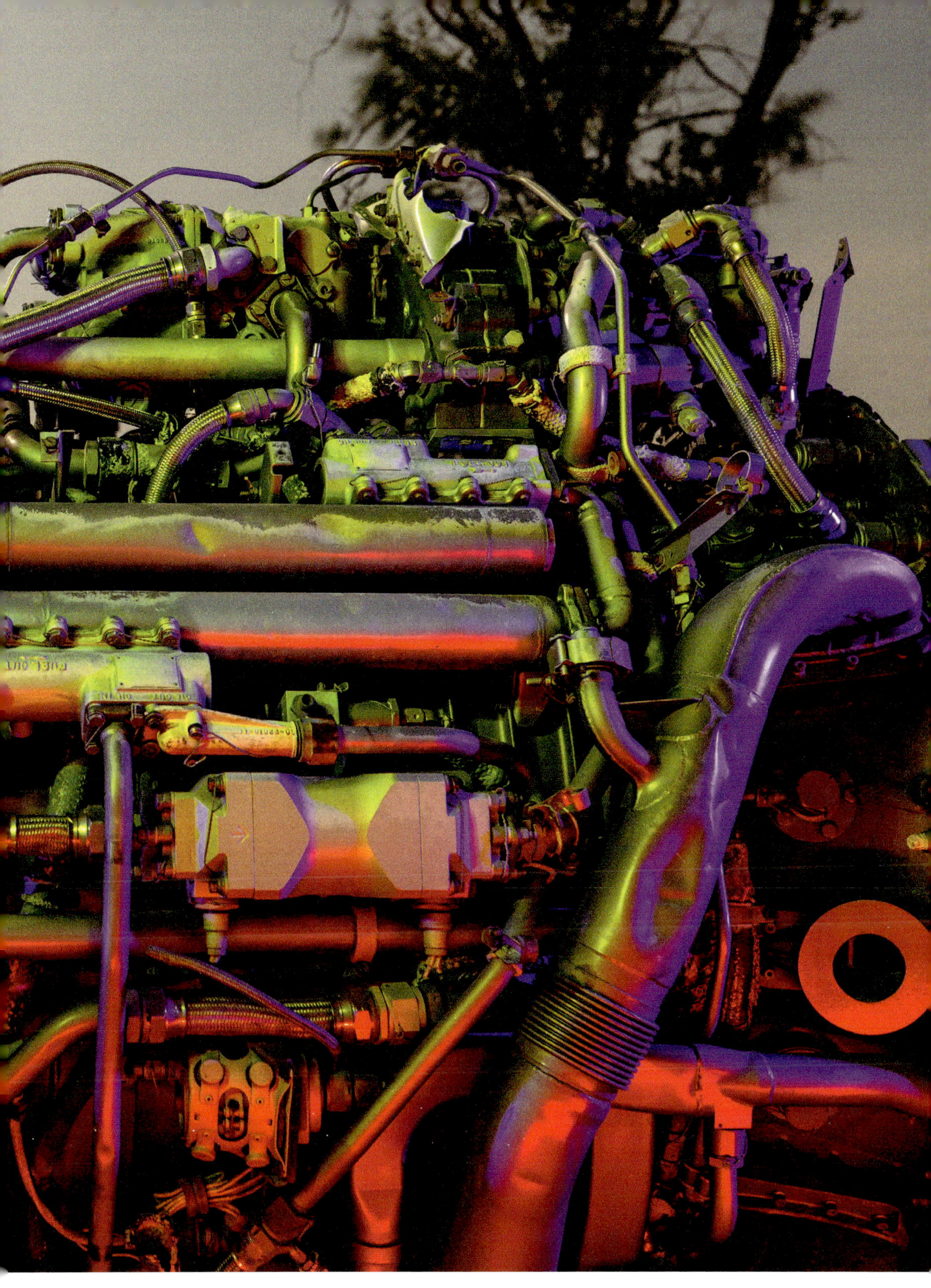

Canon 6D MkII, f/8, ISO 200. 50 seconds, 5500K WB.
Full moon / purple, lime and red Protomachines flashlight.

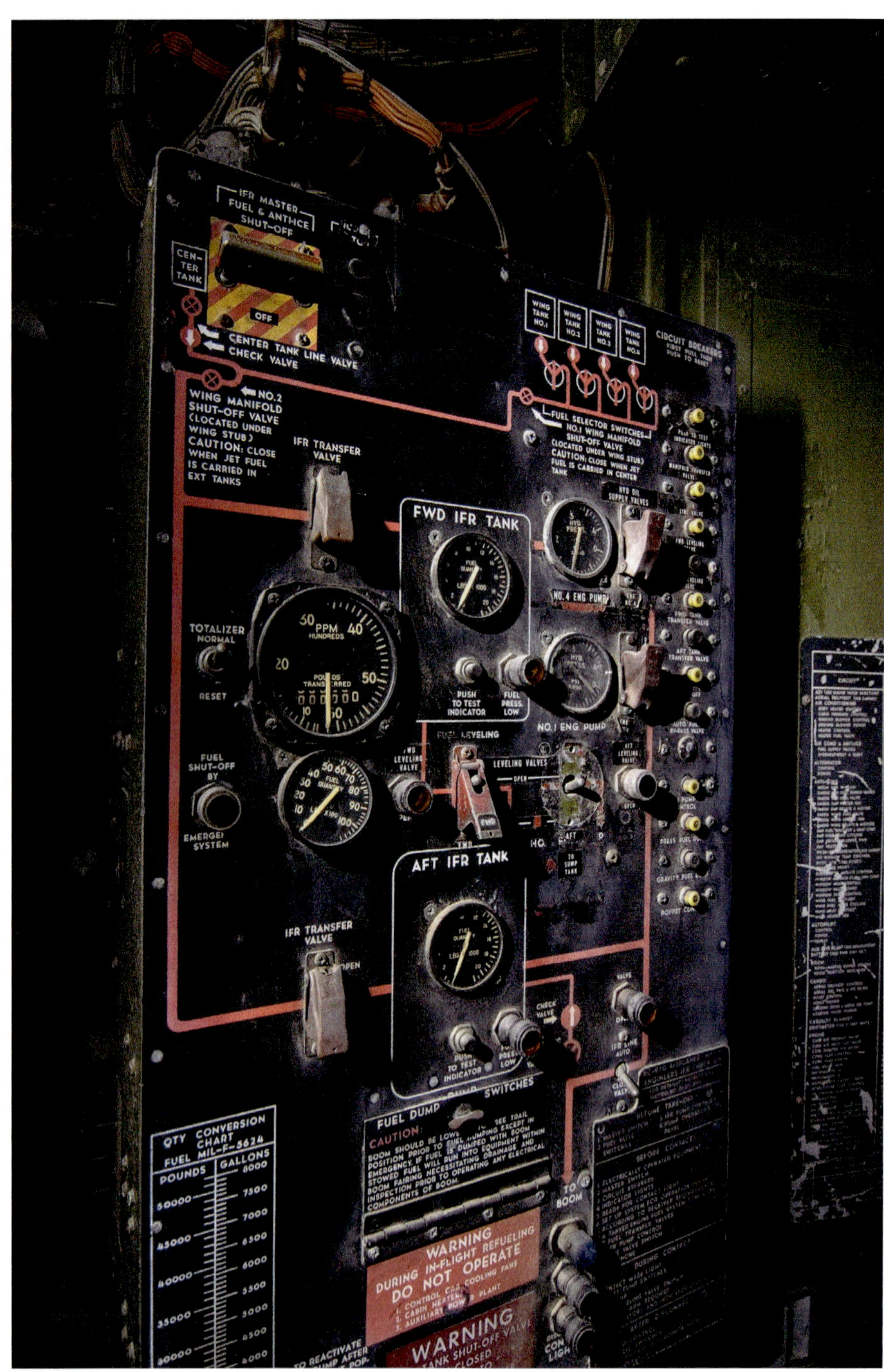

Gas Station

Aviation Warehouse. 10/25/2007, 7:48 PM.

Canon 20D, f/5.6, ISO 100. 11 seconds, 7500K WB.

Total darkness/ natural white LED flashlight.

Boeing KC-97 Stratotanker

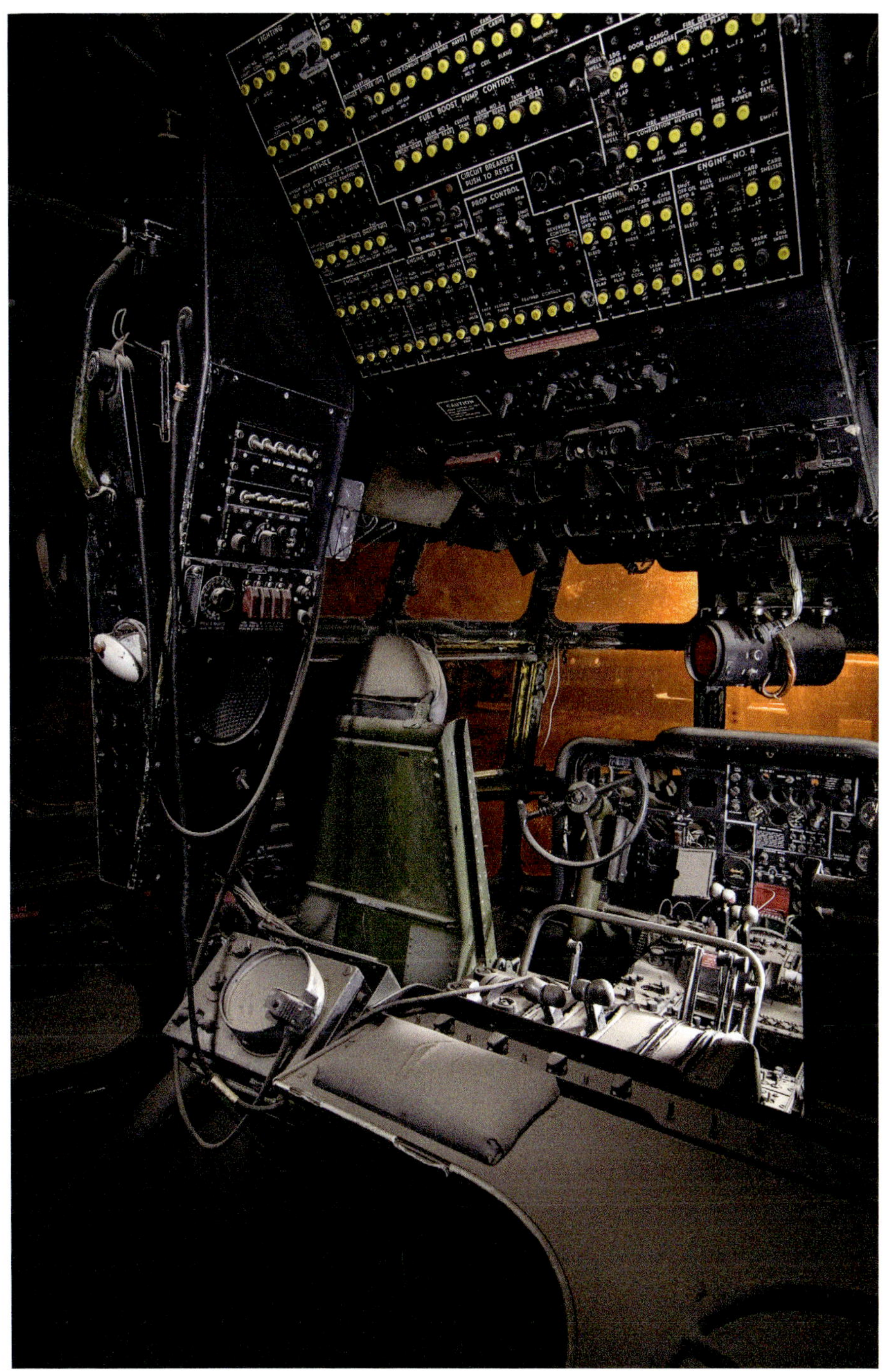

Cockpit Ashtray

Aviation Warehouse. 10/25/2007, 8:06 PM.

Canon 20D, f/5.6, ISO 100. 58 seconds, 7500K WB.

Full moon, sodium vapor streetlights / natural white LED flashlight.

Boeing KC-97 Stratotanker

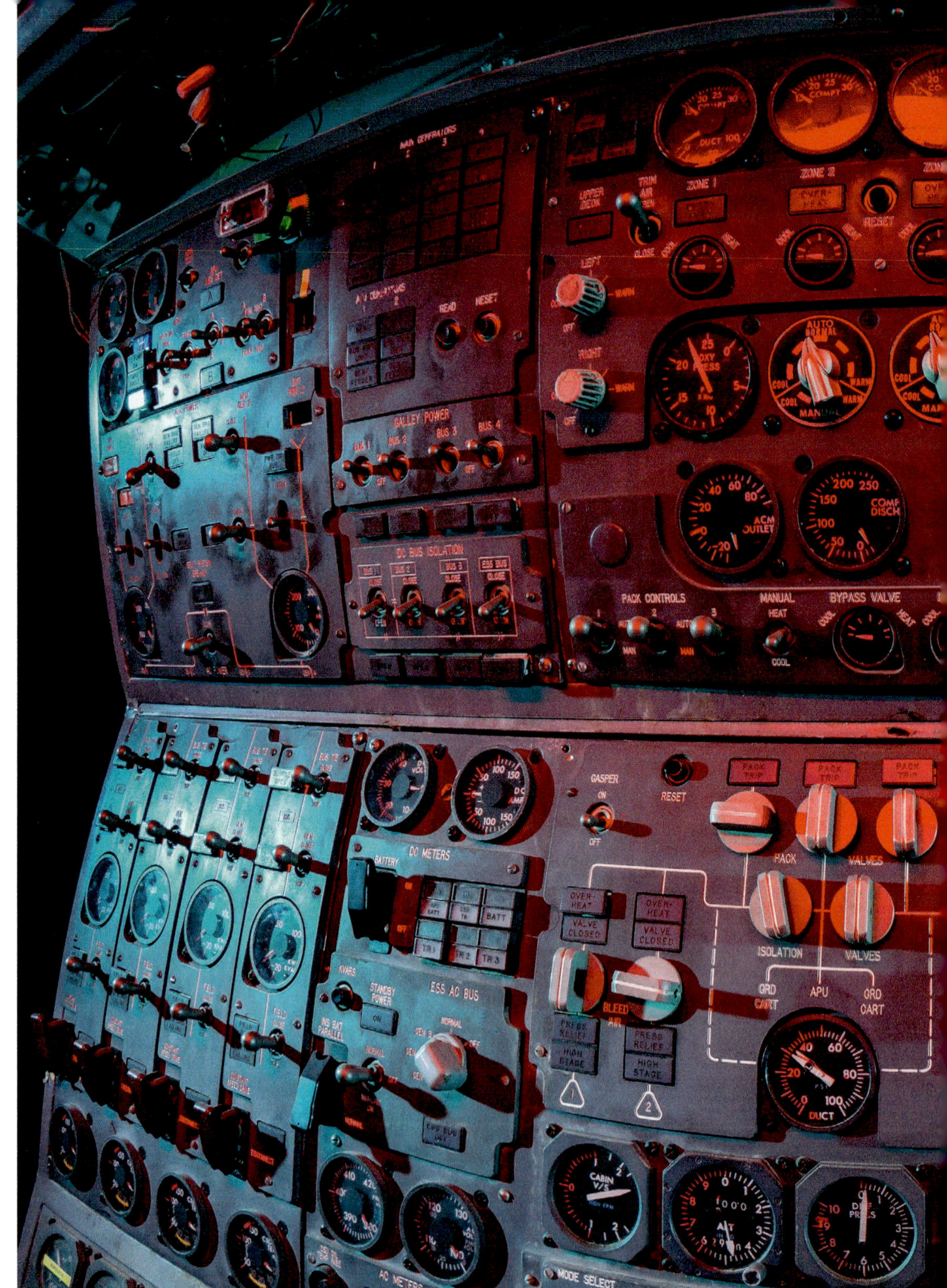

Four Engined Nightmare
Aviation Warehouse. 12/7/2014, 6:59 PM.
Canon 60D, f/8, ISO 200. 32 seconds, 5000K WB.

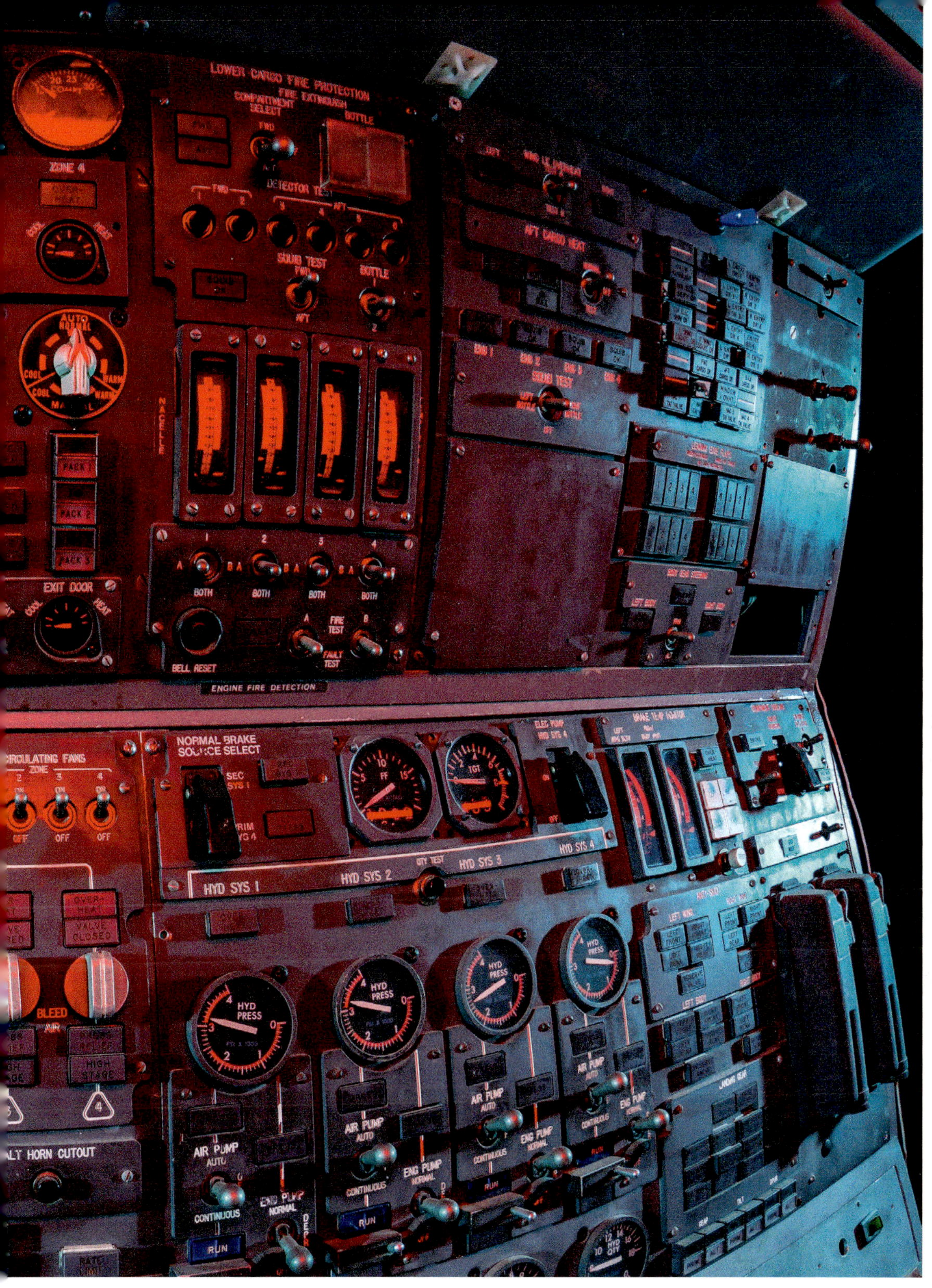

Total darkness / red and blue Protomachines flashlight.
Boeing 747.

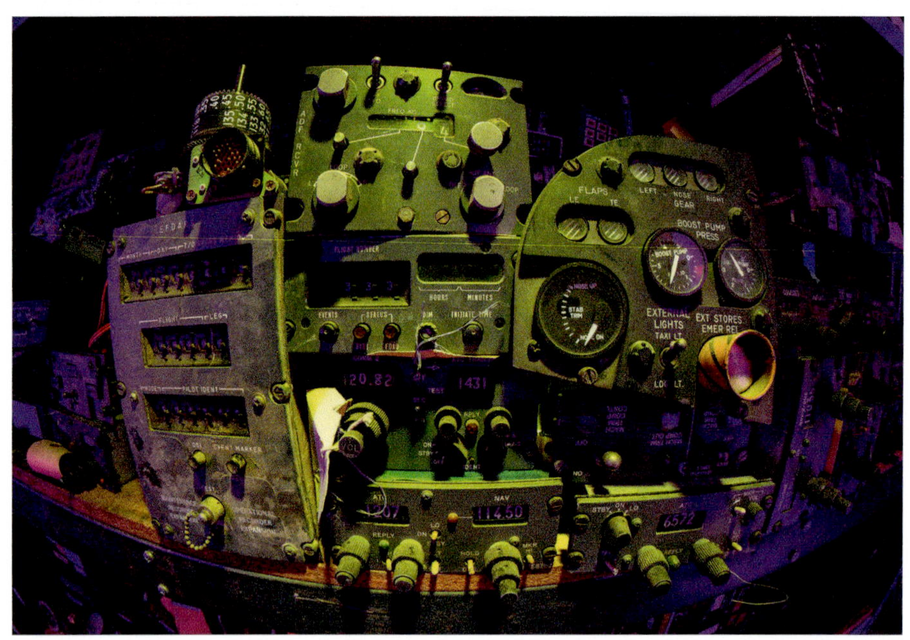

CRM114

Aviation Warehouse. 12/7/2014, 8:43 PM.
Canon 60D, f/8, ISO 200. 38 seconds, 4400K WB.
Total darkness / purple and green Protomachines flashlight.

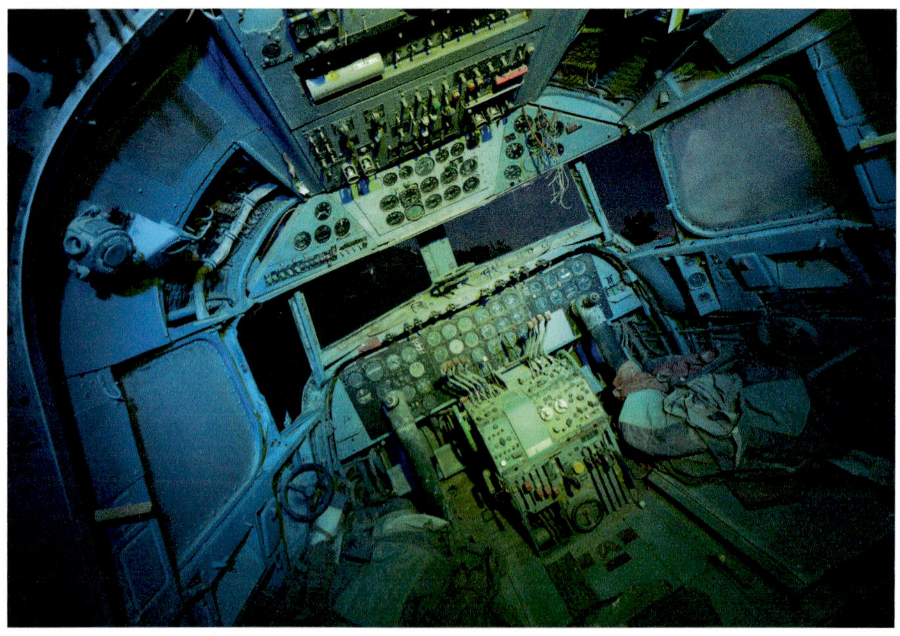

Buck Rogers

Aviation Warehouse. 2/3/2015, 7:10 PM.
Canon 5D MkIII, f/8, ISO 200. 42 seconds, 3800K WB.
Full moon / lime and blue Protomachines flashlight.
Douglas DC-7.

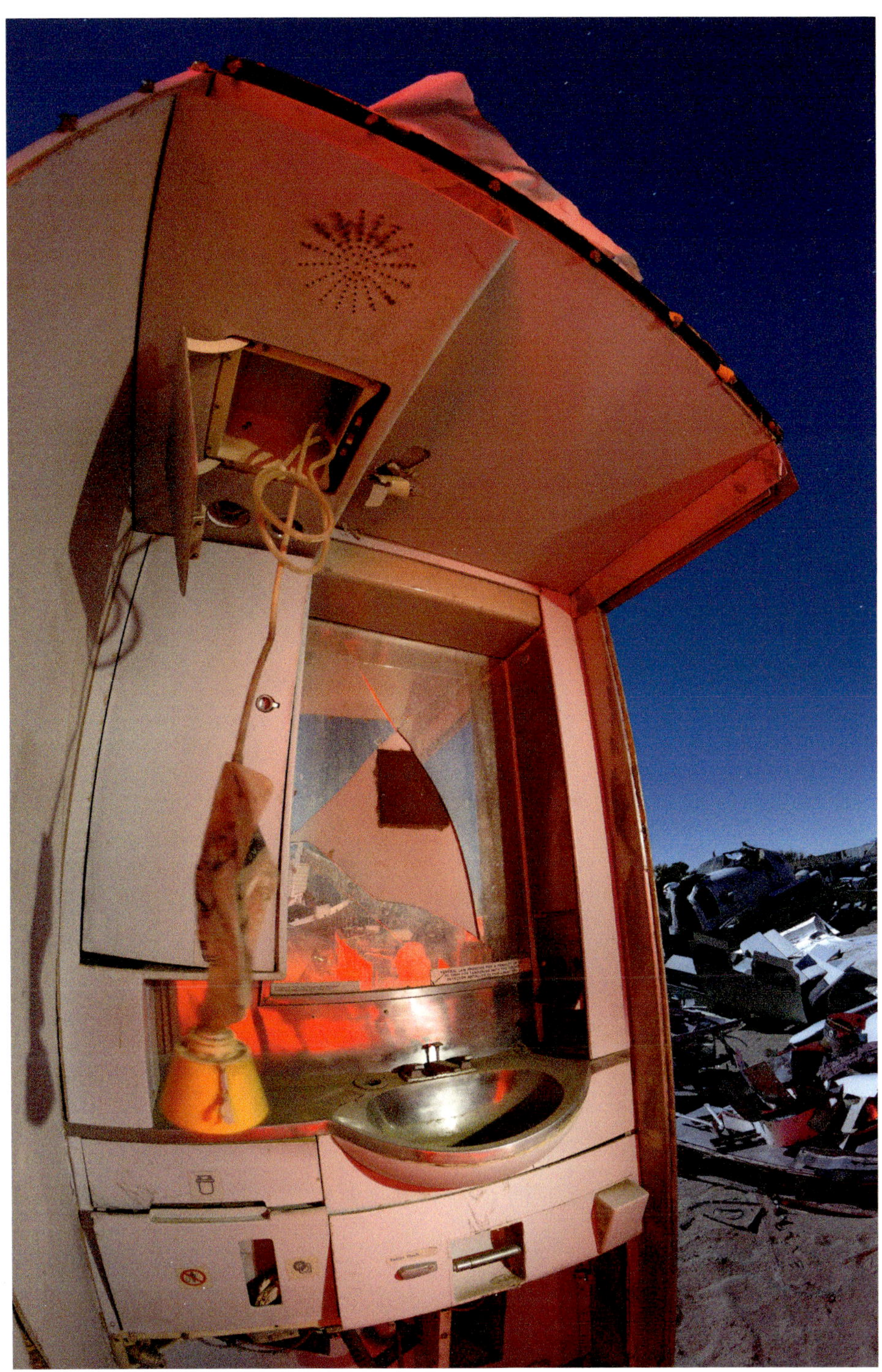

Blue Ice

Aviation Warehouse. 11/6/2014, 8:40 PM.
Canon 60D, f/8, ISO 200. 68 seconds, 3300K WB.
Full moon / red and white Protomachines flashlight.

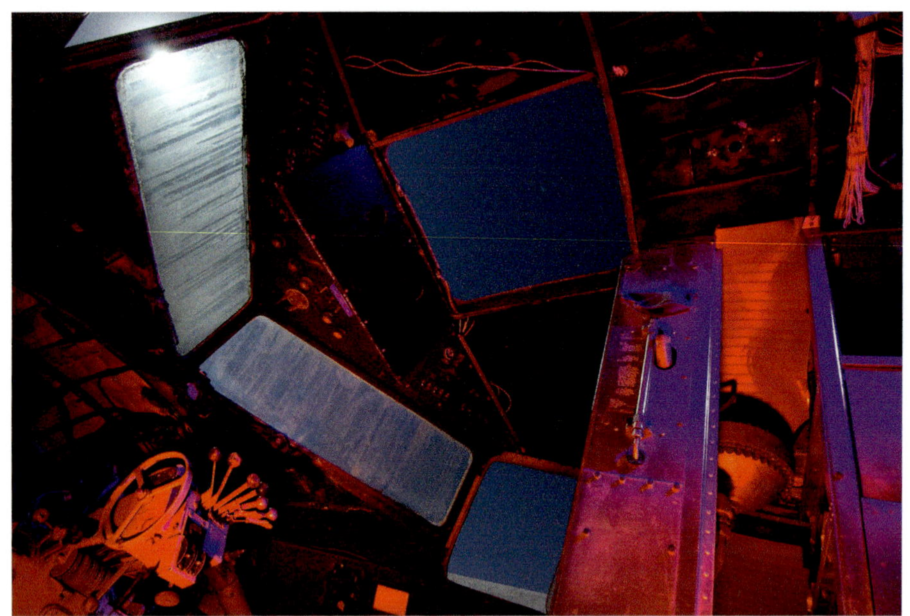

Throttle Up
Aviation Warehouse. 8/2/2012, 1:32 AM.
Canon 60D, f/8, ISO 200. 25 and 158 seconds, 3950K WB.
Full moon / purple and red Protomachines flashlight.
Douglas DC-7.

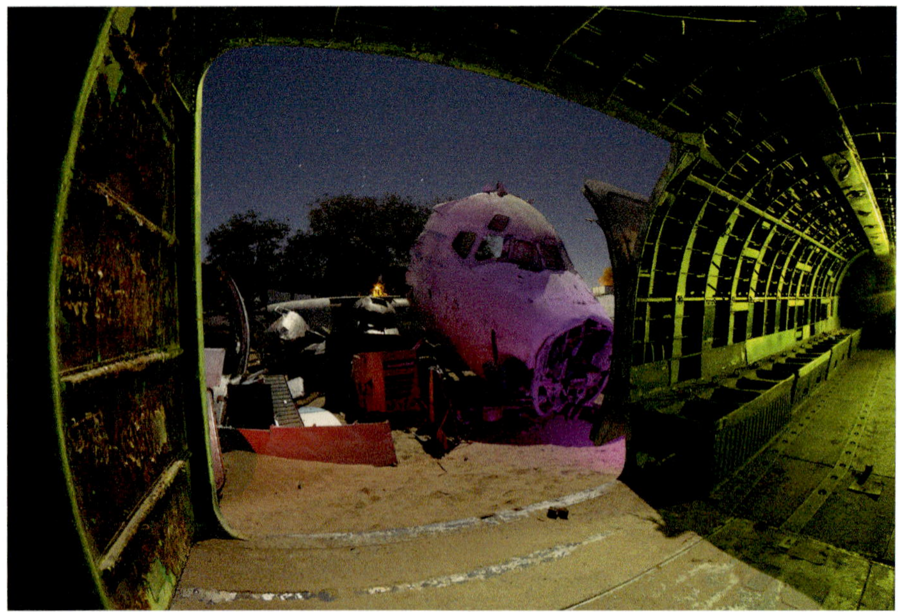

Green Light Means Jump
Aviation Warehouse. 11/6/2014, 10:20 PM.
Canon 60D, f/8, ISO 200. 130 seconds, 5000K WB.
Full moon / green and purple Protomachines flashlight.
Douglas C-74.

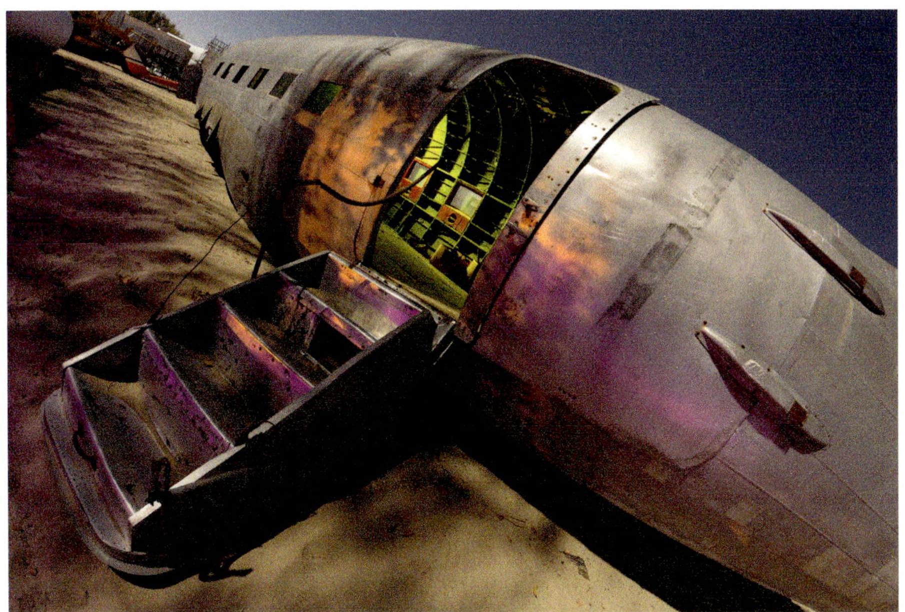

Sherbet Boarding
Aviation Warehouse. 11/6/2014, 9:58 PM.
Canon 60D, f/8, ISO 200. 339 seconds, 5300K WB.
Full moon, sodium vapor streetlights / purple Protomachines flashlight.
Douglas C-74.

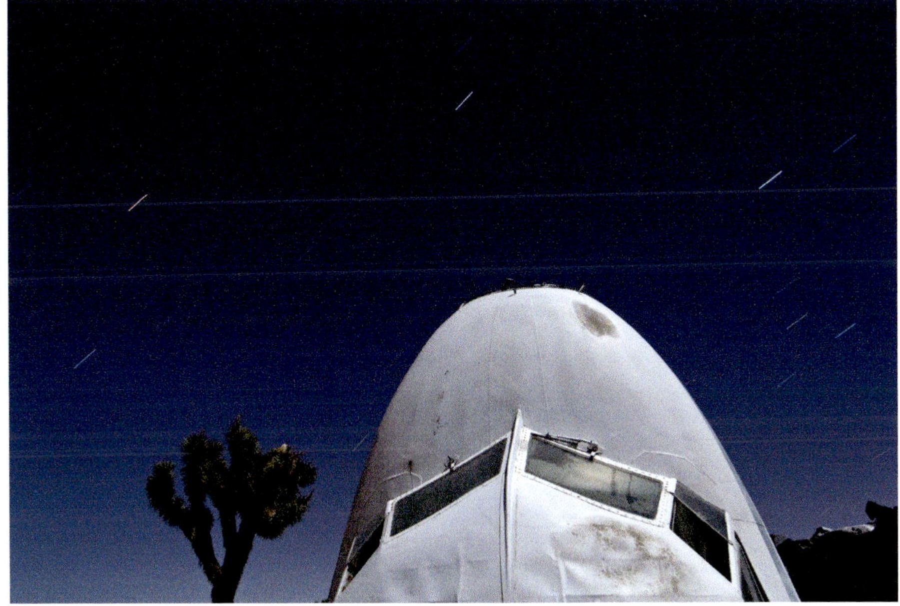

Seven Stone
Aviation Warehouse. 11/30/2009, 1:47 AM.
Canon 20D, f/5.6, ISO 100, 120 seconds, 3900K WB.
Full moon / lime-gelled LED flashlight.
Douglas DC-7.

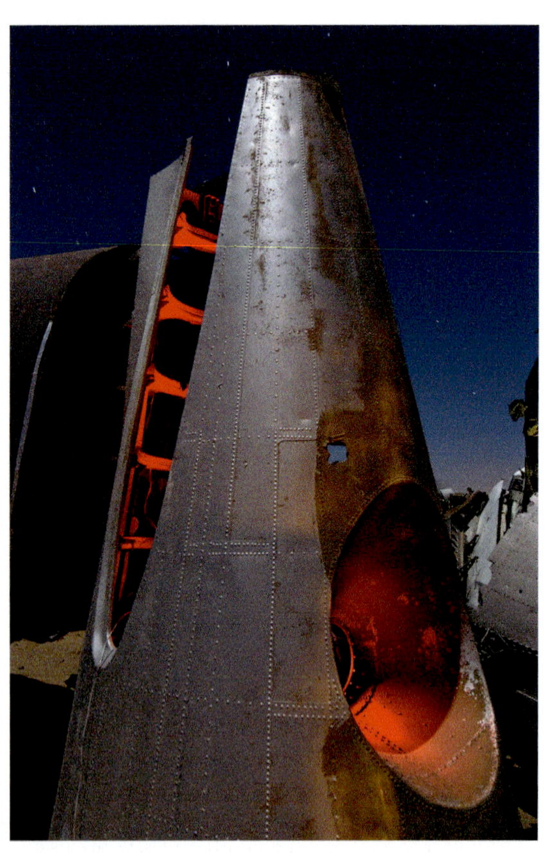

Lobo Blowhole
Aviation Warehouse. 11/28/2009, 11:18 PM.
Canon 20D, f/5.6, ISO 100, 120 seconds,
3900K WB.
Full moon / red LED flashlight.

The Edge of the Mirage
Aviation Warehouse. 7/25/2018, 7:47 PM.
Canon 6D MkII, f/8, ISO 200. 64 seconds,
6000K WB.
Full moon / white, red, purple and lime
Protomachines flashlight.
Douglas DC-3.

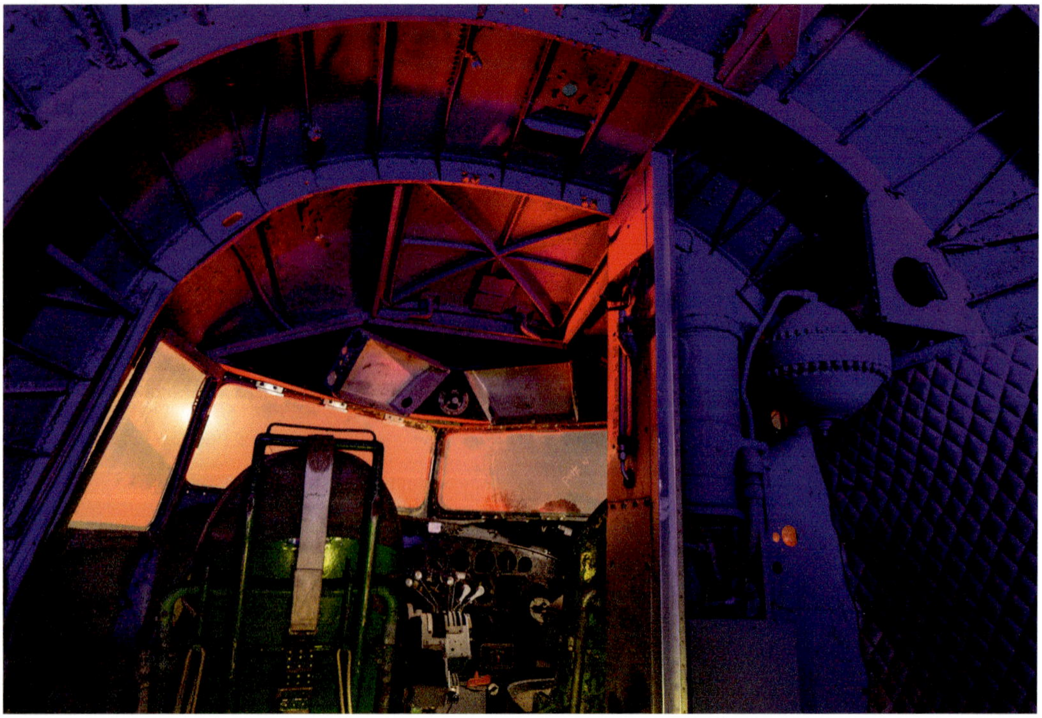

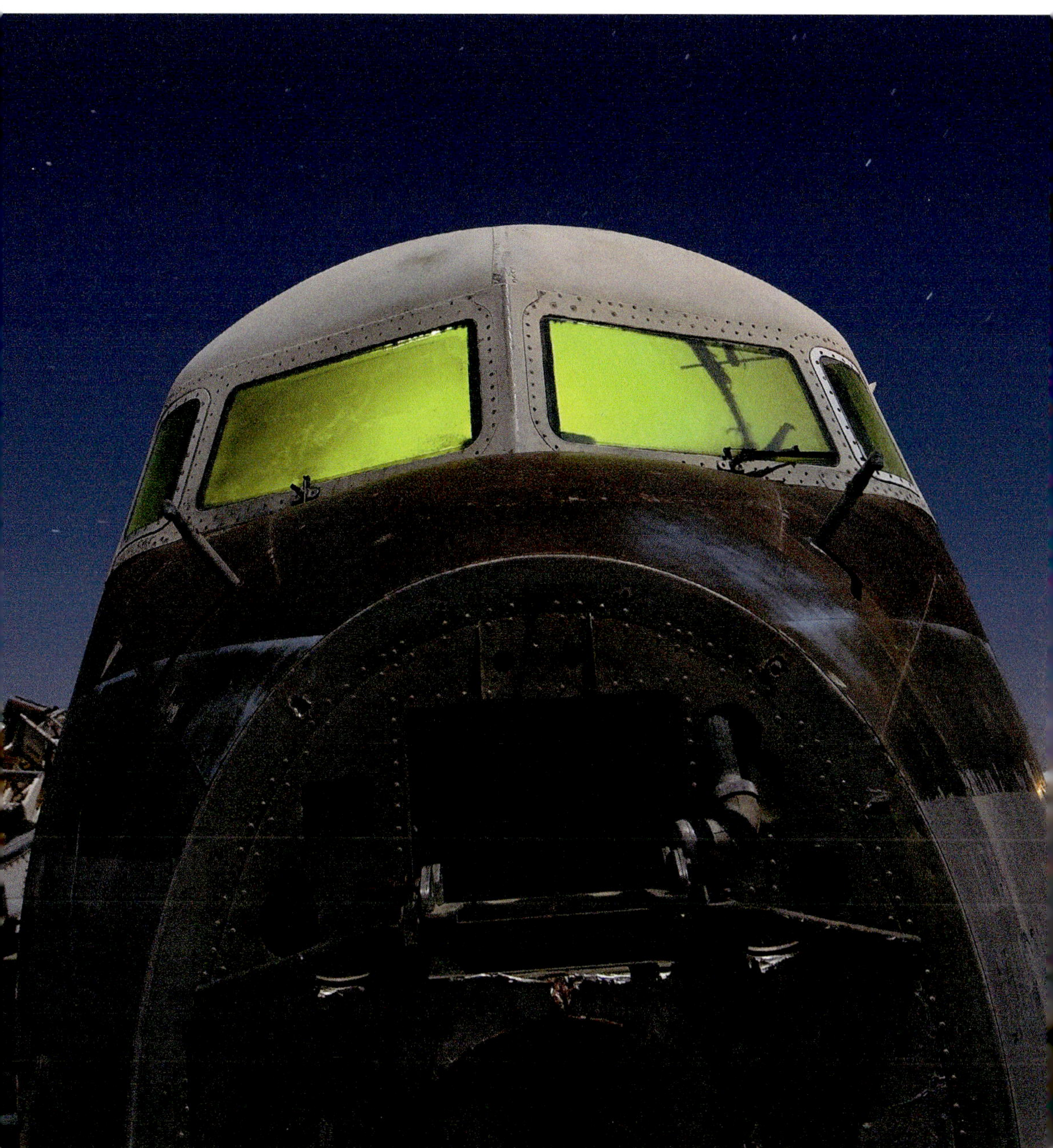

Patinateer
Aviation Warehouse. 11/28/2009, 10:35 PM.
Canon 20D, f/5.6, ISO 100, 120 seconds, 3900K WB.
Full moon / lime-gelled LED flashlight.
Douglas DC-7.

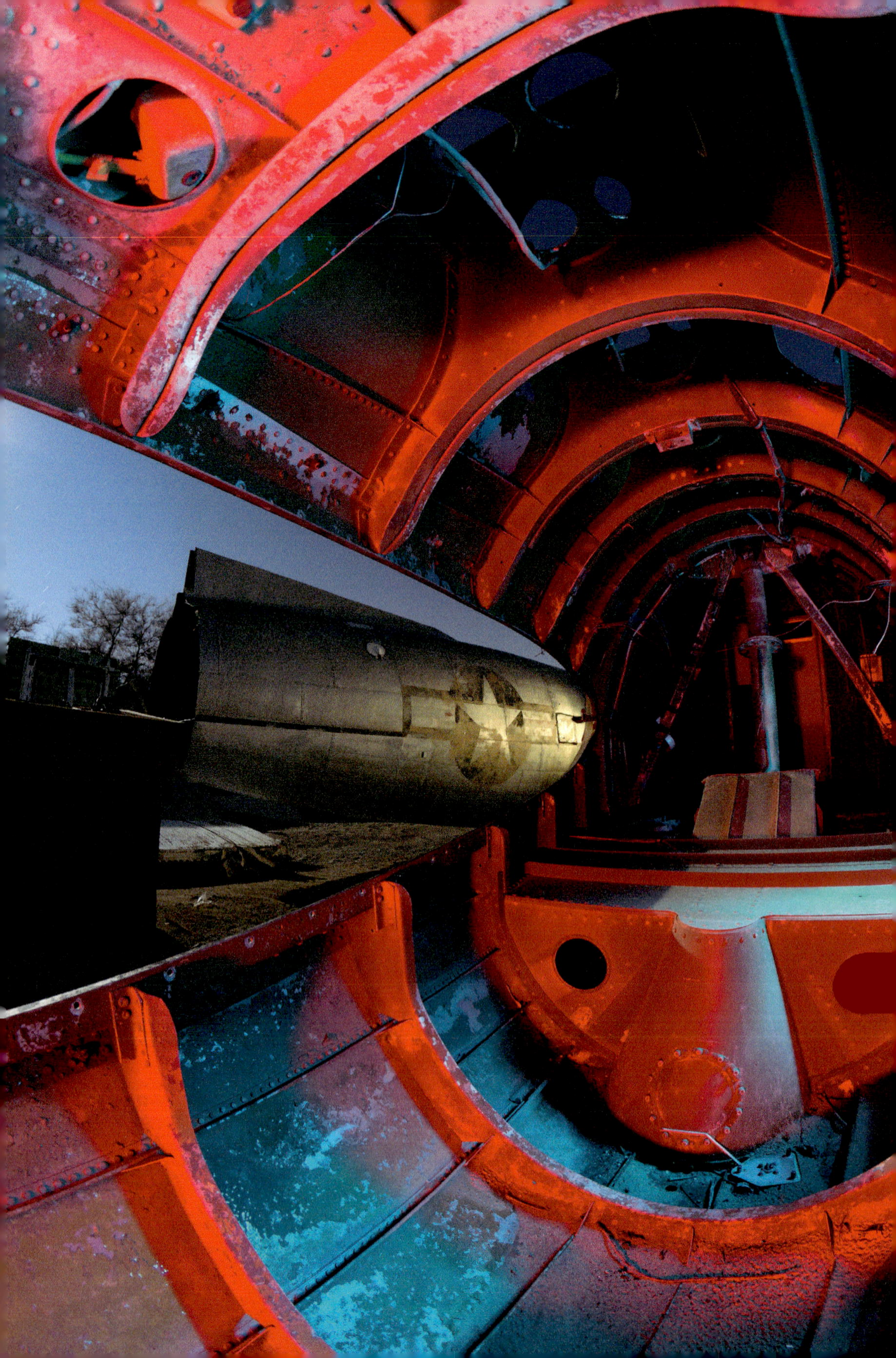

◄ **Starslot**
Aviation Warehouse.
12/6/2014, 7:49 PM.
Canon 60D, f/8, ISO 200.
237 seconds, 3900K WB.
Full moon / red, white and blue Protomachines flashlight.
Douglas DC-7.

Black Windows ►
Aviation Warehouse.
12/7/2014, 12:05 AM.
Canon 60D, f/8, ISO 200.
56 seconds, 5050K WB.
Full moon / purple and red Protomachines flashlight.
Boeing 737.

Boneyard Luchador ▼
Aviation Warehouse.
7/26/2018, 9:08 PM.
Canon 6D MkII, f/8, ISO 200.
177 seconds, 5000K WB.
Full moon / purple, lime and red Protomachines flashlight.

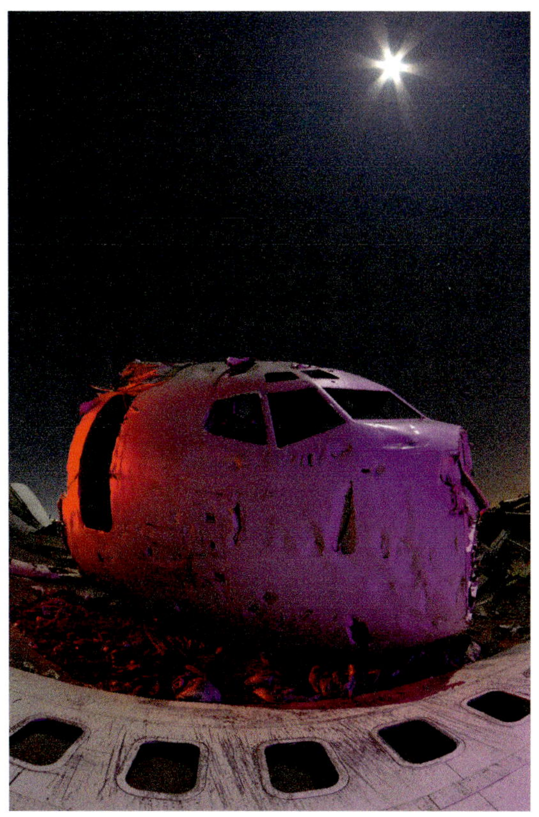

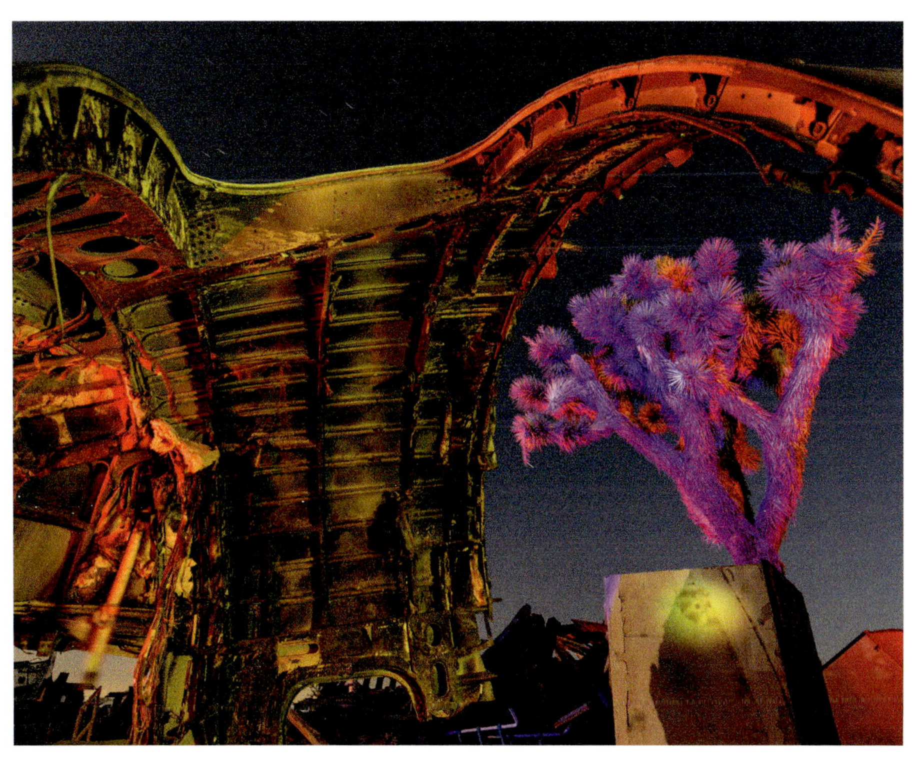

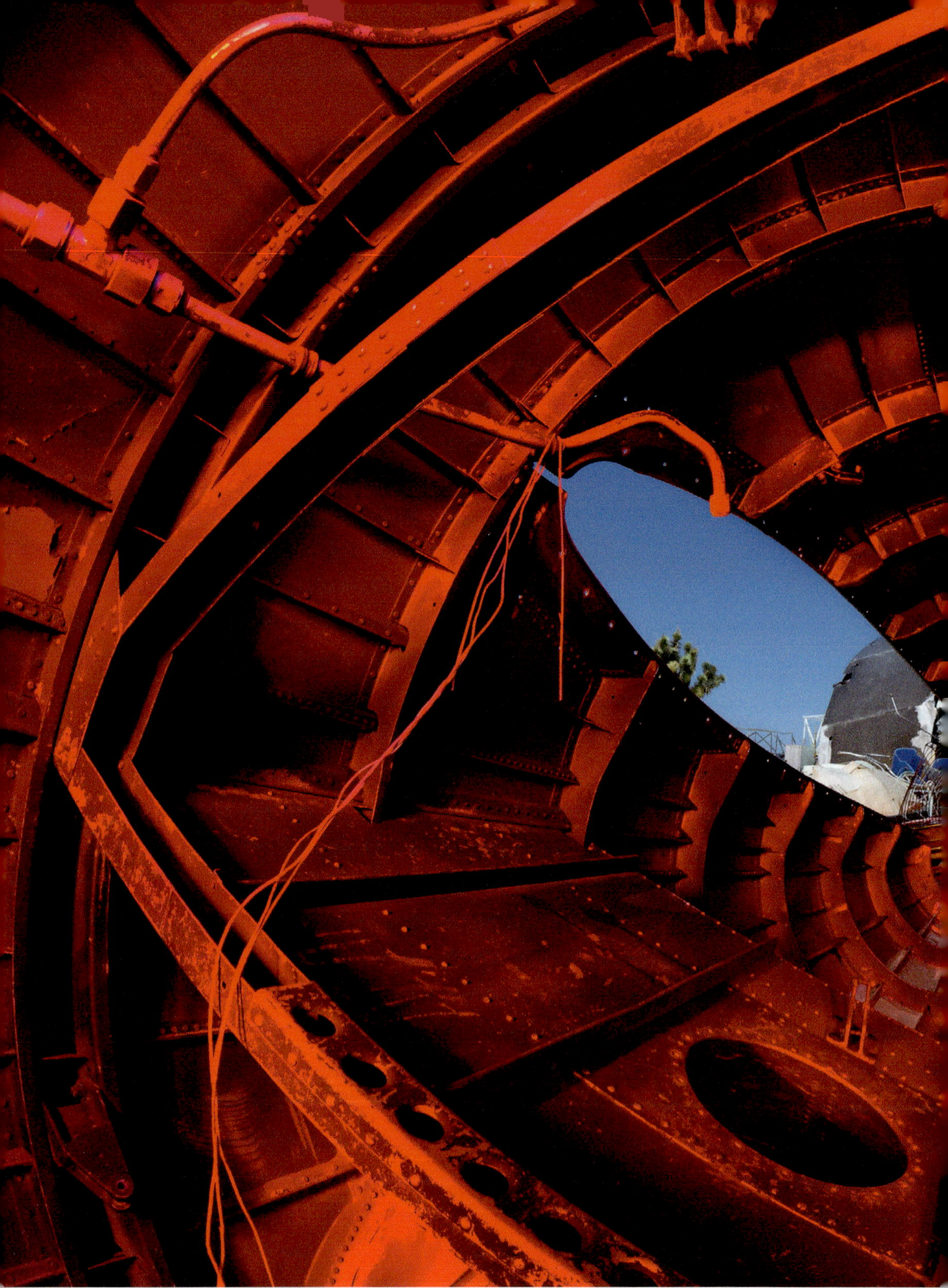

Inside the Cat's Head
Aviation Warehouse. 12/7/2014, 7:54 PM.

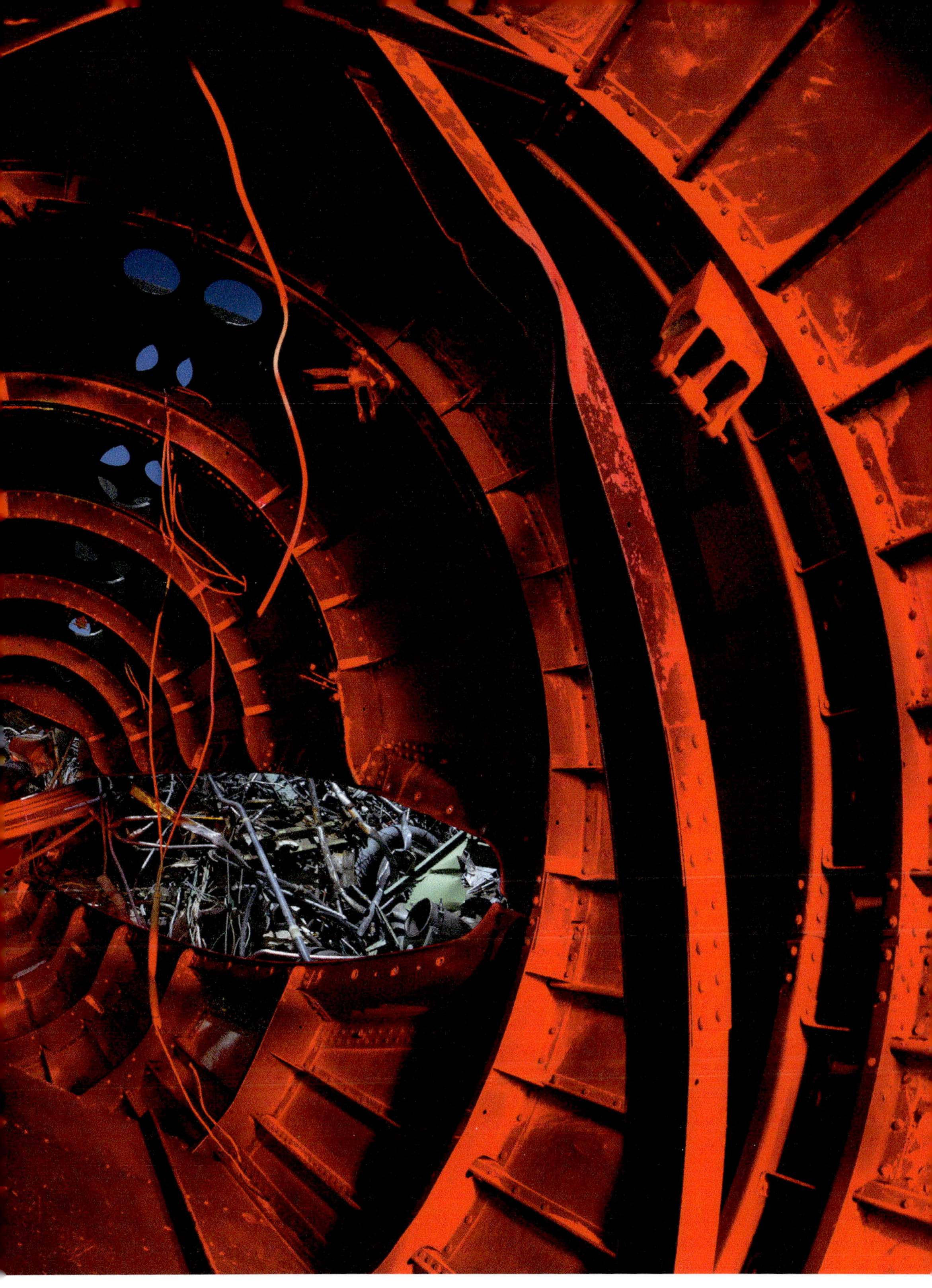

Canon 60D, f/8, ISO 200. 316 seconds, 3400K WB.
Full moon / red Protomachines flashlight.

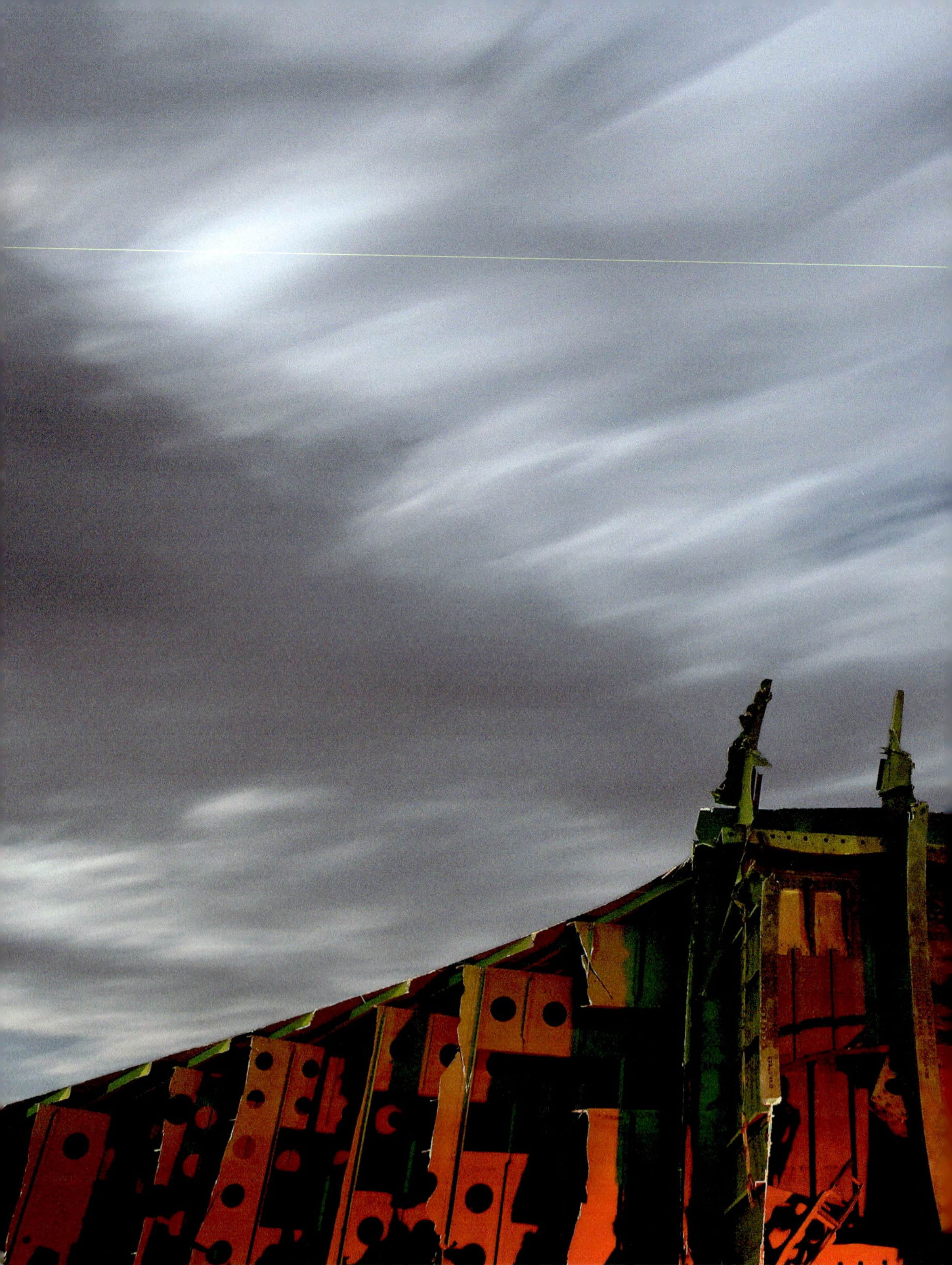

Wing Root Tor
Aviation Warehouse. 8/1/2012, 1:21 AM.
Canon 60D, f/8, ISO 200. 121 seconds, 3800K WB.

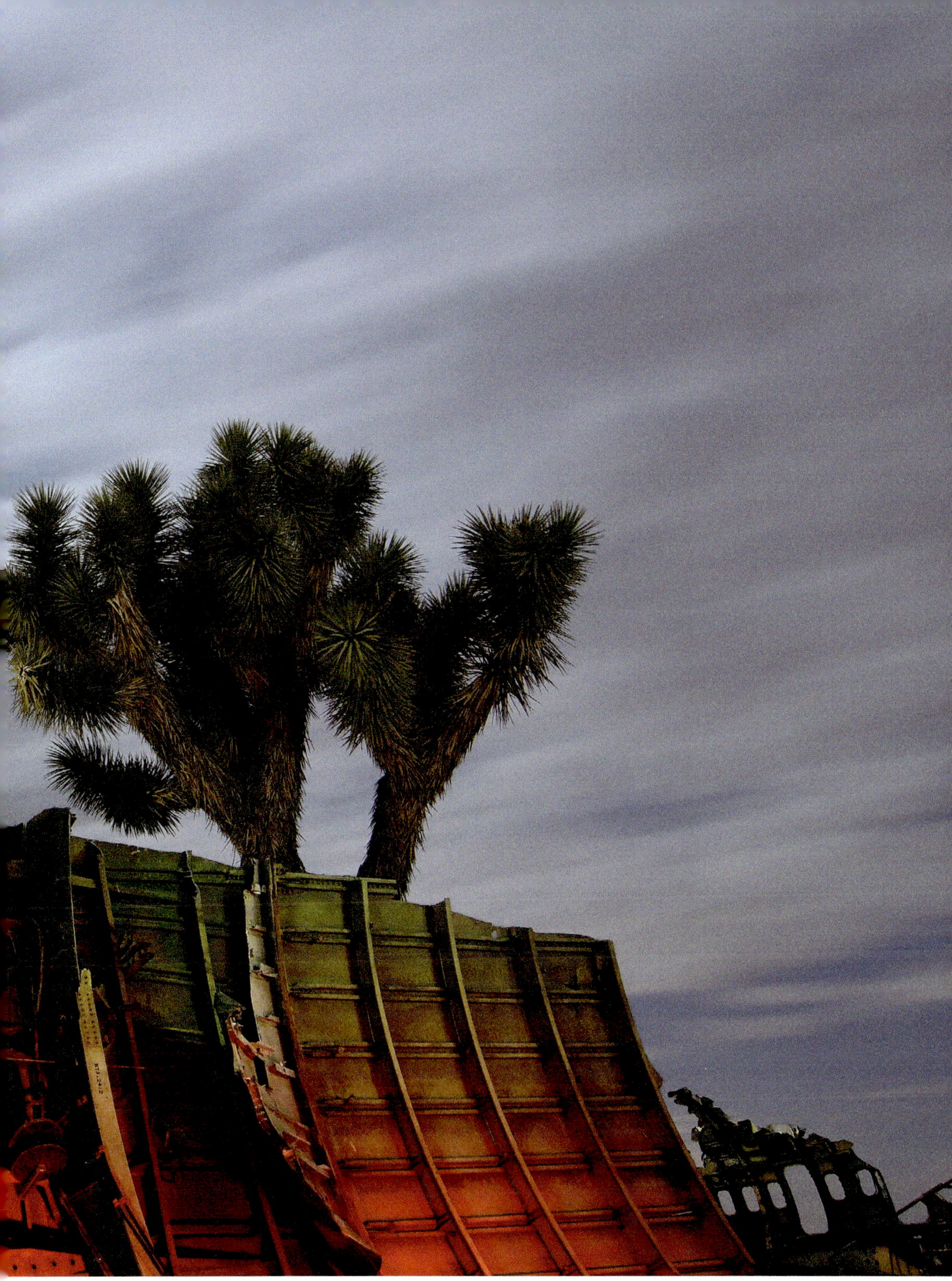

Full moon / red and green Protomachines flashlight.
Boeing 747.

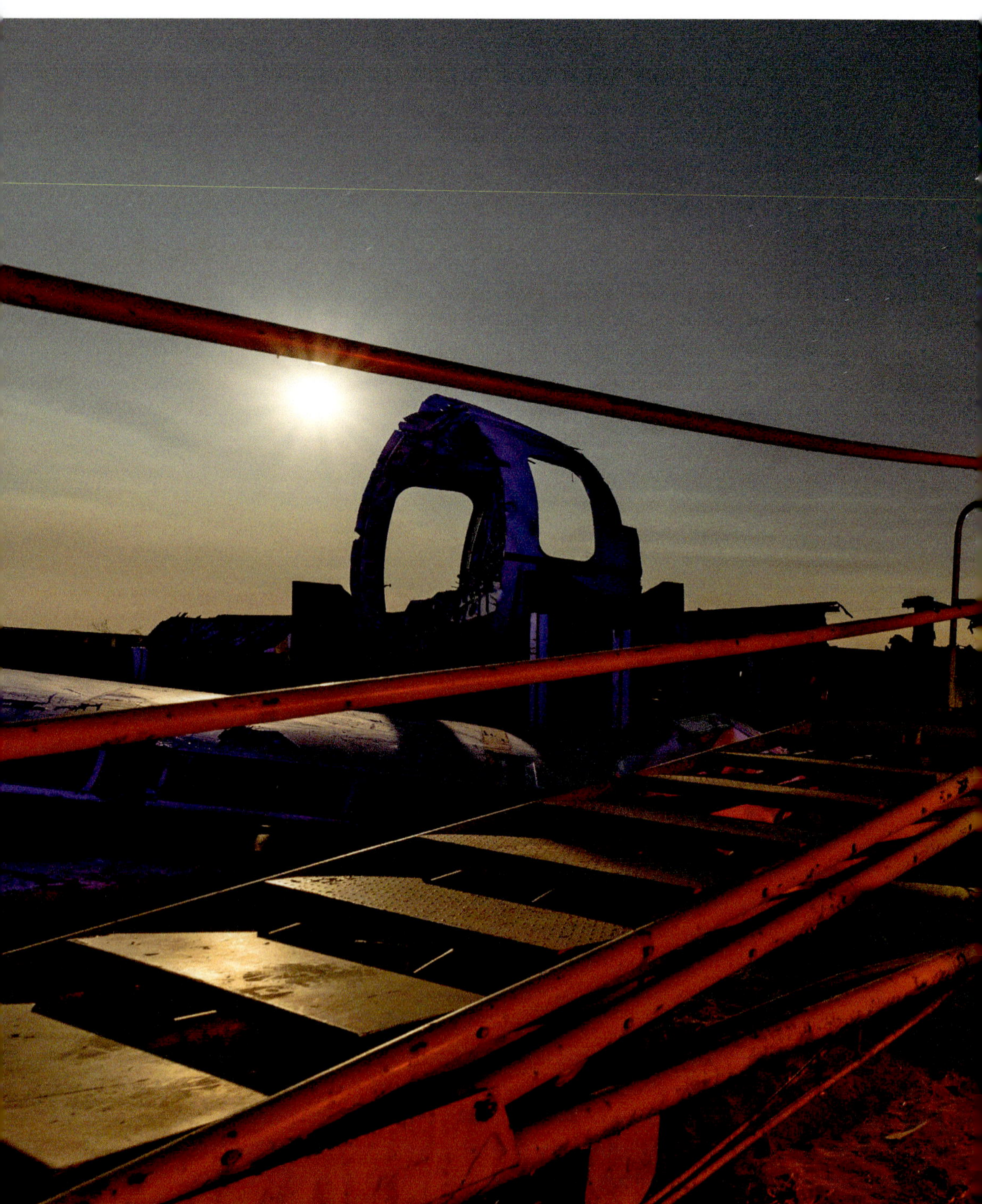

Cola War Casualty
Aviation Warehouse. 7/26/2018, 9:30 PM.
Canon 6D MkII, f/8, ISO 200. 58 seconds, 4800K WB.
Full moon / purple, white and red Protomachines flashlight.

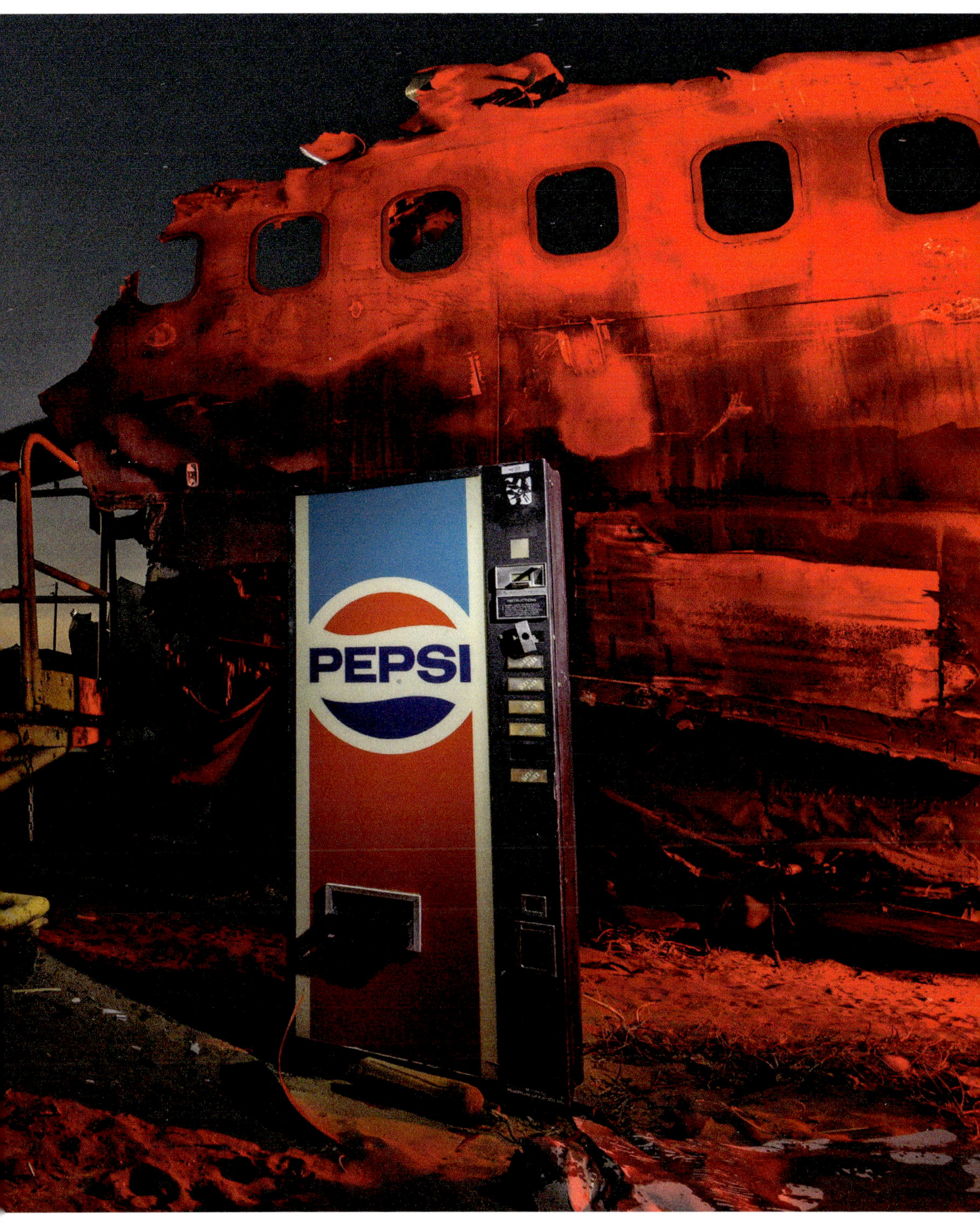
PEPSI

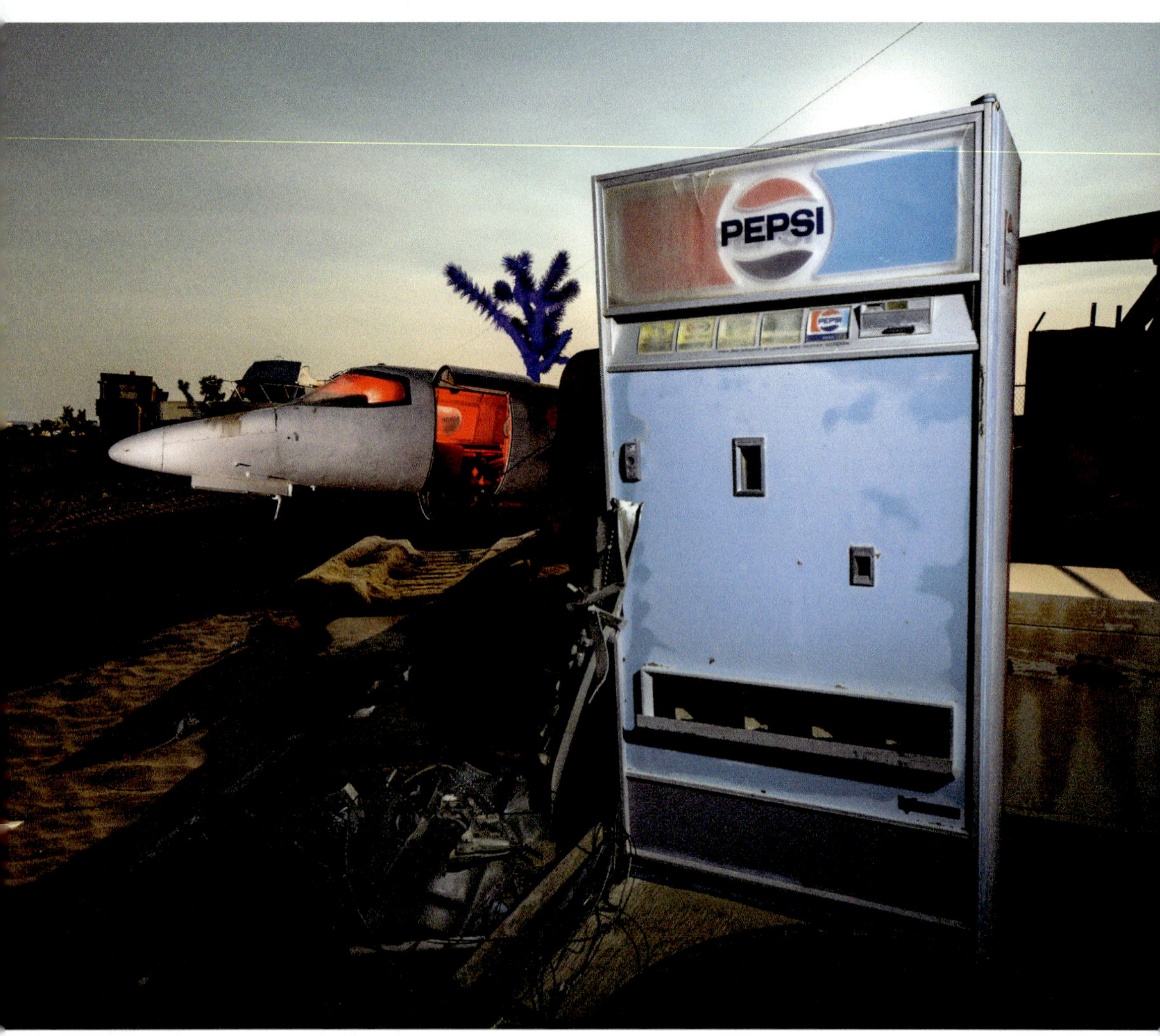

Pepsi Blues
Aviation Warehouse. 7/26/2018, 9:47 PM.
Canon 6D MkII, f/8, ISO 200. 126 seconds, 4600K WB.
Full moon / white and red Protomachines flashlight.
Learjet 24.

Chickasaw Ozymandias ►
Aviation Warehouse. 7/26/2018, 12:11 AM.
Canon 6D MkII, f/8, ISO 200. 98 seconds, 3700K WB.
Full moon / blue, white and red Protomachines flashlight.
Sikorsky H-19 Helicopter.

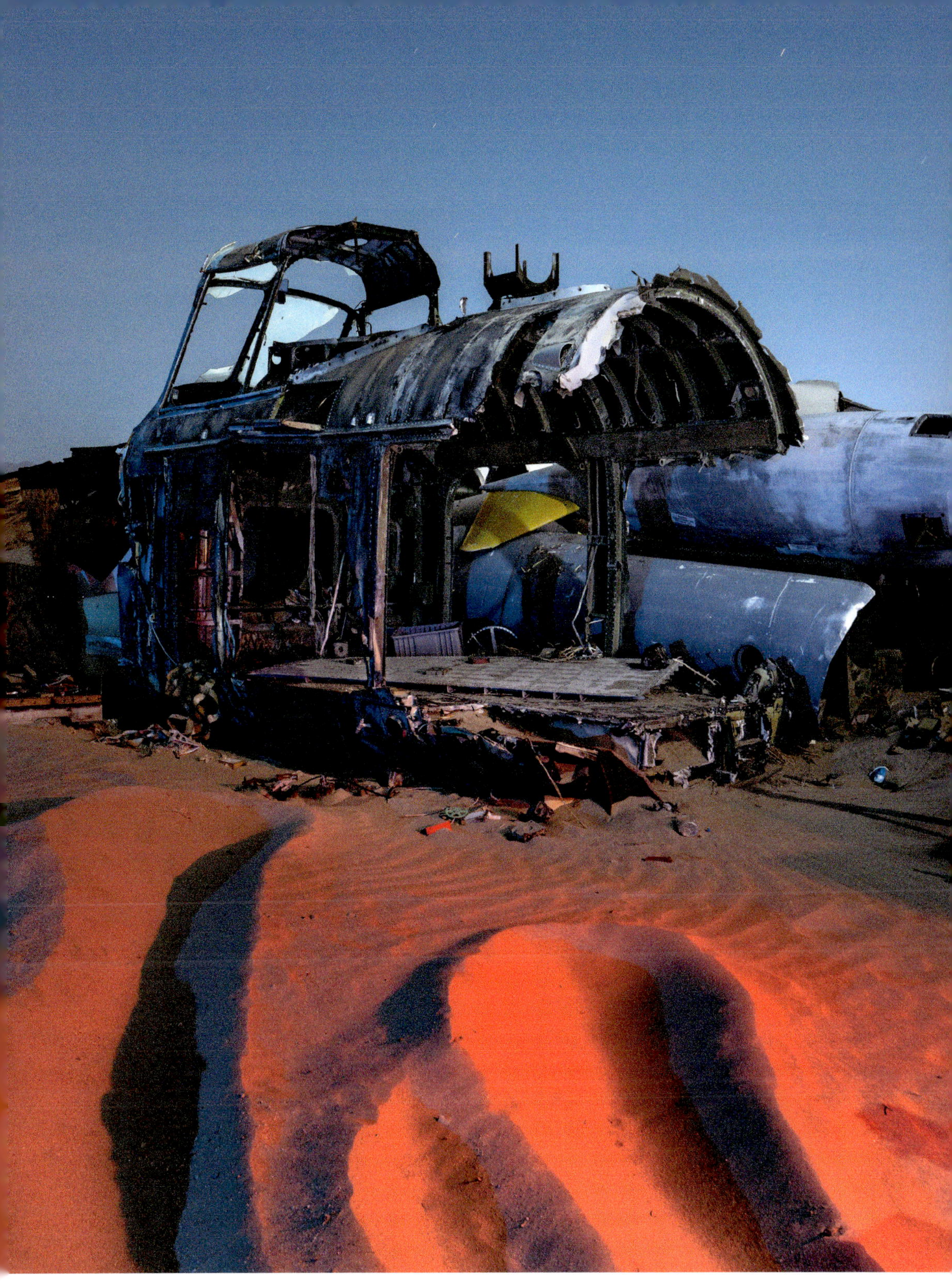

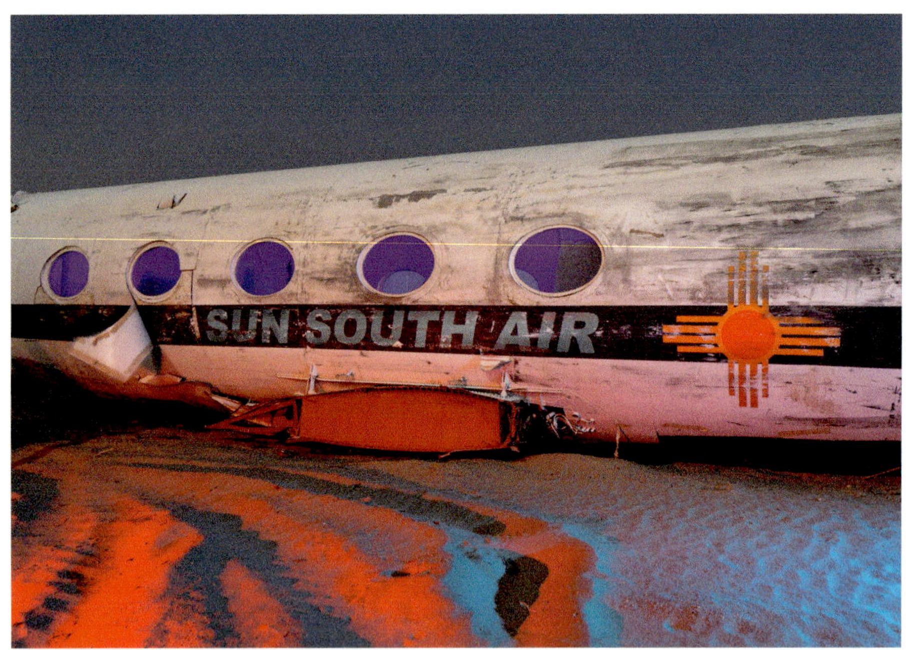

Sun South Air
Aviation Warehouse. 7/26/2018, 12:33 AM.
Canon 6D MkII, f/8, ISO 200. 128 seconds, 3900K WB.
Full moon / blue, white and red Protomachines flashlight.

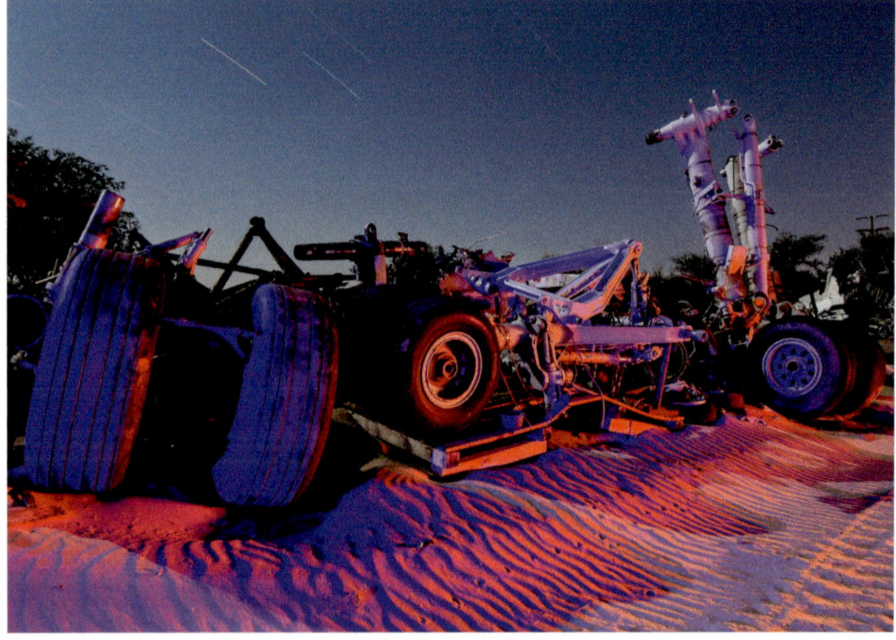

Happy Landings
Aviation Warehouse. 7/31/2012, 10:43 PM.
Canon 60D, f/8, ISO 200. 25 minutes, 3900K WB.
Full moon / red and blue Protomachines flashlight.

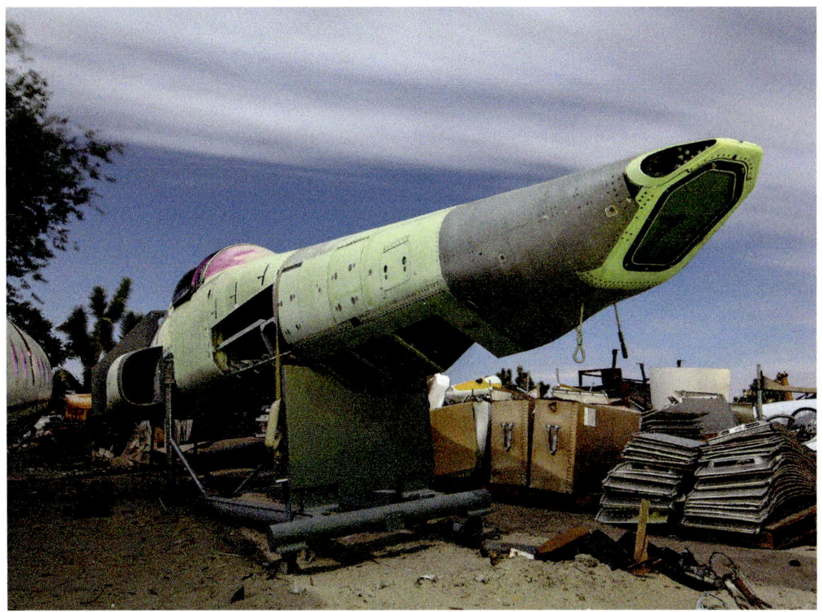

Cylon
Aviation Warehouse. 8/1/2012, 12:05 AM.
Canon 60D, f/8, ISO 200. 253 seconds, 3900K WB.
Full moon, partial cloud cover / lime and pink Protomachines flashlight.
Northrop RF-5E.

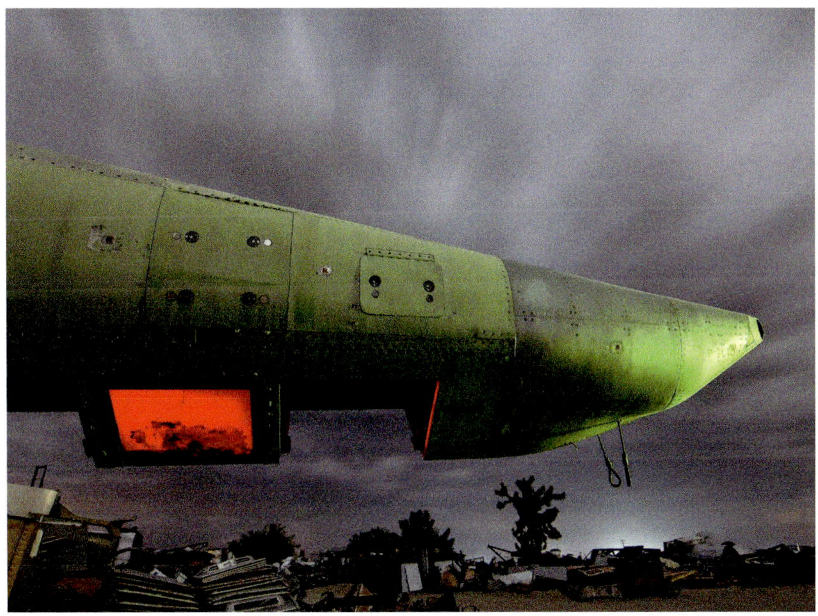

Photo Recon
Aviation Warehouse. 8/1/2012, 12:19 AM.
Canon 60D, f/8, ISO 200. 121 seconds, 3950K WB.
Full moon, partial cloud cover / lime and red Protomachines flashlight.
Northrop RF-5E.

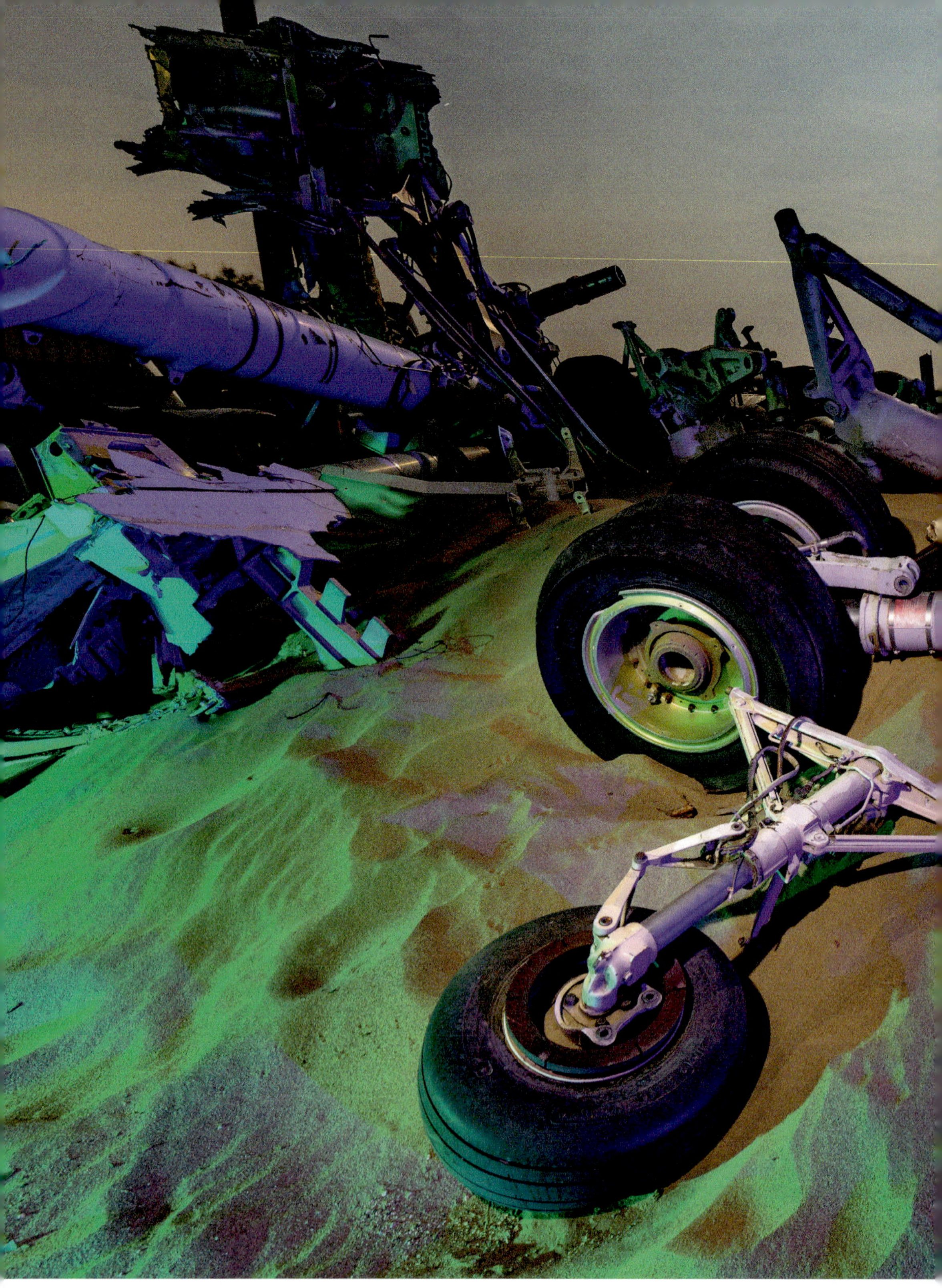

The Purple Lagoon
Aviation Warehouse. 7/26/2018, 12:52 AM.

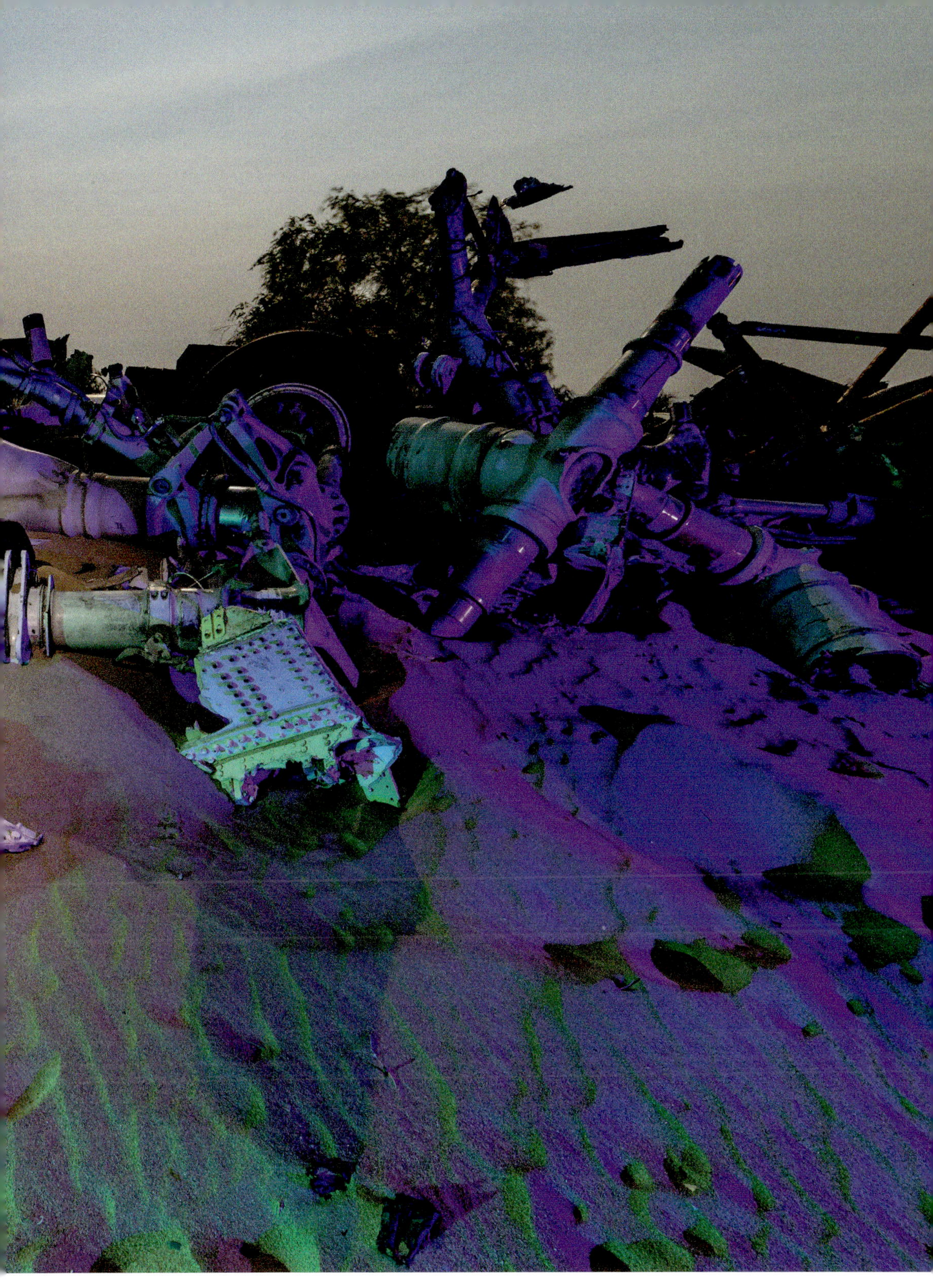

Canon 6D MkII, f/8, ISO 200. 76-seconds, 4500K WB.
Full moon / purple, green and white Protomachines flashlight.

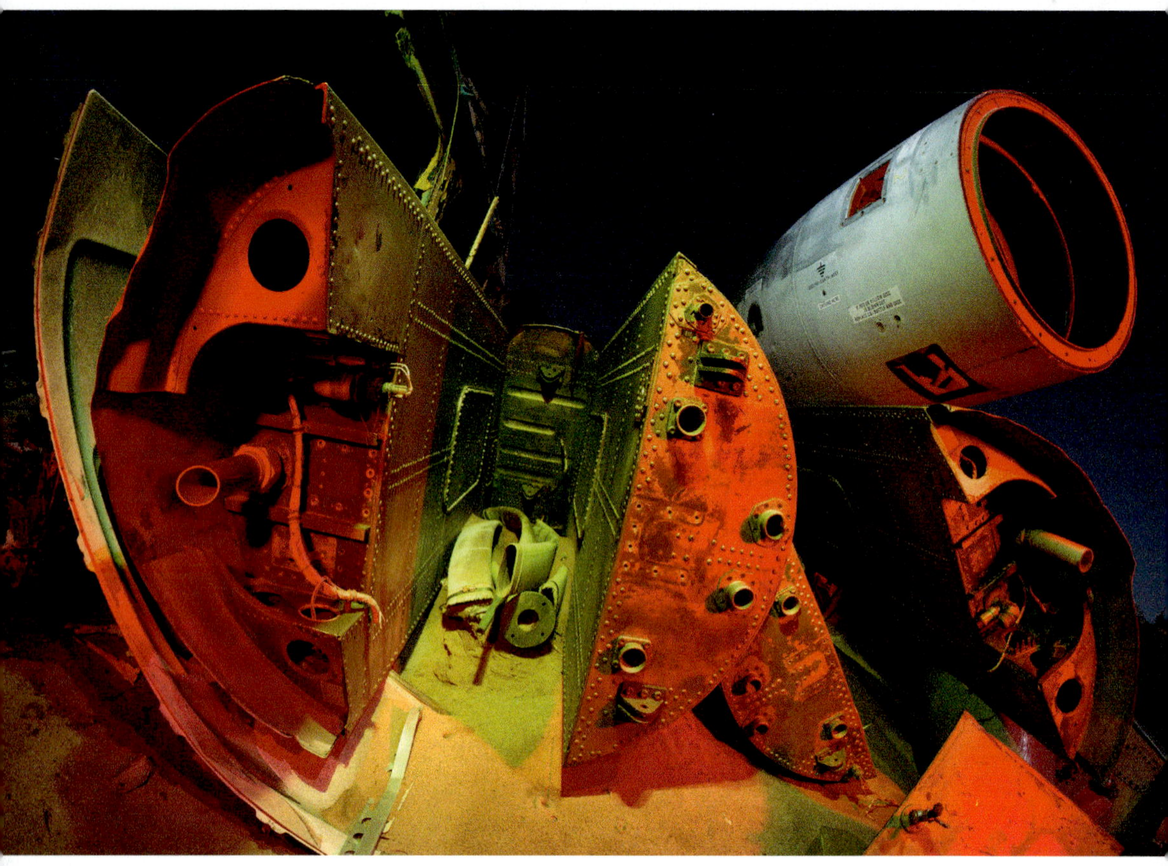

Earth Here
Aviation Warehouse. 12/6/2014, 11:48 PM.
Canon 60D, f/8, ISO 200. 66 seconds, 3800K WB.
Full moon / lime, red and white Protomachines flashlight.

A Crash in the Andes ►
Aviation Warehouse. 8/1/2012, 12:50 AM.
Canon 60D, f/8, ISO 200. 123 seconds, 5100K WB.
Full moon, partial cloud cover / purple and red Protomachines flashlight.
Fairchild FH-227.

The Trailing Edge ►
Aviation Warehouse. 8/1/2012, 12:36 AM.
Canon 60D, f/8, ISO 200. 120 seconds, 3200K WB.
Full moon, partial cloud cover / red and white Protomachines flashlight.

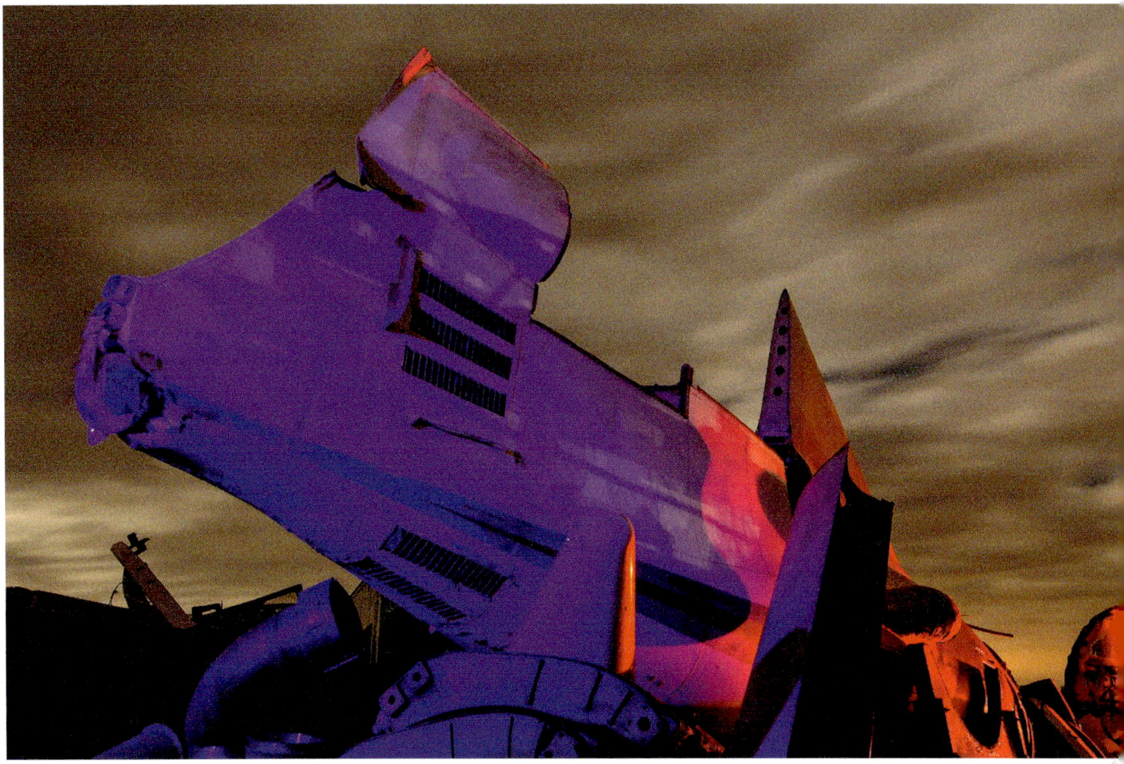

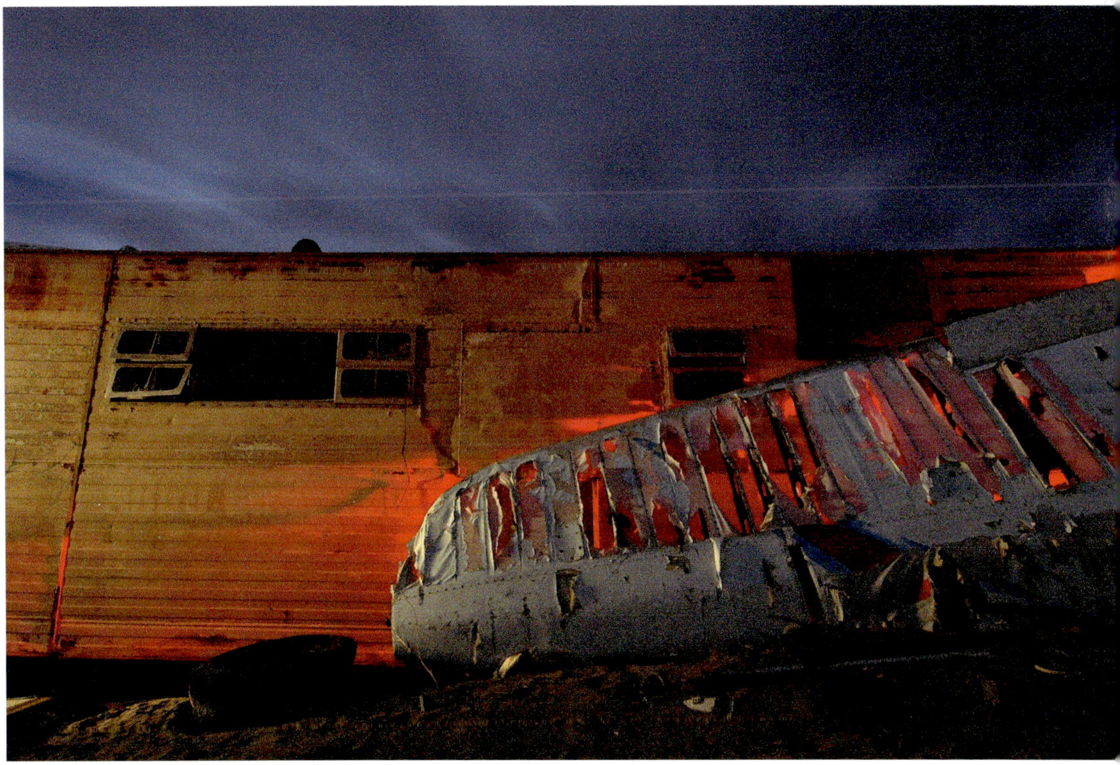

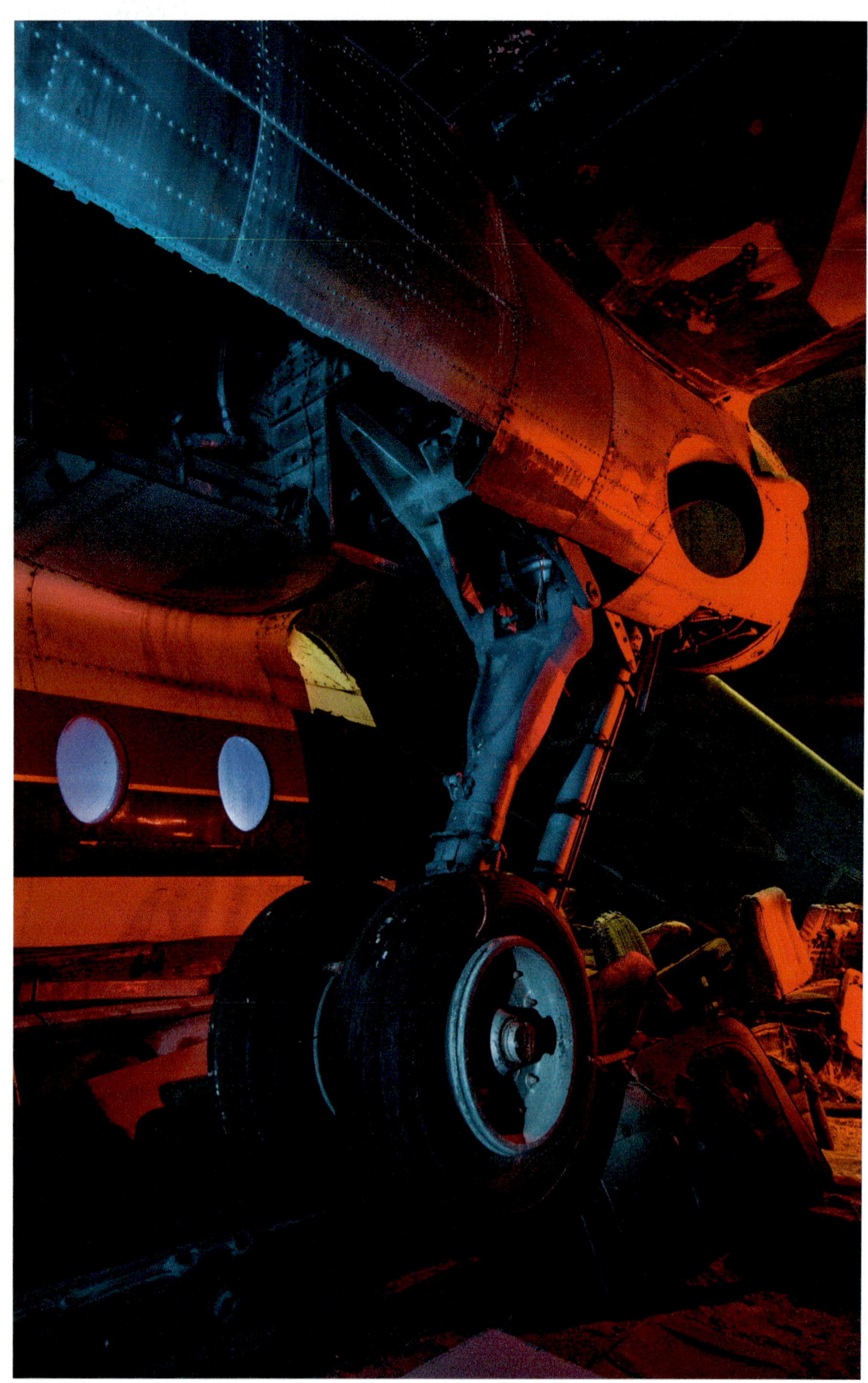

Flight 571

Aviation Warehouse. 11/30/2009, 9:31 PM.
Canon 20D, f/5.6, ISO 100, 103 seconds, 10000K WB.
Full moon / blue-gelled and red LED flashlight.
Fairchild FH-227.

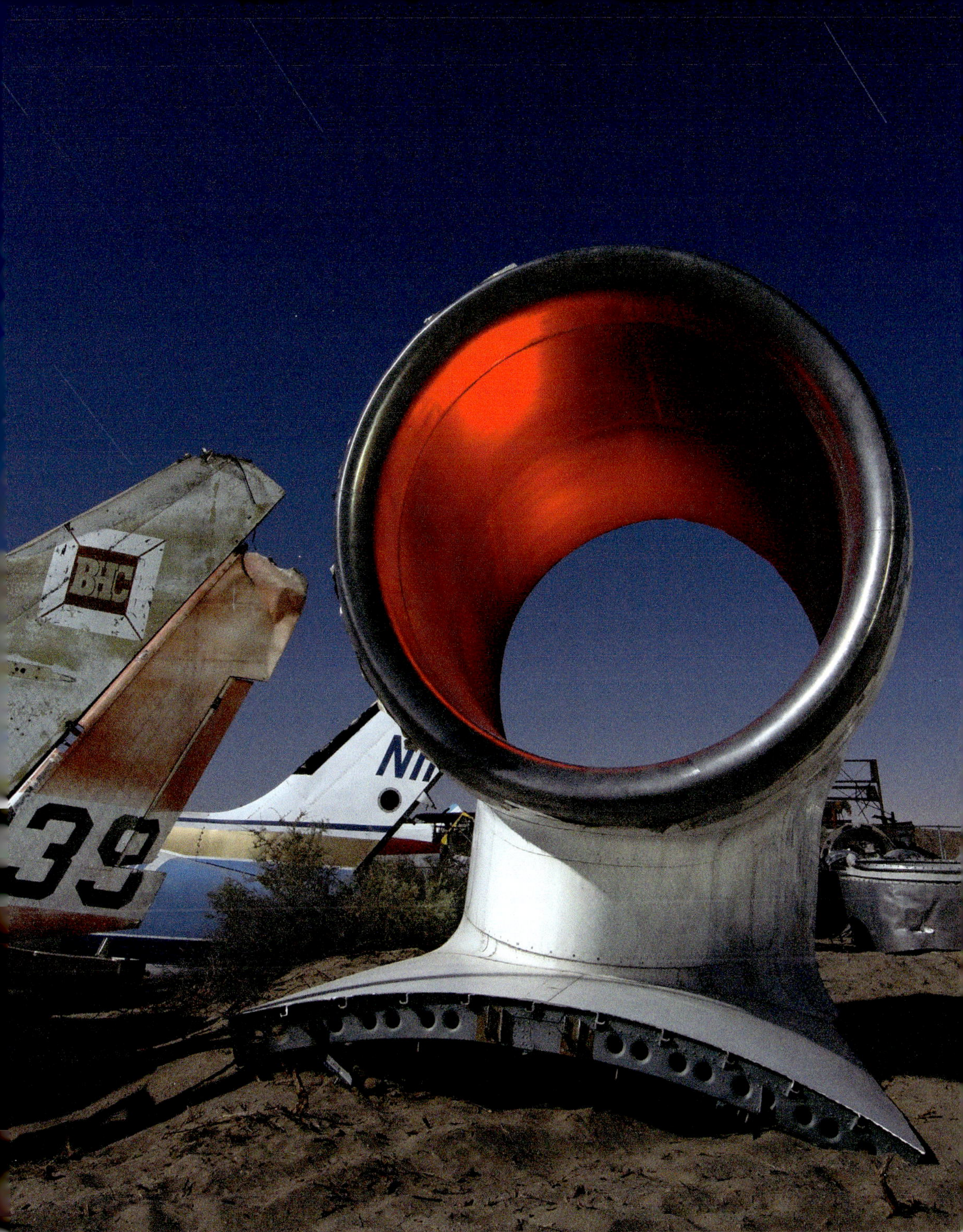

Tristar
Aviation Warehouse. 8/1/2012, 10:56 PM.
Canon 60D, f/8, ISO 200. 25 Minutes, 3900K WB.
Full moon, mercury vapor streetlights / red Protomachines flashlight.
Lockheed L1011.

4

TECHNIQUE

The photographs in this book were shot at night. The full moon serves as the primary light source in most of these images. Some were shot indoors, in total darkness.

The basic exposure formula: ISO 100 or 200, at f/5.6 or f/8, with most exposure lengths running from one to four minutes. All the images were captured with Canon 20D, 5D MkIII, 60D and 6D MkII DSLRs, and a variety of wide angle lenses, ranging from 30mm to a fisheye.

The color and light effects were all done in-camera during the exposure. I don't use light stands, umbrellas, synced lighting or external power supplies. All my lighting is hand-held and added one source at a time during the minutes-long exposures. I normally light the entire scene with a single light source, used from multiple angles.

For the 2006 through 2011 images, I used Maglite and Coast brand xenon and LED flashlights and a single Canon 430EX strobe—all frequently masked with theatrical lighting colored-gel material.

The post-2012 work was lit with the Protomachine LED, a 100% hue-, saturation- and brightness-controllable flashlight that fits in your coat pocket. Literally millions of colors, at any brightness, at the touch of a button. It's bright enough to light a whole airliner from a hundred yards away, but adjustable enough to subtly light a screw head from two feet.

I also use hand-held reflectors, snoots and gobos to manipulate the way the light falls. This simple lighting methodology allows me to travel light and work fast in these difficult, often cramped locations.

Some of these photographs were finished in the digital darkroom—making composites, or star trail stacks—using multiple exposures, from the same tripod set-up.

Amputee ▶
Mojave Airport. December 1990.
Canon AE-1, f/8, Kodak 160T film. 8 Minutes.
Full moon / pink, green and blue-gelled strobe flash.
Douglas DC-8.

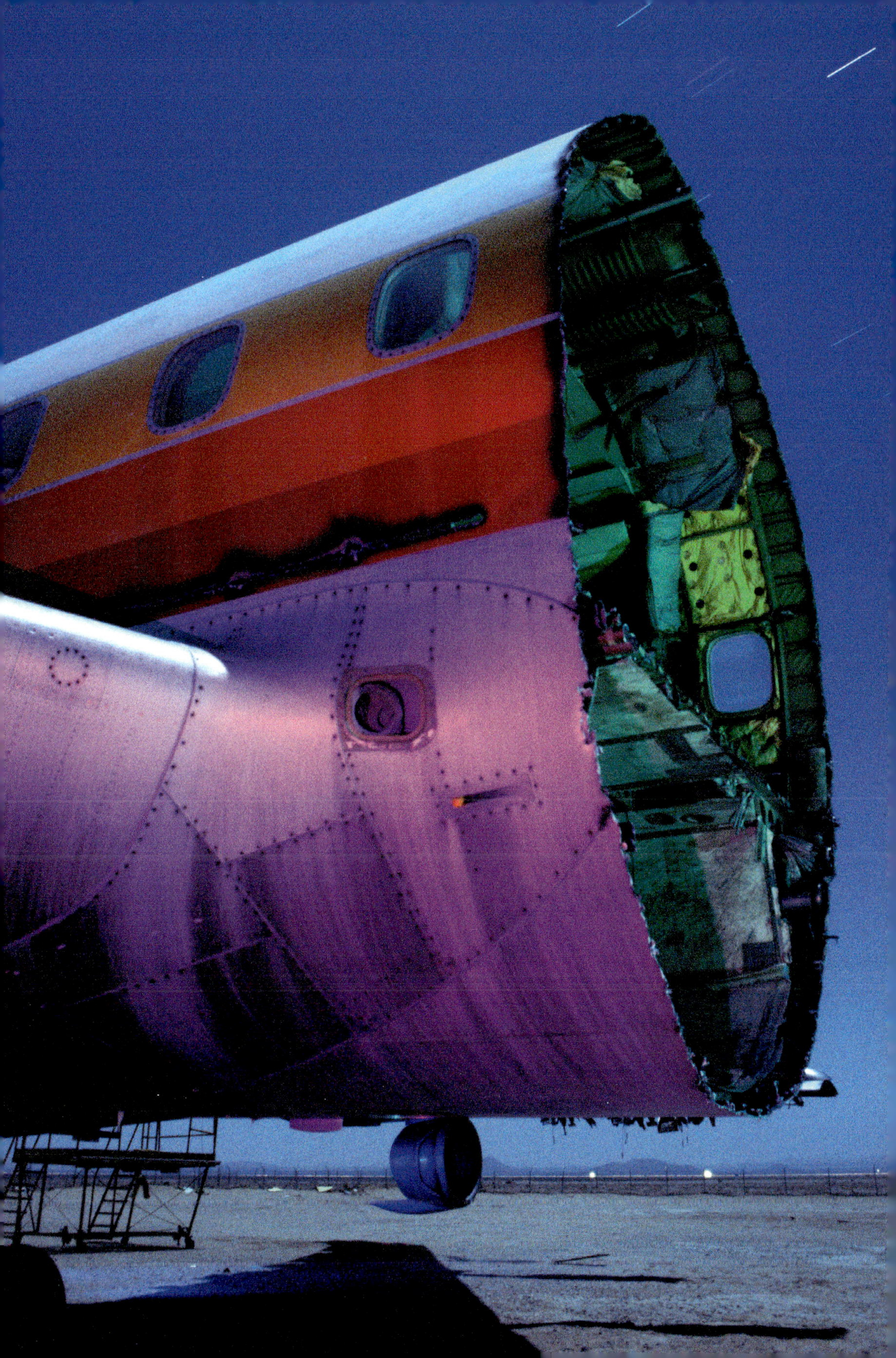

They may also incorporate more traditional, yet still digital adjustments, such as exposure, contrast, and spotting. In all cases, however, the lighting and color were done in-camera. These images are not Photoshop creations. What you see is what I saw and lit that night.

I started creating hand-lit pictures in the dark in 1989, as a *Micro Machines* designer and illustrator at Galoob Toys. While auditing a night photography class taught by Steve Harper at the Academy of Art in San Francisco, where my brother Tom was enrolled, I was immediately floored by the moonlit, time-exposure aesthetic. Having no previous experience with manual photography, I bought a used 35mm camera and made my first baby-steps under ridiculously complex circumstances: experimenting with eight-minute exposures by moonlight of abandoned Route 66 buildings. My first aviation boneyard night-shoot was in 1990.

Over the decades, I've brought this style of endless trial and error, evolution and play, to a never-ending stream of decommissioned military bases, junkyards of every description, bypassed and abandoned roadside towns, derelict amusement parks, industrial infrastructure, hospitals, hotels, and ocean liners. The *Lost America* body of work is an almost thirty-year—and still ongoing—art experiment.